Expert Obedience Training for DOGS

Left to right: OTCH Bar von Weissen-Zwinger, UD; Roger of Wynthea, UD; Randy of Wynthea, UD; Roxy of Wynthea, CD; OTCH, Ch. Joll vom Summerland, UD; Topper of Wynthea, UD.

Expert Obedience Training for DOGS

4th Edition

Winifred Gibson Strickland

HOWELL
BOOK
HOUSE

For general information on our other products and services or to obtain technical support please contact our Customer Care Department within the U.S. at 800-762-2974, outside the U.S. at 317-572-3993 or fax 317-572-4002.

Wiley also publishes its books in a variety of electronic formats. Some content that appears in print may not be available in electronic books.

Library of Congress Cataloging-in-Publication Data:
 Strickland, Winifred Gibson.
  Expert obedience training for dogs / Winifred Gibson
Strickland Fourth. — 4th rev. ed.
   p. cm.
  ISBN 978-1-63026-988-3
  1. Dogs — Obedience trials. 2. Dogs — Training. I. Title.
  SF425.7 .S76 2003
  636.7'0887 — dc21
   CIP   2002015567
Manufactured in the United States of America

10 9 8 7 6 5 4 3 2 1

Fourth Edition

Book design by Marie Kristine Parial-Leonardo
Cover design by Wendy Mount
Book production by Wiley Publishing, Inc. Composition Services

For all obedience training enthusiasts

A board meeting at Wynthea, or "boning up for the next show." Left to right: Wynthea's Donna, UD (DW); Wynthea's Roger, UD (DW); Wynthea's Pawnee Princess, UD; Wynn Strickland; Wynthea's Little Sister, (pts); Wynthea's Marsha, UD and OTCH; and OV Wynthea's Tony, UD (DW).

ALSO BY WINIFRED GIBSON STRICKLAND

The German Shepherd Today (Third Edition)

Obedience Class Instruction for Dogs: The Trainer's Manual

Joll and Me

Obedience Training Videos for Beginners, Novice Handlers, Open and Utility
(with Winifred G. Strickland demonstrating her training as outlined in this book)

Acknowledgments

Grateful acknowledgment is made to the American Kennel Club for permitting me to quote from their Obedience Regulations.

Special thanks to my friend Georgia Bialk and my son, Ronald G. Strickland, for their excellent photography.

Table of Contents

Foreword to the 4th Edition

My training method has passed the tests of time. When I started training my first German Shepherd back in the '40s, the method being used by the training instructors I knew was too harsh, so I conceived my own distinct training method, which is the same today. In the '50s I trained three German Shepherd Dogs who became the National Obedience Champions for five consecutive years. During three of those years, when I showed two dogs, I also won the Runner-Up title.

These dogs were Margelen's Chieftain, UDT (Topper); Hussan vom Haus Kilmark, UDT, (Hussan); and Alf von Kroppelberg, UDT (Arry). Arry won his UDT and passed Tracking twice in five months and three weeks with a 199-point average. This was the greatest record ever made in Obedience history, and it still stands today. People loved to watch them compete because they were such happy, exuberant workers.

Over the years, although I moved a few times, I continued to compete with my dogs in Obedience Trials. In the '60s I started raising German Shepherds and concentrated on temperament, intelligence, and conformation. I wanted all of my dogs to earn Utility titles. It was, and is, equally important that they enjoy and excel in their work and earn high scores. So far, as a result of this, I have earned two hundred eight Obedience titles, forty perfect scores, and hundreds of High in Trial awards.

I have trained all breeds of dogs privately and in the Obedience classes and clinics I have given both at home and all over the United States and Canada. A good number of these dogs were shown in competition, so I proved to myself that my method works with any breed of dog. I also judged all AKC Obedience Classes and Tracking Trials for eighteen years, and believe that perfection and precision are synonymous with good training.

The American Kennel Club changed their Rules and Regulations a few times over the course of the years to accommodate the new exercises that were introduced in their Obedience Trials. Despite the new exercises and various changes, I was able to continue winning with all of the dogs I showed in competition. My method of appealing to a dog's finest instincts has always worked.

Whether you are just interested in training your dog to be well-mannered or would like to earn Utility Dog Excellent and Tracking titles, this book will help you achieve your goal in the shortest possible time. You will find my method uses a great deal of common sense. There are no gimmicks, prong collars, or shock collars. All you will need is your dog, a simple lightweight collar, a leash, and a genuine desire to train your dog.

I can personally attest to the fact that the exercise you get from training your dog every day will be beneficial to your general well-being. In January 2001 I had a triple coronary bypass. I was in such terrific physical condition that I was back training and competing with my dogs a few months later.

Winifred Gibson Strickland

In 1953, Winifred Strickland and Hussan vom Haus Kilmark, UDT, won the National Obedience Champion Award. Sgt. Preston of the Yukon, the popular television star, made the presentation at the Eastern Kennel Club Show. Hussan won fifteen perfect scores in one year and never failed in competition.

Foreword to the 1st Edition

In 1941, there arrived on the Obedience Trial scene a reserved, infinitely patient young woman who was, within the next decade, to gain international renown for herself and the dogs she trained and handled. Now, after many years of experience both with her own dogs and those owned by others, Winifred Strickland is sharing her *Expert Obedience Training for Dogs* so that her own successful methods may aid others to attain training titles in the shortest possible time and with the faultless precision necessary to win top scores.

There have been many good trainers and handlers since Obedience Trials were adopted in 1936 by the American Kennel Club. However, none has attained the records of Winifred Strickland's dogs, nor have other trainers received continual acclamation of their dogs' eagerness and willingness to work. Top scores and mental attitudes both were gained through methods of training that employ the magic of praise, patience, understanding, and respect by the trainer-handler for each dog's individuality.

The joy with which the Strickland dogs always work emphasizes the fact that no force training is employed; the dogs work because they have been taught to enjoy learning. Gay, willing workers can be yours, too, if you will follow the methods explained in detail in this book.

So successful has Winifred Strickland been that her methods, thoroughly tested by her and proven so successful by her enviable record, have been adopted by many Obedience advocates who, as a result, have themselves been most successful. None, however, has attained her great overall record, compiled prior to her retirement from extensive showing in 1955. Up to that time, Winifred Strickland had earned the greatest record in Obedience history, and many of these records still stand.

For five consecutive years, three of the German Shepherd Dogs Mrs. Strickland trained and handled were named Top Obedience Dogs of the Year in the United States. In 1952 and 1954, while showing two dogs at the same time, she captured Top Obedience Dog of the Year and Runner-Up. Four dogs have been trained through the Tracking title by her. One German Shepherd Dog earned all his degrees, including Tracking, in the record time of five months, three weeks, with an average score of 199, for which he received a special award. Another earned his CD, CDX, and UD in exactly five months with an average of 195.

We mention these achievements and records of 231 First Awards, 91 Highest Single Scores, 68 Highest Combined Scores in Show, 35 Perfect Scores, citations from various clubs, including the German Shepherd Dog Club of America, Inc., for service to the breed and the Verein für Deutsche Schaferhunde for outstanding success in training, and numerous honors from dog magazines, to point out that the methods presented in this book have succeeded hundreds of times.

Winifred Strickland's approach to training and handling gave Obedience Trials a much-needed lift in the late '40s and early '50s. The team of immaculate handler and well-groomed dog working almost as one gave other handlers a goal of perfection at which to shoot; thus many tried to emulate her performances. This writer described one such performance in 1951, after watching *this* Obedience artist at work at the Obedience Trial Specialty of the German Shepherd Dog Club of America, Inc. We quote: "However, the highlight of the day was the perfect 200 score earned by Winifred Strickland's ever reliable Margelen's Chieftain (Topper). Topper and his handler-owner work with a precision and mutual understanding attained in few dog-owner combinations. Watching this team is a thrill, although the observer may miss the merit of the work because of the ease with which the exercises are completed. Topper and his owner are to be complimented by German Shepherd Dog advocates for bringing before the public the precise work of an Obedience Trial dog, while at the same time displaying the rapport and complete understanding which is needed to put Obedience Trial exercises to practical use."

Readers will find that *Expert Obedience Training for Dogs* will do more than any other book on the subjects covered to assist them in attaining faultless performances at Obedience Trials, *and* practical obedience away from the show ring.

—Jane Gawthrop Bennett
Former editor of the *German Shepherd Review*

Howell Book House
Published by Wiley Publishing, Inc., Hoboken, NJ

For general information on our other products and services or to obtain technical support please contact our Customer Care Department within the U.S. at 800-762-2974, outside the U.S. at 317-572-3993 or fax 317-572-4002.

Wiley also publishes its books in a variety of electronic formats. Some content that appears in print may not be available in electronic books.

Library of Congress Cataloging-in-Publication Data:
Strickland, Winifred Gibson.
Expert obedience training for dogs / Winifred Gibson Strickland Fourth. — 4th rev. ed.
p. cm.
ISBN 978-0-7645-2516-2 (alk. paper)
1. Dogs — Obedience trials. 2. Dogs — Training. I. Title.
SF425.7 .S76 2003
636.7'0887 — dc21
CIP 2002015567
Manufactured in the United States of America

10 9 8 7 6 5 4

Fourth Edition

Book design by Marie Kristine Parial-Leonardo
Cover design by Wendy Mount
Book production by Wiley Publishing, Inc. Composition Services

For general information on our other products and services or to obtain technical support please contact our Customer Care Department within the U.S. at 800-762-2974, outside the U.S. at 317-572-3993 or fax 317-572-4002.

Wiley also publishes its books in a variety of electronic formats. Some content that appears in print may not be available in electronic books.

Library of Congress Cataloging-in-Publication Data:
  Strickland, Winifred Gibson.
  Expert obedience training for dogs / Winifred Gibson
Strickland Fourth. — 4th rev. ed.
     p. cm.
  ISBN 978-0-7645-2516-2 (alk. paper)
  1. Dogs — Obedience trials. 2. Dogs — Training. I. Title.
  SF425.7 .S76 2003
  636.7'0887 — dc21
     CIP   2002015567
Manufactured in the United States of America

10 9 8 7 6 5 4

Fourth Edition

Book design by Marie Kristine Parial-Leonardo
Cover design by Wendy Mount
Book production by Wiley Publishing, Inc. Composition Services

Chapter 1

Should You Own a Dog?

Consider these facts if you are contemplating the purchase of a dog. You must give him a well-balanced diet if you want him to be healthy. He must have combination shots of distemper, parvo, adenovirus type II, and parainfluenza. He will need a rabies shot at five months of age.

If you have neighbors, you should fence in your backyard so the dog can get plenty of exercise on your own property. A dog needs as much love and attention as a child.

Think twice about getting a dog "just for the children." It will mean that you will not only have to train the dog, but, what is harder, you will have to train the children to respect the dog's rights. Children should be taught to be gentle with dogs. They should not be permitted to pick them up by their legs or carelessly drop them. They should be taught to walk around the dog and not step on him thoughtlessly. The dog should be permitted to eat in peace and should not be teased when he wants to sleep.

In a special ceremony at the Eastern Kennel Club Show in Boston, Winifred Strickland and her German Shepherd Margelen's Chieftain, UDT (Topper), were invited to receive several awards. All judging was stopped when Vaughn Monroe, the famous television star, presented them with the National Obedience Champion awards for 1950, 1951 and 1952, the President's Award, and the Schacht Memorial Trophy. Her Hussan was named Runner-Up in 1952.

At the prestigious Westchester Kennel Club Show in Rye, New York, all judging was stopped when Jack Baird (left), the award-winning sportscaster, presented a Special Award of Canine Distinction to Winifred Strickland and Alf von Kroppelberg, UDT (Arry). To the right of Baird are Wynn, who trained and handled Arry; Len Carey, Show Chairman; and Gustave Schindler, owner and importer. Arry won his CD, CDX and UD, and passed Tracking twice in five and a half months with an average of 199 points.

Parents have a wonderful opportunity to do a little character building when they introduce a puppy into their home. It is a pleasure to watch children grow up with a dog when they have been taught to be kind and considerate of the dog's feelings. Encouraging a child to help take care of a dog is fine, but it should not be the sole responsibility of the child unless he or she is over twelve years of age. Even then, the child will need supervision and guidance from the parents. It is the parents' responsibility to see that the dog is fed, sheltered, and trained. Children who learn to take loving care of their own dogs and, in many cases, train their own dogs, become very fond of all animals. Thus a child's love for his dog will often awaken other virtues in him. On the other hand, children who are permitted to torment, tease, or needlessly neglect their dogs will become so hardened to cruelty that they may someday turn their vindictiveness upon their fellow man.

Dogs are wonderful for children not only because of the companionship they provide, but also because they can protect them from harm. I know of instances when German Shepherds have saved the lives of children by: preventing toddlers from walking into the street, rescuing them from drowning, protecting them from strangers, and sounding the alarm when they discovered a house was on fire.

It has been proven that dogs are an excellent means of therapy when working with chronically ill patients, elderly people in nursing homes, or terminally ill children and adults. The condition of emotionally disturbed patients has been known to improve noticeably when they had a dog to love.

Dogs are being used to good advantage in all walks of life. They can be trusted to guide the blind so that these people can lead normal lives, and dogs can now serve the deaf. Each year dozens of lives are saved by Search and Rescue dogs and avalanche-trained dogs. Police use dogs for sniffing out illegal drugs or bombs and explosives, while other dogs are used to detect gas and pipeline leaks.

If you train a dog to be your companion, be assured he will be loyal and trustworthy. Unlike humans, dogs probably will not disappoint you in the way some friends might. Your dog will be content to share your life with you, whatever it might be.

Dogs are fun to own. Their antics are a constant source of entertainment, their companionship can dispel any feelings of loneliness, and their loyalty and devotion are unparalleled. All this can be fact, not fancy, when you care enough to train your dog and treat him like a member of the family.

Hitching a ride.

Chapter 2

Choosing a Puppy

Every puppy has so much appeal that it takes all the willpower you command not to succumb to his charms. Any breed of dog can be irresistible as a puppy, but when full grown may not be exactly suitable for your needs or taste. If you are undecided about the breed of dog you want, it's a good idea to go to a dog show and get acquainted with all the various breeds.

If one particular breed appeals to you, speak to a breeder and find out its characteristics, virtues, and limitations. You will see it shown in the Conformation Classes where dogs are judged for beauty, structure, and gait. The dogs that place in the ribbons are usually good representatives of their breed, and you should keep their appearance in mind later on when you are selecting your pet. You may also watch your breed shown in the Obedience Classes where the dogs are judged for their ability and intelligence. Almost all the different breeds can be successfully obedience-trained and shown in American Kennel Club licensed Obedience Trials. Many Obedience enthusiasts have become interested in training their own dogs after watching an Obedience Trial at a dog show.

When you choose a particular breed, consider the following: its overall characteristics, personality, general behavior pattern, temperament, size, required amount of care, and acknowledged intelligence. To get a clear picture of any breed, study a sound, normal animal. You can make the right decision only after observing a true representative of the breed. There are good and bad individuals in all breeds, so be sure the one you choose is sound, physically and mentally. Sex is also a matter of choice, because both male and female are equally intelligent and affectionate. Give either sex a good home with care and personal attention, and the response will be the same.

I knew for many years which breed of dog I wanted, and as soon as I was in a position to give the dog the care he needed, I bought one. I chose a German Shepherd dog because I had wanted one since I was a little girl. I had seen all the movies in which they were featured and read everything printed about them. I was greatly impressed by their courage and intelligence as well as their noble appearance and size. I spent many hours planning what I would teach my dog someday. I have never regretted my choice.

At about the same time, good friends of mine chose a Miniature Poodle for his size, appearance, and gaiety. They wanted a dog that did not shed hairs and one that they could carry. They did not mind the extra expense involved in getting him clipped every six weeks. They have been just as happy as I am. Choose your breed to suit your taste. If you buy a certain breed because the Joneses have one, you may end up giving your dog to the Joneses.

Wynthea's Jack of Hearts, UDX, at six weeks of age.

Once you have made up your mind what breed of dog you want, go to a reputable breeder. He can show you his breeding stock and some young dogs so that you will have an idea what your puppy will look like when he is mature.

If you are interested in training and showing your dog in Obedience Trials, be selective in your choice of a kennel. Many kennels breed dogs for intelligence and physical soundness as well as for temperament and conformation. These conscientious breeders have spent considerable time and money in developing a strain that is way above average in intelligence. Only superior dogs are used for breeding purposes, and these highly trained dogs can be traced back five or more generations.

I know from personal experience that this is true, for here at Wynthea we have developed a strain of show dogs that is remarkably intelligent and sound in every way. By selective breeding, these dogs are consistently expert at scent work and tracking, and all display an amazing ability to jump effortlessly and fluidly.

There is nothing quite so wonderful as a sound, healthy puppy that delights you each day with proof of his intelligence. You will probably have your dog for at least ten years, so choose one that will be a joy to own.

It doesn't cost you any more to buy a puppy that has generations of selective breeding behind it. Many people who decide to get a dog rush out and buy the first cute puppy they see because he is a bargain. Most of these bargain puppies require medical attention and special diets to keep them healthy. Later they have countless training problems because the dog turns out to be below average in intelligence or unsound in temperament.

The first thing you will notice is the puppy's temperament. If he comes running to greet you wagging his tail, it is a pretty good indication that he is sound. If he stays back and tries to run away from you when you approach him, he is probably shy. Shy dogs do not make the best pets or Obedience workers. It takes the most expert training and patience, plus endless hours in building up the dog's confidence in himself and the world, to obtain satisfactory results. The dog will grow up giving strangers the impression that he has been beaten by you or his former owner, when in fact he is, frankly, neurotic. The quiet puppy who approaches you will be easier to cope with than the extrovert who is the boss of the litter. The latter will always be trying to keep one step ahead of you, and you will need a great deal of determination and experience to master him.

Your puppy should give the impression that he is well fed; he should have a glossy coat, healthy skin, and clear eyes. He should be sturdy, alert, and unafraid. When you buy him, ask for a copy of his pedigree, a record of the inoculations he has had and those he needs, and inquire about a proper diet for him.

Determine if the litter has been registered with the American Kennel Club. If it has, the breeder will give you a registration slip to fill out and send to the American Kennel Club with a small fee, which will enable you to have the puppy registered in your name. If not, be sure to get the necessary information needed to register your puppy on the day you take him home. You will need the sire's and dam's registered names and numbers, the date your puppy was born, and the name of the breeder. If the sire of your puppy at birth was owned by someone other than the breeder, you will need his signature. Do not put off obtaining this information. The breeder may move away or die, and it may be difficult, a year or two later, to trace your puppy's ancestry.

You should be able to purchase a purebred puppy for about one thousand dollars if you just want a pet. If you are interested in a puppy that is a show prospect, be prepared to pay more.

A purebred puppy is sold as a pet when he does not quite measure up to the standard for that particular breed. He may be overshot (the top teeth may protrude over the lower), or he may have another fault that would prevent him from becoming a champion. You could, nevertheless, own a purebred dog with good bloodlines that might make a name for himself in Obedience or become a happy addition to your family.

Chapter 3

Choosing a Name for Your Puppy

When choosing a name for your puppy, try to find one that is original. If you don't, you may find yourself doing a Long Sit exercise with your dog in a ring while next to you a handler is doing the Recall with *his* dog using the same name as yours. This can be confusing to say the least.

Remember that when you register your dog with the American Kennel Club you cannot use more than twenty-five letters for his name. I think it is nice to include the dog's call name in the registered name so that everyone will become familiar with it. For instance, if I wanted to call a dog Hussan, I would include it with my kennel name. For example: Hussan of Wynthea. It becomes less confusing later on when the dog is well known. The call name will be easier to use if it is only one or two syllables. The name should not rhyme with any of the commands, such as "Neal, Heel," or "Day, Stay." Keep it distinctive, and the dog will not be confused.

Here are a few suggestions:

Amber	Cookie	Fancy	Harry
André	Countess	Flaxe	Holly
Andy		Flint	
Annette	Danny	Fran	Ilsa
Asta	David	Frieda	Inca
	Diane		India
Barney	Dierdre	Gaby	Ingo
Bart	Dinah	Gary	Ingrid
Bernice		George	
Berry	Easter	Gerry	Janette
Brandy	Edo	Ginny	Janice
	Elmer		Jill
Candy	Elsie	Hans	Jimi
Captain	Eric	Hansel	Joni
Chieftain		Happy	

Karen	Odon	Sally	Waco
Karl	Oka	Sammy	Wilbur
Karol	Opal	Simon	William
Kimmy	Oscar	Slim	Wotan
Kris	Otto	Sunny	Wyatt
Ladd	Pat	Terry	Xanth
Lana	Patience	Tiger	Xenon
Larry	Paul	Timm	Xeres
Lori	Perry	Tucker	Xerus
Luke	Polly	Tula	Xylan
Mandy	Qazak	Uca	Yamin
Maple	Quacker	Udall	Yankee
Mark	Quail	Ufa	Yola
Mickey	Quantum	Ugric	Yolann
Mister	Questor	Ulan	
			Zena
Naida	Raven	Varro	Zeus
Nanette	Rita	Vaux	Zorn
Nero	Robin	Vega	Zulu
Nina	Rocky	Vera	Zyggy
Noble	Ruby	Verdun	

Chapter 4

When to Start Training Your Dog

It is important to you as a new owner to know when to start training your dog. You have just bought a new puppy, paid what seemed to you a good price, and you feel that he deserves the best care and training that you can give him. Naturally, you wonder when you should start training him, what you should do first, and how you should go about it.

You will hear all sorts of conflicting stories, words of advice from friends, and a barrage of warnings from well-intentioned souls who all have one thing in common: They are self-appointed experts.

The training program I am outlining in this book is simple and direct and covers all phases of training from housebreaking to the most advanced exercises. It discusses all the problems that will crop up sooner or later. The only thing it will not cover is the human element. If you wish to achieve success in training your dog, stick to the method of training described in this book and ignore any outside attempts to try something else. By switching from one method to another and then back again, you will break the perfect harmony and consistency necessary to achieve success. My method is highly successful and well proven; this is primarily due to the fact that I am consistent in my training from the very first lesson throughout the advanced work. Praise, reprimands, tones of voice, and gestures should remain consistent. From the moment you buy your puppy to the day he receives his Utility degree, your method of handling him should be the same. As you advance from the preliminary training to the more formal training, your dog should know what to expect if he does well or if he misbehaves. The whole period of training should proceed smoothly and harmoniously. The degree of success that you achieve can be measured by your own ability to follow instructions carefully.

A well-trained dog does not become so accidentally. It takes careful planning, close adherence to details, and the patience to progress one step at a time. If you start training your dog when he is between twelve weeks to six months of age, he should be fully trained when he is fourteen months old or less.

Your puppy can start his training as soon as you get him; that is, any time after seven weeks of age. People may tell you that you will break the dog's spirit if you start training him so early. Naturally, you are not going to start with scent discrimination or any other advanced work at this tender age. Would you expect a child in kindergarten to learn

11

algebra? You merely give the puppy his training in simple stages, remembering at all times that he is a baby. If the lesson is short and pleasant, the puppy will retain it.

Teaching your puppy to Sit on command is very important. This is very easy for him to learn and very beneficial if he is going to be obedience-trained some day. He can learn to do this any time after he is seven weeks of age. At this age your puppy will be fed three times a day, and he will look forward to each meal. When his dinner is ready, ask him, "Do you want your dinner?" He will be so excited he will jump around eagerly anticipating his dinner. So say "Sit," and if he doesn't do so, reach down and push him into a sit. Repeat the command two or three times and when he Sits, immediately give him his meal. If you do this every time you feed him, he will soon Sit when he sees you making his dinner. This is great. Also, teach him to Sit for a treat if he has come in the house when you called him. Things like this will be a great help to you later when you start his formal training.

At the Hatboro Kennel Club show in October 1999, Wynthea's Liesl (right) won her CD, with first place in a class of thirty-two, 198 points and High in Trial. Her brother, Wynthea's Georg (left), won his UD at the same show. These two titles gave Wynn her 200th Obedience title. In the *AKC Gazette* under "Great Achievements," it was noted that Wynn was the first trainer in this country to reach this level of achievement. Six months later, Georg won his UDX title before he was two years old.

Let your puppy live in your home and don't be afraid to love him and pamper him. You won't spoil him by doing so. You can train him not to be destructive, or bite, or be rough or noisy. If the puppy has his own toys, it is easy for him to understand that he is allowed to chew only these or a beef bone. Because puppies must chew, especially when they are cutting their second teeth, give them toys or beef bones. Large, hard rubber balls make excellent toys. Puppies also enjoy soft squeaky toys, but once they start to tear them apart, throw them away or your puppy will swallow the small pieces. In fact, some puppies seem to have a penchant for swallowing anything from stones to razor blades. If you have noticed your puppy eating a variety of stones or litter in your yard, give him a dose of Phillips' Milk of Magnesia every two weeks until he gets over the habit.

Don't allow the puppy to bite or to be rough. It will become a habit and will be hard to break later on. If he persists in jumping up against you, catch him in the chest with your knee, and after he has lost his balance two or three times, he will stop. Follow through immediately by calling him back to you and petting him while he is standing still. He should not be discouraged from greeting you. He jumps simply to attract attention, so the act must be accompanied by something unpleasant. If you get in the habit of bending over to pet your puppy before he gets too close to you, he will soon learn to stand quietly. Don't be timid about bumping your knee into his chest. One or two good jolts will break this bad habit where dozens of futile attempts will make no impression whatever. This method will work with either a puppy or a full-grown dog.

Don't step on your puppy's toes when he jumps up on you. You may step too hard and break his toes. Imagine how you would feel if someone tried to step on your bare toes.

I start a puppy's formal training at fourteen weeks of age. Up to this time he has been learning many new commands and tricks that will help him later on. The first week he gets ten minutes' training a day, and this should gradually be increased to fifteen.

If you plan to show your dog in Obedience, and you want to win with him, my advice is to make a companion of him. The dog that you keep by your side, that will work for you always just for the joy of pleasing you and being with you, is the dog that will win consistently.

Chapter 5

Care and Grooming

I am not going to delve too deeply into the subject of general care. I will cover those phases which I feel are of extreme importance to the person owning a pet. If you are interested in training your dog, you are undoubtedly concerned about his welfare. A dog in good health and top condition will respond much more readily to training than one neglected by his owner. Any dog shown in Obedience Trials should be shown at his best. He does not need to meet the breed standard, but he should be a shining example of good care and grooming.

You have the opportunity to mold an even stronger bond between your dog and yourself by this evidence of loving care. He will respond with a full measure of devotion.

The benefit you both derive from this daily ritual is twofold. Aside from the obvious benefit to your dog's health and appearance, you can learn to employ the first subtle approach to training. In other words, you can train your dog to understand simple commands without his becoming aware of them, for his attention will be centered on the actual act you are performing — bathing, brushing, combing, and so on. Take these moments to understand your dog better. To train him successfully, you must understand him thoroughly, his moods and reactions, and this is a splendid opportunity to do so.

Cleanliness is as important to your dog's general health and well-being as a good diet. Your dog should be brushed or combed every day. Even though it may appear unnecessary, it still should be done. Dust particles, skin scales, and dead hair accumulate and make the dog want to scratch to get rid of them. If he scratches, he may do so too vigorously and break the skin, thus leading to skin infections. If you give the dog a sensible diet and groom him every day, his coat will acquire a high gloss that is beautiful to behold.

Make it a practice to do this every day at the same time. By doing so it will become a good habit, and when it becomes a habit, you will not consider it a chore.

If you are grooming a puppy, start by having him sit in a corner. Press down on his rear to make him sit, and then quickly brush his neck, shoulders, and chest. If he gets up, caution him with the command, "No, Sit," in a pleasant tone of voice. When the brushing is finished, have the puppy stand. (Show him how to do this by supporting him with your hand under his stomach.) Then quickly brush him again to center his attention upon the act. Brush his back, sides, and hindquarters. If he moves, caution him to "Stand"; and then pause and say, "Stay."

The puppy will learn quickly what is expected of him, and he will absorb the four words, "No," "Sit," "Stand," and "Stay." By the time you are ready for formal training you will have accomplished a great deal. When the puppy responds nicely, talk to him and praise him for his good behavior in a pleasant tone of voice. If you have to correct him, change your tone of voice, speak firmly and with authority, but do not raise your voice. Use any of these commands whenever it is necessary so that the puppy will really understand their meaning, and be quick to show him what any command means. This applies to mature dogs as well.

Dogs do not need many baths in the course of a year. Still there may be times when it is necessary. If they should soil their coats, whether in winter or summer, give them a bath. Small dogs do not present a problem because they can be washed indoors with little or no trouble. The important things to remember in washing any dog are to RINSE HIS COAT THOROUGHLY with clear water, dry it just as thoroughly, and make sure that he is warm and away from drafts.

In my home I have a special room where I groom my dogs. They have their own bathtub that is raised up off the floor so I won't have to bend over to wash them. Two cement steps have been built against the far end of the tub so the dogs can step into the tub. There is a telephone shower attached to the wall, which is just the greatest thing I have ever seen for bathing dogs. It is a glorified hose attachment that resembles a telephone and, when it is not in use, hangs up out of the way like a phone. The hose is made of flexible chrome tubing to match the rest of the fixtures.

Joll steps into the tub.

I bathe my dogs one at a time, and because German Shepherds are too heavy for me to lift, I have taught them to step into the tub. I did this by lifting their front paws into the tub, saying "Hup," and then lifting their hind legs in. With a little urging I soon had them stepping in themselves by just saying "Hup." Of course I praise them a great deal, letting them know the instant they start to get the idea that they are really clever. I believe in being extravagant with praise.

I get my dog's coat completely wet with the shower, then I pour a mild shampoo lightly over all of him except his head. If your dog has a skin problem, use pHisoderm, as it will get him very clean, combat skin problems, and make his coat glossy. I have never had a dog with a skin problem of any kind when I used this. Then I spray my dog lightly and rub his coat vigorously until I have worked up a thick lather that penetrates the fur. Last of all I rinse him thoroughly with the shower to remove all traces of lather. I wash his head and face with a damp sponge.

Winter or summer I rub the dogs as dry as I can, using plenty of towels. The toweling also serves to bring a beautiful sheen to their coats. In summer I make them run by playing ball; the heat from their bodies dries their coats faster. In winter I keep them indoors until they are completely dry.

After you remove the excess water with a towel, comb your dog so that his coat will be neat. If your dog has a short coat, finish grooming him by rubbing the towel over his coat to make it lie flat and smooth. Later, when the coat is dry, brush it with a clean brush. A daily brushing will keep his skin healthy and his coat glossy. There are new products coming out on the market, such as Frontline, that protect your dogs against fleas and ticks. Consult your veterinarian to determine which product is best for your dog.

Check your dog's ears every week to be sure they are clean. If they are not, wipe them out very gently with a piece of cotton moistened lightly in alcohol. If you see that the inside of the ear is red and swollen, spread Vedco ointment on the area very lightly. You can purchase this ointment from your veterinarian. Many dogs seem to get a fungus disease in their ears at certain times of the year. Some dogs are bothered with ear canker; others need your help to get rid of excess wax that hardens. If your dog is scratching his ears constantly and shaking his head, he may have ear mites; have your veterinarian check him. If you are alert, you can catch these things in the beginning when they are simple to cure.

Your dog's toenails should be clipped regularly, depending upon the type of exercise he gets. Dogs that run on cement do not need their nails cut as frequently as those that exercise on grass. When using a nail clipper on your dog, try to cut off just the portion of the nail that extends beyond the quick. If you should happen to cut off too much nail and it bleeds, do not get upset. Stop the bleeding by holding some Quik-Stop powder to the nail. After the nails have been cut, file them off smoothly with a dog file or a file from your workbench. If you have made a nail bleed, do not file it for several days. Some dogs object strenuously to having their nails cut but do not object to having them filed. Hold the nail firmly between your two fingers as you file with the other hand. To file the nail down fast, go sideways, then, to finish it off smoothly, file in one direction away from the paw.

I have found that the simplest way to cut a mature dog's nails is to do it while he is lying on his side. Have your dog sit; then pull his front paws out from under him, saying "Down." When he is down, roll him over on his side and gently scratch his stomach. When he is relaxed, go ahead with the clippers or file. If you talk to your dog while filing his nails, he will probably go to sleep and make your task a simple one.

Your puppy will begin to cut his second teeth when he is about four months old. The second teeth, or permanent teeth, will force out the baby teeth. The puppy should be given beef bones to help him with this process. Occasionally, the second fanglike teeth have trouble coming in straight because the baby fangs are in the way. If this should be the case, you should try to loosen the baby teeth when you are playing ball or tug-of-war with the puppy, as you could do it at this time without antagonizing him.

Hard rubber balls or bones make excellent teething toys. Raw beef marrow bones are the best, as they will not splinter, and the puppy will spend hours licking the marrow out of the bone. You might find one or two baby teeth on the floor, but the puppy will swallow most of them. This will have no ill effect on him.

A young puppy is able to keep his teeth clean and white until he is nine months old, if he has not been ill. At this time, if you clean the teeth at two-week intervals, the tartar will not harden. Moisten a piece of cotton in water, dip it in baking soda, and rub each tooth clean. If your puppy's teeth are already caked with tartar, pry it off with a tooth scraper, which you can obtain from any pet store. Your dog will not object to having his teeth cleaned if you are very gentle with him and do not stick your fingernails or a scraper into the gums or pinch his lips.

There are as many well-balanced diets for dogs as there are different opinions on the subject. The following is the diet I give my own dogs and is a wholesome diet for any breed.

A puppy up to five months of age gets three meals per day. The morning and late afternoon meals consist of a top quality baked dry kibbled puppy food mixed with good quality ground beef. The noon meal is cottage cheese or vanilla yogurt. After he is five months of age, he will thrive on two kibble and meat meals per day. Hardboiled eggs are good for him twice a week. Raw vegetables are also excellent for dogs. Mine just love broccoli and cauliflower. After their last meal of the day, my dogs love to get a large raw carrot. They hold it between their paws and chew it from the top. They enjoy their carrot so much it is fun to watch them.

Before closing this chapter I want to mention one source that can raise havoc with a dog's health. Almost every puppy has worms. The litter should be wormed by the breeder when they are three weeks old and again at five weeks. Have your puppy's stool checked for worms by your veterinarian every few weeks until he is six months old. This is of the utmost importance: Worms can rob a dog of all the nourishment that you are giving him and can sap his strength and vitality literally as you watch. If you have the slightest suspicion that your dog has worms (poor coat, finicky appetite, sometimes a ravenous appetite, or loose stool), have him checked immediately. By means of a floatation test in which the worm eggs in the stool float to the surface and are then examined under a microscope, the veterinarian can determine what type of worm is present. It could be roundworms, hookworms, or whipworms. By taking a blood test the veterinarian can determine whether your dog has heartworms. If heartworms are not detected in the early stages, they can prove fatal to the dog. Heartworms are found in areas that are heavily infested with mosquitoes. Keeping your dog in a screened enclosure or spraying him with a mosquito repellent will help. If your dog has fleas, he may get tapeworm from them. If you should look at a fresh stool and notice small white segments in it that look like rice, it means that your puppy has tapeworm. In administering medicine to rid the dog of worms, the most important point is to be careful to follow your veterinarian's advice.

Every puppy should be inoculated for distemper, adenovirus II, parvo, parainfluenza, and, at five months, for rabies. Your veterinarian will advise you how often they should receive these inoculations.

Chapter 6

Housebreaking

Housebreaking is the first lesson your puppy must learn. You can teach him in any time after you bring him home. The length of time it takes usually depends on your determination to put up with the inconvenience of watching him constantly. A concentrated effort over a few days on your part is better than any sporadic method that may last for months. A puppy should be let out the first thing in the morning (try to sneak up on him before he wakes up), after each meal, after each nap, after he has been playing, and the last thing at night.

When you get your puppy home, give him a bowl of water; and when he has had all he wants, take him outdoors so that he can relieve himself. Wait until he does, then praise him and take him back indoors. Thereafter, when you let him out, take him back to the same spot and give him some command such as "Hurry up." Use the same words each time so that the puppy will associate the act with the words. Months or years later, if you travel with your dog, he will understand what you want when you tell him "Hurry up" in a strange place.

It is best to teach your puppy to go outdoors, but if you should prefer to break him on newspapers, start him off in one room with newspapers covering the whole area. When he gets used to soiling the papers (probably in two or three days), gradually reduce the area until only one square of newspaper remains. The puppy will still go over to it. This arrangement will work at night for the puppy who is trained to go outdoors in the daytime. For this little fellow, wait until he is reduced to one square of newspaper for several nights, then do not put any down. Try to get up earlier than your puppy does each morning, and he will soon learn to wait for you to let him out.

If your puppy makes a mistake, be sure to clean the spot thoroughly with soap, water, and ammonia. If there is any odor left, the puppy will feel it is permissible to return to the same place. When he soils the floor in your absence, take him over to the spot, saying in a disgusted voice, "What did you do? Shame. Go out." Besides being trained, he will learn the word "out." Eventually he will look at the door and whine if he needs to go out or if the word "out" is mentioned.

Puppies entirely broken to newspapers sometimes refuse to go outdoors when they get a little older, and when you yourself are tired of this whole procedure. If this is the case, take a soiled newspaper outdoors, and when your puppy decides to use it, slip it away from him. Once he has soiled the ground, take him back to the same spot each time.

It will help with the puppy's training if you take his water away from him at 5:00 p.m. If you notice him circling the floor and sniffing it, he probably wants to go out. A very young puppy has difficulty going through the night without relief. If he should get up during the night and soil the papers, don't scold him. The average puppy is anywhere from twelve to fourteen weeks of age before he can go from 10:00 p.m. to 6:00 a.m. comfortably. For the older puppy that is slow in going through the whole night, tie him to your bed; if he should have to relieve himself, he will whine and ask you to let him out. Another method is to tie him to a radiator or some stationary object, with a four-foot leash or light chain. A puppy rarely soils his bed, and this prevents him from straying far enough to feel comfortable.

The fastest way to housebreak a puppy during the night is to tie him to your bed. If he has to do his business, he will either whine or jump up against the bed to tell you. You should take him outdoors on a leash, tell him to "Hurry up," then praise him when he goes and bring him back indoors again. He will gradually learn to wait until you get up. I always housebreak my puppies this way, and they rarely ever make a mistake in the house.

If your puppy soils a rug, wash the area immediately with warm soapy water and rinse thoroughly with clean fresh water. Then apply a good brand of rug shampoo, which is available in a spray can. The soiled area has to be covered with the foam, which should be rubbed into the rug with a clean cloth and left to dry. Later the spot should be vacuumed. By cleaning the area this way there should be no telltale spot. Dog owners who have wall-to-wall carpeting in their homes will appreciate this foamy rug cleaner. A soiled area left uncleaned is an open invitation for a puppy to soil again even though he was punished earlier for his mistake.

Summing up, the simplest way to housebreak your puppy is to watch him constantly for a period of at least two weeks and take the time to take him out whenever necessary.

Chapter 7

Should a Top Obedience Dog Live in Your Home?

Some people feel that if a dog lives in the home, he will be spoiled for the precision work needed to win high scores in Obedience competition today. Their argument is that if the dog is kept in the kennel, he will be so glad to see the handler that he will work more enthusiastically. A number of handlers kennel their dogs for just this reason. I do not agree with this cold, insensitive approach to training your dog. I have known a good many handlers who leave their dogs on the bench at the show in the morning and purposely keep away from them all day with the hope that the dogs will be happier to see them on their return and work better in consequence. But this method of training results in no bond between the dogs and their owners. The dogs are trained only for Obedience competition and cannot be called obedient dogs in the true sense of the word. A properly trained Obedience dog who is still a pet in the home will obey his owner's commands all or almost all of the time.

I can offer three excellent examples of my theory that pets make the best Obedience dogs. My three German Shepherd males, Topper, Hussan, and Arry were all pets who lived in my home and were with me constantly. They were my constant companions and would follow me all day from room to room or accompany me on errands. If I was gardening, each would carry something I needed — a tool, a pail, or a basket. If we went to the grocery store they would each carry packages into the house from the car. They were true companions in every sense of the word and made life much more fun for all of us. Yet each became the Top Obedience Dog of the United States and among them held the title for five consecutive years. They worked in the show ring with the utmost precision and had consistently high scores including twenty-eight perfect scores. What is most important, they enjoyed every minute of it.

These three were males but of different ages, yet they loved one another and would eat from the same dish. They would invariably lie down at my feet and rest their heads on each other. As each joined the family, he was taught to be friendly to the others. They were loved equally and for themselves, and felt so secure and happy that they never found any cause to fight.

Topper was two years old when I bought Hussan, and although Hussan was only six weeks of age, Topper was very gentle with him. In the weeks and months that followed, Hussan was a bundle of energy, but Topper was always tolerant with him. I was very

Wynn always has company when she cooks. OTCH Wynthea's Ace, UD; Wynthea's Falco, UD; Wynthea's Holmes, UD; Wynthea's Jack, UDX; and Wynthea's Jet, CD.

careful to give them an equal share of affection and praise. If Hussan was naughty he was promptly scolded. A trained dog such as Topper would not understand it if a new dog was permitted to get away with misdemeanors. When the scolding was over I would pet Topper and say, "But you were a good boy." He seemed to understand.

Hussan was two years old when Arry, who was also two, was brought into our home. Arry was an aggressive dog, very self-assured and fearless. He was very rambunctious and had every intention of bossing the other two dogs around. Whenever he tried to assert himself in an unpleasant way such as growling whenever the other dogs came near him, or pushing them aside in order to get all the attention for himself, he would be tapped on the nose and scolded. He soon learned that it was more fun to be gentle and friendly. In just a few days they were all playing outdoors together having a wonderful time.

If you introduce a second dog into your home, insist that he behave himself. Don't do anything to make either dog jealous of the other. If you handle the situation sensibly and show no impartiality there will be no misunderstanding.

During the past forty years I have bred and raised German Shepherds. All the dogs that I keep for myself are highly trained, so I generally enjoy having five or six dogs in the house. They are of different ages and both sexes, and they all get along together very amiably. The oldest male is the boss, and the other dogs realize this instinctively. He never has to prove his leadership beyond a quiet growl or a fixed stare. Because dogs communicate with each other by thought transmission, no other outward signs are necessary. Even though the house dogs might change from one week to the next, there is a definite pecking order, and it applies according to the age of the dogs. The older dogs are always encouraged to be tolerant of the youngsters, and the puppies are taught not to pester the older dogs. It is easy to keep peace among so many dogs if you treat them as individuals and respect their rights.

So by all means let your puppy or grown dog live in your home with you, and never fear to love him and play with him. By making a companion of your dog you are cementing a bond between you and him that will last a lifetime. It does not mean that, because you keep him with you, your dog will be spoiled. He will learn much more quickly if you are there to encourage him along the right path.

Chapter 8

Preliminary Training

TEACHING YOUR DOG NOT TO BITE

Never allow your puppy to bite or become obstreperous. This sort of thing will become a bad habit and be hard to break later on. If he bites your hands, give him a tap on his nose or under his chin. He will probably yelp, but he needs this lesson as early in life as you can give it to him. A puppy that is allowed to nip and bite becomes very bold and aggressive as he grows older. Then when he gets to be over a year old, the harassed owner takes him to a professional trainer to be tamed down. Such dogs present a problem to both their owners and society in general. It takes a firm, experienced trainer to get them under control. Many owners are so upset by their dog's uncontrolled behavior and aggressiveness that they decide to give him away. Unfortunately, what they do not realize is that the next person does not want a problem dog either. So take my advice and control your puppy while he is young and trainable.

Teach him to be gentle by offering him tidbits in your hand. If he snatches the tidbit say, "No. Ow." If he continues to grab for it, give him a tap on the nose with your fingers, and then offer him the tidbit again saying, "Easy," in a soft voice. If he takes it gently, praise him. Repeat this lesson over and over again. After a lesson or two you will note that if you say "Easy," and pause for a second before giving the tidbit to him, he will be gentle. This is a valuable lesson that can be learned easily and retained.

A variation of this lesson will be very useful from time to time. For instance if, when you are playing with a toy, the puppy gets excited and starts to bite, just say "Easy," softly. If he has learned his tidbit lesson well, he will relax and play gently.

TEACHING YOUR DOG NOT TO JUMP UP

Puppies and dogs that jump up on you are only looking for attention, and it is your duty to give it to them. If, when you enter a room, your puppy dashes over to greet you, bend over to pet him. If you simply stand where you are, he will probably want more of a greeting from you and speaking to him is not enough. Remember that this display of affection is one of the ways your puppy will show that he loves you, and your affectionate response will assure him of your devotion. Dogs are gregarious creatures and enjoy your company. Don't be surprised if your dog greets you with the same abandon with which he greeted you only a few minutes ago; it is a compliment.

25

If your puppy jumps on your friends or strangers when they come to visit you, another method must be employed. Because you could hardly expect anyone else to use the knee method to prevent the puppy from jumping on them (described in chapter 4), it is up to you. Have the puppy on a leash when a caller comes to the door and as the puppy starts to jump up, pull him back. Ask your friend to reach down and pet him. Any time you pull your puppy back off balance, say "No, easy," to him. It is best to have a choke collar on your puppy at this time. The collar should not be heavy and it should fit properly.

If you wish to teach your dog later on to stand up against you, try this. Encourage him to stand against you by saying, "Up," and patting your chest. If the dog jumps and leans on you too heavily, hit him in the chest with your knee. Encourage him to try again, and when he leans against you lightly, praise him with your voice and pet him. Here is another opportunity to use the word "Easy."

USING DIFFERENT TONES OF VOICE

Your puppy can learn many things at a very early age by the different tones of voice you use and by the different inflections you give your words. He may not understand your new word commands until you have repeated them over and over, but he will instantly recognize your different tones of voice.

He will soon learn to recognize words when they are used in the form of a question. This is especially true when an act is performed each time a question is asked. Here are a few examples:

Do you want to go out? (As you go to the door.)

Do you want your dinner? (As you pick up the puppy's dish.)

Do you want a drink? (As you turn on the faucet.)

Do you want a cookie? (As you take the cover off the cookie jar.)

Do you want to go for a ride? (As you walk toward the car.)

Do you want to go to bed? (As you pat the dog's bed.)

Do you want to go for a walk? (As you pick up the leash.)

If you repeat these questions and go through the motions a great number of times, your dog will soon learn to understand all the words. At first upon hearing a question, he will look at you expectantly and may wag his tail with anticipation. Later he may speak, and still later he may bring you his dish or leash. When your dog's training is completed, you can sit in your living room and ask any of these questions and your dog will reply by acting out the answers. So, at first when you ask your dog questions, use a pleasantly excited tone of voice and emphasize the last word of the question.

When you use the word "No" to correct your dog, lower your voice, making it sound authoritative and firm.

When reprimanding your dog, lower your voice and draw out the words. "S-h-a-m-e. B-a-a-a-d d-o-g."

The tone of voice that is most important in training is the one you use when you praise your dog. Make it gay and full of good spirits. Include a laugh here and there and be sincere, for a dog can spot insincerity easily. Put on a little act for his benefit, for this is his real reward for being obedient. Put your heart in your voice and watch your dog respond.

If you give commands to your dog in actual training, use a moderately pitched, pleasant voice that is both firm and authoritative.

There is absolutely no reason to shout at your dog if he is working near you. A dog's hearing is at least sixteen times better than that of a human being. With such acute and sensitive hearing there is no excuse for you to speak to your dog above a moderate tone. If you wish to attract his attention, clap your hands, say "Sssst," or call him by name. Even at a distance raise your voice just enough to be heard above the crowd.

If you find yourself continually shouting at him, it would be better to turn your dog over to another member of your family for training because you are probably temperamentally unsuited for the job. If you find yourself confronted with a problem, the dog seems to be getting stubborn, and you find yourself shouting at him, stop. Repeat a simple exercise the dog knows and understands, praise him, and then stop for the day. Always end the day's training on a pleasant note. Next day you will accomplish more when you are both rested.

You may have attended Obedience Trials and noticed that some of the handlers were shouting at their dogs. This is generally most noticeable on the Long Sit and Long Down exercises, but with many handlers it continues through every exercise. It certainly puts Obedience in a bad light when the noise erupting from the Obedience rings carries all over the show grounds. Obedience handlers should set a good example at all times and not invite ridicule. The type of handling where shouting is used is a form of intimidation. Instead of appealing to the dog's finer instincts and using various quiet tones of voice to control him, the loud voice is intended to bully him into obeying. By yelling at the dog in this rude manner, some handlers expect to command the dog's attention, but in so doing they eventually lose the dog's respect. Only the most placid breeds will meekly tolerate this type of training. It is an insult to a dog's intelligence to expect him to respond to this crude method. Contrast this type of handler with one who asks his dog to Heel in a pleasant, quiet tone of voice. The quiet handler in setting a standard of perfection would, by contrast alone, expose the loud handler's imperfections.

To quote from the American Kennel Club's Obedience Regulations, "Commands which in the judge's opinion are excessively loud will be penalized." When handling your dog be gentle, make a companion of him, talk to him as you would to a friend, conversationally. You won't spoil him by doing this, but will gain your dog's respect. Your dog will be your best friend if you will just consider his feelings at all times. If you train him with patience and establish a mutual feeling of companionship, he will be eager to work just to please you. A well-trained dog will execute any command perfectly, even if the order is given in a whisper. Gentleness and smoothness of handling can be acquired only through constant practice.

TEACHING YOUR DOG TO LIE DOWN

One of the first things to teach your puppy is to lie down upon command or signal. If you can teach him to do this at an early age, life will be much easier for both of you. There will be many times during the course of the day when this simple exercise will prove its worth.

Have a nylon choke or buckle collar on your puppy and attach a short leash to it. Have your puppy Sit as you stand directly in front of him. Hold the leash short in your left hand as you give him the verbal command "Down" in a quiet but firm tone of voice. Also give him the Down signal by raising your right hand where he can see it as you pull him down with the leash. Quickly place a treat between his paws as you stroke him on the withers saying, "Down, good, Down, good." Try this three more times, giving him a treat

Give your dog the Down signal where he can see it, as you say "Down."

each time and praising him in a happy tone of voice. The fourth time you try it he will probably go down by himself. Get excited and tell him what a good boy he is, using a very exuberant tone of voice accompanied by a treat. Just be sure that your puppy looks at the palm of your hand when you give him the Down signal.

This exercise will make your puppy feel very special. Just be sure that he doesn't crawl forward but Drops straight down. Try this several times the first few days so that he will learn to Drop on either your voice or the hand signal. A week or so later try giving him the Down command a few feet from you. Then gradually increase the distance until you are about ten feet from him. You must continue to run up each time he Drops and praise him very enthusiastically and give him his treat reward.

When you have accomplished this, try training him to lie down off leash. You must continue to praise him extravagantly and give him the treat. At first it is best to train him to Down indoors. Then, when he is reliable, train him outdoors. Several months later you can teach him the Drop on Recall, but be careful *not* to overdo it. Puppies should be very eager and willing to do straight Recalls before they are taught the Drop on Recall.

In the beginning it will be necessary to bend over a little as you give the signal. Later when he knows the exercise, you can stand up straight and give the signal. When you pull the puppy down, you should pull the leash either straight down or slightly back away from you. If you pull the leash down toward you, the puppy will move forward. You do

Praise your dog when he lies down, as you stroke him on the withers saying, "Down, good, Down, good."

not want him to do this or he will crawl between your feet. He should go down exactly where he is sitting without moving forward.

TEACHING YOUR DOG TO RIDE IN A CAR

If you take your puppy home with you in your car, he will feel much happier if he can cuddle up next to you on the seat. It will give him a sense of security and make his first ride a pleasant experience. Have an old blanket or towel handy in case he drools or is sick. Hundreds of puppies take to riding the first time they are in a car and are never sick, but many others get used to riding only by countless short trips. As they get accustomed to the car's motion, the excursions can be gradually lengthened. Keep your windows open so the puppy will have plenty of fresh air.

It is a good idea to teach the puppy to Sit quietly in the car right from the beginning. Dogs that dash from one window to the other or that jump from the front to the back seat, or those that are allowed to bark, soon become a nuisance and a driving hazard. If you want your puppy to ride in the car, it is up to you to make him behave. Have someone other than the driver in the car and every time the puppy stands up, say "No, Sit," and make him Sit by pushing his rear down. When he Sits, praise him quietly. This will probably have to be repeated dozens of times, but it is worth it to have a well-mannered dog.

In teaching an older dog to ride in a car, follow the same routine unless you have a dog who is actually afraid of cars. In this case you must gain his confidence. First, you should put him on a leash and give him the idea that something special is going to happen by asking in a pleasantly excited tone of voice, "Do you want to go for a ride?" Take him into the car with you and have him Sit on the seat with you for ten minutes, talking to him and petting him. Repeat this the second day, and on the third day try it with the engine running.

Keep this up for a week, and then try it while you back the car out of the garage; park it in the yard for ten minutes and then drive back in the garage. This slow method is the easiest and brings the best results. When you have worked up to a two-mile ride around the block, you can gradually increase the ride to ten miles. If you plan to drive more than fifteen miles, it is a good idea to give your dog some carsickness pills an hour or so before starting. It will probably be many weeks before he is actually a good rider, but it will be worth the effort to have the pleasure and protection of his company.

Teach your dog to Sit by the car and wait for your command to get in. Also, after a ride, have him Sit patiently inside while you step out and until you have given him the command to get out. Everyone appreciates a well-mannered dog, and a few minutes' practice each time he goes for a ride assures you of owning one.

If you take your dog on a long trip, be sure to carry his water dish along. Dogs get thirsty more quickly than human beings. Keep a leash in your car at all times. You never know when you may need it on a trip. If you should have to stop to exercise your dog, always put him on a leash.

If you have a dog that barks madly when he is in the car, it is fairly easy to stop him. Purchase a water pistol and squirt the dog in the face with it whenever he barks, saying "No barking."

TEACHING YOUR DOG TO STAY AT HOME OR IN THE CAR

Once your puppy is housebroken and is trusted enough to be allowed the freedom of the house, it is time to train him to stay alone.

Begin by leaving him in a familiar room that can be shut off from the rest of the house. Be sure to leave his toys in the room. Leave him for only a few minutes the first time and gradually increase the time as he behaves.

If he scratches the door, open it quickly and slap him with your hand, saying "No, shame." Repeat this as often as necessary.

To correct a puppy that has been getting into mischief by chewing things, set a trap and come upon him in the act as if by surprise. After you have scolded him a few times he will behave. If you do not want your puppy to get up on furniture, refuse to allow him to get up from the first day. To prevent him from climbing up on furniture when you are away, set mousetraps on the chairs and sofa.

If a dog doesn't get carsick, it is easy to teach him to stay in a car because he loves the car so much that he is perfectly happy to sit in it. Leave a window partly down on each side so he will have plenty of fresh air. If he starts to bark, go back quickly and reprimand him with your voice, or if this is not sufficient, use the water pistol on him.

TEACHING YOUR DOG TO COME WHEN CALLED

It is *very* important to teach your dog to come when called. You can accomplish this in one lesson if you treat it as if you were teaching your puppy a new trick. If you make it routine after that, it will make formal training much easier.

Give your puppy the Stay signal and go back three feet. If someone is nearby, ask her to hold the puppy until you call him. Say the puppy's name and the word "Come" in a happy tone of voice. When the puppy runs to you, say "Sit" and push him into a straight Sit. Give him a reward treat for doing so. Repeat this procedure several times and gradually increase the distance between you until you are twenty feet away from him.

It is important that he learns to Stay when he is told, Sits straight in front of you, is praised and petted, and gets his treat reward immediately. Puppies learn this lesson quickly and will learn to do it without anyone holding them after ten minutes.

It is a valuable lesson that a puppy can learn after he is eight weeks of age.

TEACHING YOUR DOG TO WALK ON A LEASH

I put a thick round nylon choke collar on a puppy when he is about three months old, and this is the only type of collar that he ever wears. To form a collar, just slip the cord through one of the rings and draw it all the way through to the other ring. If you do not wish to use the collar as a choker, you may attach your leash to the stationary or dead ring. If fitted properly, that is a very comfortable collar for a dog to wear as it is never rigid but is strong and lightweight.

Dogs that are permitted to run free should wear a leather or nylon buckle collar. The dog's license and rabies tag should be attached to it. A dog running in the woods or jumping against a picket fence could catch his choke collar and hang himself. A loose, ill-fitting choke collar is dangerous, and many dogs bite at a collar that hangs too low on their necks. It can get caught in the dog's mouth, and no amount of pawing or headshaking will free it. If any length of time passes before his predicament is discovered, the dog's gums may start bleeding, and he will have a sore, tender mouth.

When walking on a leash for the first time, a puppy may pick up the leash and carry it along. This makes it much more fun for him, so don't correct him. Hold the leash in your left hand and try to keep the puppy by your left side. If he moves over to the right side, guide him back gently and pet him with your left hand.

By reaching down and petting him occasionally as you walk along, and by calling him back to you when he runs out to the end of the leash, you will be able to keep him near you. The first few times the puppy is on leash, limit him to five minutes.

It is fairly easy to teach a puppy to walk on a leash. Use a lightweight nylon buckle collar and a five-foot leash. You can start training the puppy when he is three months old, provided you praise him in a happy tone of voice and make it a fun experience. Walk out in a field and make several turns. Each time you take a sharp right or left turn, give the puppy a tug with the leash, clap your hands, and laugh to get his attention. He will be willing to follow at heel if you make it interesting. Let him stop and smell a big weed or investigate a bush or stump, but then teach him that the word "Heel" means for him to stay with you. Each day he will do a little better. Soon you will not need to give him a little tug when you make a turn. You will get results if you slap your leg and persuade him to stay close. You must always show puppies exactly what you want them to do. They are willing to do anything if they think it is a game. The tone of your voice is most important; make it pleasant so your puppy will know that you love him.

TEACHING YOUR DOG TO SWIM

Not all dogs know how to swim, but it is easy enough to teach them how to do so. I have seen several older dogs jump into a swimming pool and immediately sink to the bottom. Someone had to jump in the water to pull them out.

When Hussan, Topper, and Arry were alive I lived in New England on one of the lovely lakes, and I taught each of them lifesaving in the water. After a long lapse of time I am now able to continue training dogs to work in the water. A few years ago I built a two-acre pond on my property and since then all of the puppies have learned how to swim. Once they learn how to swim, they learn to dive off our dock, retrieve articles from the water, and learn how to bring a supposedly drowning person safely to shore from the middle of the pond.

At first when teaching a puppy to jump in the water, the leash should be taut enough to keep his head from going under the water. Later, he won't mind dunking himself.

Summer fun! Wynthea's Elsie, UD; Wynthea's Big Foot (at five and a half months), Ch.; Wynthea's Julie, CDX; Wynthea's Elissa, UD; Wynthea's Jasper, UD; Can. Grand Victrix Ch.; Fara v.d. Erika-klause, CDX; and the author.

I had a narrow platform built one step down from the dock at the end of the fifty-five-foot pier. Stairs lead up to this platform so the swimmers can climb onto the dock without going in to shore. It is at the end of this platform that I lower a puppy into the water on leash, being careful to keep his head above water. The puppy is encouraged to swim toward the shore, and I hold the leash taut enough to keep his head above water. The experience is a pleasant one, and after it has been repeated twice, the puppy will swim to shore on a very loose leash. Then the puppy is placed on the platform and told to "Jump in" as he is guided forward with the leash. He soon gets the idea and is jumping in off leash on the verbal command.

The next step is to have him jump to a person who is standing in the water and learn to swim nearby him without scratching or climbing on him. Swimming is the best form of exercise, and once a dog has learned how to swim, he loves every minute of it.

There are many things to teach a dog in the water, and it comes under the word "fun." I taught my dogs to jump off the dock, swim out to the raft in the middle of the pond, climb the raft ladder that is vertical, climb the vertical ladder to the upper platform that is ten feet from the water, and dive on command. They all love to retrieve pond toys from the water. I also taught my dogs how to ride quietly in my canoe so that I could enjoy their company and they could enjoy riding with me.

Wynthea's Victor, UD, climbing the ladder.   **Reaching the platform.**

Diving into the pond.

Chapter 9

Practical Tricks

At first glance, these tricks may not seem to be worth your attention. However, if you will read this chapter you will discover that I have a definite reason for suggesting you include them in your dog's training program.

Each one will be of great value to you as the training progresses. By this I do not mean that it is necessary to teach your dog tricks in order to train him to be obedient or prepare him for the Obedience Trials. He can earn his Obedience degrees without any preliminary training, but it will take longer.

I look at it this way. The more exercises you give your dog to help him develop mentally and physically, the better off he will be. Compare the English student who studies only what is required of him with the student who not only keeps abreast of the required work, but also crams extra hours of reading into his daily schedule because he has a thirst for knowledge. Obviously the latter will soon be mentally superior.

This is equally true of dogs. If you want to give them the extra time it takes to teach them practical tricks or small chores, they will develop faster and become more responsive and alert to commands. They will gain coordination and agility, and the exercise will be good for them.

I taught my first German Shepherd these simple tricks back in 1941 before she was seven months old. I realized later that they had helped her to master the advanced work much more quickly. I have followed the same procedure with all my dogs, and I advise others to do the same.

Dogs that are alert mentally do not become bored. A wise trainer will prevent boredom by introducing a change of pace in his dog's exercises. Some dogs that are shown in Obedience become mechanical workers because their handlers have never taught them anything else. Dogs, like people, learn that variety is the spice of life. These Practical Tricks are the elementary steps in teaching a puppy the useful and practical exercises to come later.

When teaching your puppy some of these tricks, it is wise to offer him food as an inducement. Puppies are very fond of tidbits, and if they are rewarded with a dog cookie or a piece of meat, they will be eager to try something new. This applies to puppies only, because they become bored and restless very quickly; the food will maintain their interest until they have learned the trick. Later, when your puppy is older, he will be happy to do the tricks for praise alone.

"Speak." Topper of Wynthea, UD.

SHAKING HANDS

Shaking Hands is the prelude to the Stand for Examination exercise. It teaches the dog to accept the attention of strangers at an early age. It is essential for shy dogs.

It is a very simple trick and can be learned in one or two lessons. Start by having your dog sit in a corner; he is less likely to walk away. As you offer your hand to your dog say, "Shake hands," and touch his right foreleg. If the dog doesn't raise his paw, lift it yourself. Repeat this until the dog understands you. To make it easy, as you offer your right hand, gently shift the dog's weight over onto his left foot by pushing his shoulder gently with your left hand. As soon as the dog lifts his paw, praise him and give him a dog biscuit.

Have your friends shake hands with your dog so he will learn to do it for anyone. This trick is especially good for dogs that are shy of people. If the shy dog does not respond to the command, lift his paw yourself and ask your friend to take it. A shy dog will back away; put your left foot behind him to prevent this. Once a shy dog will permit strangers to shake hands, he will soon allow them to pet him.

ROLLING OVER

Rolling Over is excellent therapy for tense, nervous dogs. If they can be persuaded to relax by this exercise, formal training will be much easier.

Begin by having your dog sit, then having him lie down, and next pushing him over on his side. When the dog is lying flat on his side, say "Roll over," making a circular motion with your right hand. At the same time, grasp the dog's paw in your left hand and help him to roll over. Once he has rolled over, say "Roll back," and help him to do so as before.

Once the dog has mastered this you can vary the trick by saying, "Roll over and over and over," and then, "Roll back and over and over." Eventually you can give the dog the verbal command and the hand signal without helping him at all. Many dogs are afraid to roll over on their backs themselves because this places them in a rather helpless position. This will teach them to have faith in you and to overcome their natural reluctance to get in this vulnerable position. Be sure to praise your dog each time he performs correctly.

SITTING UP

Sitting Up teaches a dog to sit squarely on his haunches (see p. 40), and the dog that can Sit Up is less likely to Sit crooked later on. In the Obedience ring your dog will be penalized for crooked Sits.

This will be fairly easy to teach your dog, provided you always try it on a rug or a floor that is not slippery. Start by having your dog sit in a corner; persuade him to Sit Up by holding a choice morsel of food just above his nose. He will learn to maintain his balance if at first you let him lean a paw on your left hand. When your dog Sits Up, give him the food, and then praise him. Soon he will be doing this the moment you say "Sit Up" and hold your right hand above his nose.

Once he Sits Up in the corner, bring him out into the middle of the room. Go through the same procedure. Remember that dogs with long tails should always have them straight out behind them to help maintain their balance. Dogs that are fully trained will do these tricks without food as a reward.

SAYING HIS PRAYERS

This trick follows the last and is easily learned. Once a dog has learned to Sit Up, he will naturally come over to you if you are eating something and beg for a piece. If you are sitting down, he will Sit Up and place his paws against you. This is the position he should be in to learn this trick.

"Say Your Prayers." Wynthea's Topper, UD.

"Sit Up." Can. Ch., OTCH Wynthea's Joll vom Summerland, UDT.

Say "Stay," to the dog and gently push his head between his paws. Hold it there for a minute until you say "Amen." Then praise the dog and give him a biscuit. The dog will learn by repetition. Small dogs can do this trick by sitting on a chair and placing their paws on the back.

My first Shepherd always enjoyed this and would say her prayers repeatedly without being told if anyone was eating peanuts. She had a passion for peanuts and realized she would always get some with this trick for no one could resist her plea.

There is a very useful side to this exercise. A dog does not like to hide his eyes; he prefers to see what is going on. "Saying his prayers" teaches him to be obedient and gives you more control over him.

CATCHING A BALL

Dogs do not have good eyesight. My firm belief is that if you teach your dog to catch a ball, he will watch for it so intently that the exercise will be beneficial for his eyes. One of my German Shepherds became so adept at catching a ball that anything else in the air fascinated him. He would sit in the yard and watch a hawk circling in the sky, a plane passing overhead, or birds flying by. These innocent periods of watchfulness gave his eyes much-needed exercise. One of the prescribed exercises for nearsightedness is to look at an object close to you and then at one at a distance. Because dogs are notoriously nearsighted, this trick is an excellent method to improve their eyesight.

It will be easier to start in the house, because the dog will not be so apt to run away with the ball. I must caution you first not to use a ball that is too small for your particular dog; he may swallow it or get it caught in his throat. The exercise is perfectly safe provided the ball is small enough to be caught and large enough not to be swallowed.

To begin, have the dog Sit. Get him interested by pretending to throw the ball. Do this several times. Then throw it directly at the dog's mouth saying "Catch." The dog will make a grab for the ball, and if he catches it, praise him. Take the ball away immediately and try again. Remember to have him Sit each time. If you make this fun, the dog will soon be catching the ball and bringing it back to you each time for another try.

Once the dog has learned the trick in the house, move the game outdoors. This is a very good way to exercise the dog with very little work for you. A dog that will retrieve a ball in your yard will generally retrieve a ball floating in the water. The first time you try it, be sure to throw it near shore where the dog simply has to wade in to reach it. As he gets used to retrieving from the water, you can gradually throw the ball farther out. Swimming is excellent exercise for dogs, and retrieving makes it fun.

Many busy people who do not have time to walk their dogs find that retrieving a ball gives them sufficient exercise.

BACKING UP

This exercise is especially beneficial to the dog that will someday learn Utility. The dog will learn to Sit upon command at a reasonable distance from you. Even though your dog will Sit and Heel, it doesn't follow that he will Sit at a distance from you on command. By teaching your puppy this trick, he will learn to Sit anywhere. If you teach him to Back Up he will have no difficulty going away from you on the send-out portion of the Directed Jumping exercise. If he doesn't go out far enough, you simply tell him to "Go back." He will back up until you tell him to Sit. Next time he will go out farther of his own accord.

Once your puppy has learned to catch a ball, he can learn this trick. If you have made it a point to have your dog Sit and wait for you to throw, he now understands the word, "Sit." When your dog brings the ball to you, wave him back with your right hand saying "Go back," and after he takes several steps back, say "Sit." When he Sits, throw the ball. If your dog does not understand immediately, walk into him and push your knees against his chest, gently forcing him to step back. If you have a small dog you can push him back gently with your foot, but give him the hand signal at the same time so he will get used to it. After he has backed up several paces, say "Sit. Stay," return to your original position, and throw the ball. Always praise the dog. Repeat the routine until the dog understands.

My Topper picked up this trick practically by himself. After I got tired of throwing the ball for him I would sit down and read. He would come over and place the ball in my lap, back away, and Sit, waiting expectantly for me to throw it. We would play a little game. Sometimes I would pretend not to see the ball, and after a minute he would come over, pick it up, and drop it in my lap again. Then he would back up with quite a flourish and speak softly. This version of playing ball was so intriguing that I taught it to my other dogs.

One day while playing with a large beach ball, I threw it to my German Shepherd, Jerry. She bounced it back to me with her nose, and a new trick was born. After that she would keep the beach ball going back and forth by stopping it in the air and bouncing it back to me with her nose. She never tried to catch it in her mouth or to bite it, figuring in her own mind that it was too big. She was so eager to retrieve balls that she would dive under the water and retrieve those that wouldn't float. This was up in New England where the water was very clear. At times she would even dive in after a fish that she could see swimming by. She never was able to catch a fish, but she did corner a turtle against the ledge that bordered the shore and brought it to the surface. She played with the turtle the whole day as if it was her most prized possession. That night when we left camp I put it back in the water and it swam away, none the worse for its experience.

One day I looked up from my desk and noticed my Shepherd, Topper (named after my first Topper), sitting in the yard outside my window looking up intently at the house. Just then someone threw a ball to him from the window upstairs. He caught it and ran over to my window with it. As I was about to say something, a basket was suddenly lowered on a string from the window upstairs, passing by my window to the ground below. As I stood up to watch, Topper put the ball in the basket, and as it was pulled up to the second floor, backed up excitedly across the yard. Upon investigation, I found that my daughter was playing ball with him in this way.

Rather than run downstairs each time to get the ball, she had devised the idea of lowering the basket. Topper knew instinctively what to do, and though at first there had been a miss or two when the ball didn't land in the basket, he would pick it up and try again until he was successful. After a while he became very proficient. This little game is a good example of a dog's intelligence, for he was completely controlled at a distance. Topper was ten months old at the time, and by learning to play ball he had begun to think for himself.

JUMPING

There is no reason why your dog should not learn to Jump when he is a puppy. Once he understands the word "Hup," it can be used to advantage on countless occasions.

This trick is best suited for medium- or large-sized dogs, but many of the small breeds love to show off their versatility by jumping gaily. Large dogs should not jump the full height required in shows until they are at least eleven months old. When you are teaching him, do not ask your dog to Jump more than two feet. If your dog is small, begin by setting the jump at one-half the height required in shows.

For a large- or medium-sized dog, set the bar jump at twelve inches and keep the dog on a leash. Run up to the jump, say "Hup," and jump over it with the dog. He will learn faster if you jump with him the first few times. If your dog balks at the jump, lift him over with the leash the next time you run up. Soon he will be Jumping by himself as soon

"Hup."

as you run up to the jump and say "Hup." Next, teach the puppy to Jump by himself. Have him Sit about six feet from the jump and tell him to Stay while you take a position behind the jump. Say "Come. Hup," and clap your hands over the jump, beckoning him toward you. Try always to keep his attention focused on a point higher than the jump so that he will clear it.

Once the puppy has learned to Jump by himself, take off the bar and hold it in your hands. If he refuses, put him on leash and encourage him to Jump. From this you can progress to a short bar or a hoop or have him jump over your arm.

**Wynn and Can.
Ch. OTCH
Wynthea's Joll vom
Summerland, UDT.
Joll enjoyed jump-
ing through the
hoop.**

My three dogs, Topper, Hussan, and Arry, learned to play leapfrog after they learned to Jump. Arry would sit while Topper and Hussan would stand in position about twenty feet apart. Arry would jump over the other two, and then take a standing position while Topper would jump over Arry and Hussan. They became very proficient and would enter into the spirit of the game with much gaiety, producing gales of laughter from the gallery.

Chapter 10

Dog Shows

There are hundreds of licensed dog shows held throughout the country each year, so you should have no difficulty in finding one close enough to you in which to compete.

These shows are licensed by the American Kennel Club and are permitted to give championship points in the Conformation Classes and legs toward an Obedience title in the Obedience Classes. It is possible in one day at an all-breed show that holds classes both in Obedience and in Breed to gain points toward a Breed championship and a qualifying score toward an Obedience title.

Dog shows are put on for the individual dog clubs by licensed superintendents. A list of coming shows is published in the dog magazines. The American Kennel Club compiles this list and publishes it in the Events Calendar, a supplement to the *AKC Gazette* magazine. You will find the date of the show, the judges, the name of the club, the superintendent, and one of the officers and his address. Occasionally a dog club puts on its own show, and in this case you should write to its secretary for the premium list.

If you write to the superintendents listed in the Events Calendar and ask them to put your name on their mailing list, they will send you premium lists for the coming shows.

The premium lists will give you all the pertinent information about shows such as the location, date, judges, prizes, closing date, classes, and so on. You then fill out the form included in the premium list that asks for your dog's name, breed, registration number, birthday, sire, dam, breeder, class, and your name and address, and send it back to the show superintendent with the stipulated fee. Most shows also accept faxed entries with a credit card number, and many now take entries online. The premium list will give you all the pertinent information.

The fee varies from show to show, but is generally about twenty dollars for each class. The closing date is three weeks prior to the show, so you must plan to mail your entry a few days earlier to get there in time. A week before the show you will receive an entry slip which is your admission ticket. A schedule will also be included that will tell you at what time the various Conformation and Obedience classes will be judged, your dog's number, and the number of entries in each class. If the show is benched, your entry slip will give your bench number. (Shows licensed by the American Kennel Club are for purebred dogs of breeds recognized by the AKC only; dogs must be eligible for registration or an I.L.P. number.)

Point shows are held indoors and outdoors and are benched or unbenched. When they are benched it is necessary to keep your dog in a stall except when he is being shown or exercised. Dogs of the same breed are benched together in adjoining stalls which are separated by partitions. Take a rug four feet by twenty-six inches for your dog to lie on; he will be more comfortable. You will find a metal ring in the back of the stall and you may secure your dog to it by means of a bench chain. These chains are sold at all benched shows and come in different lengths. Dogs must be kept on leash except when being shown.

Match shows are put on by the individual clubs and can be entered the same day as the show. There are no championship points or Obedience credits given, as these shows are for practice purposes only. They are always unbenched, and you may leave when you wish. There are three kinds of Match shows. Plan A is given by the club that is trying to get permission to hold a Point show. The club publishes a premium list and conducts the show like a Point show. No points are given. Plan B is purely for fun, and the atmosphere is one of informality. You will find nonregular classes in Obedience at these shows, such as Sub-Novice (all the work is done on a leash), Graduate Novice (a Drop is included in the Recall exercise), and the Long Sit and Long Down, which are the same as in the Open exercises. The Graduate Open and Graduate Utility classes are for the dogs that have their degrees. Plan C Matches are in the nature of informal training classes. Any of the regular or nonregular classes may be offered. In addition, "run-throughs" may be offered where the exhibitor may do all or some of the total exercises from a given class. They are offered by all-breed clubs, and obedience clubs.

Novice handlers should try competing in Match shows before going into Point shows. The experience gained at Matches will be of great value to them later. If you want to know when and where there will be a Match show, ask someone who is participating in dog shows. They will be able to supply this information. In the Northeast area a Match Show bulletin is sent out each month that gives the Matches for the next two months. This handy bit of information is sent out by Myrna Lieber, Box 314, Massapequa, NY 11758.

In the Breed Classes a dog is judged against the standard of his particular breed, and the judge determines which of the dogs present is the best representative of his breed in type and temperament. The judge examines the dogs for soundness while they are gaiting and posing.

There are five regular classes in Breed — Puppy, Novice, American-Bred, Bred-by-Exhibitor, and Open, and the dogs and the bitches are judged separately. If your dog wins his class he will then compete against the winners of the other classes for Winners Dog. It is the winner of this class that will win points toward his breed championship. The bitch classes are then judged and the Winners Bitch is chosen. If there is a special entered (a dog that already has won enough points to gain his or her championship), he or she will now compete against the Winners Dog and Winners Bitch for Best of Breed and Best of Opposite Sex. When this is decided the Winners Dog and Winners Bitch will compete against each other for Best of Winners. If the Winners Bitch has earned more points than the Winners Dog, he automatically gains the same number of points by defeating her.

If he wins Best of Breed he is now eligible to compete in his Variety Group. There are seven Variety Groups and a miscellaneous classification for rare breeds. For instance, if you were the owner of a German Shepherd, he would be in the Herding Group. If by some good fortune you were to win this group, you could then show him with the winners of the other groups for the top honor, namely Best in Show. During this competition if your dog were to win over another dog that had picked up more points that day, this would entitle your dog to the same number of points. The largest number of points that can be acquired at one show is five, and if you have a popular breed of dog this means that a large number of dogs will be competing against one another. A dog needs to gain fifteen points in order to become a Champion, but he must have won two major shows worth three points apiece under two different judges.

The Conformation Classes have nothing whatever to do with Obedience, and a dog can become a Champion without displaying any signs of intelligence. The Obedience Classes have a definite purpose because each exercise clearly shows the dog's ability to work and obey under difficult conditions. If you have a purebred dog, it does not matter if he has a foul that would disqualify him in the Conformation Classes; in Obedience it is the dog's working ability that counts. Spayed or castrated dogs can be shown in Obedience. It is a pleasure to live with an obedience-trained dog when his good behavior is a way of life.

Obedience Trials are held in conjunction with most all-breed shows. There are also Obedience Trials held separately and sponsored by training clubs. The latter cater to the Obedience exhibitors and feature such niceties as large rings, close-cropped grass at outdoor shows, efficient stewarding, and an impressive trophy list.

There are three regular classes at an Obedience Trial: Novice, Open, and Utility. The degrees that correspond with these classes are CD (Companion Dog), CDX (Companion Dog Excellent), and UD (Utility Dog). A perfect score in each of these classes is 200 points, and in order to gain a qualifying score your dog must earn 170 or more points and more than 50 percent of each exercise. When you have received three qualifying scores in the Novice Class under three different judges, the American Kennel Club will send you a Companion Dog Certificate with the name of your dog and the title CD after his name. This makes it official, and you may now compete in the Open Class whenever you are ready. (A dog may continue to compete in Novice B until he receives a qualifying score in an Open class or until he has won one High in Trial.) You need the same number of qualifying scores to earn a Companion Dog Excellent and a Utility Dog certificate. Once you have the CDX title you may compete in the Open B Class as often as you wish, and you may go ahead and try your dog in the Utility Class. Later when he has his UD title you may wish to compete in both the Open B and Utility classes just for the fun of it. You can earn the title UDX (Utility Dog Excellent) by competing and qualifying in *both* Open B and Utility B, in ten trials.

Use the titles CD, CDX, and UD after your dog's name as soon as he earns them. They represent a great deal of work and are a badge of distinction. A very small percentage of the dogs in this country have earned the right to use them.

Once a dog has earned his Utility title, he may continue to compete in Open B and Utility B (if divided) to earn points toward his Obedience Trial Championship. He must accumulate 100 points by winning First or Second Place in these classes, and a total of three Firsts under three different judges, including a Utility First, an Open B First, and another First.

In order to accumulate these points, a dog must compete against other dogs who have already acquired their OT Championships and who are making a career of competing for points. This is unfortunate as it gives them an unfair advantage, and it discourages competition.

Chapter 11

Equipment

In the Novice Classes your dog will need a choke collar and a leash. When you compete in the Open Classes your dog will need a dumbbell similar to that shown in the photograph on page 107. He will retrieve this on the flat, which means he will get it in an open area where there are no jumps. Then he will retrieve it over a high jump. This is a solid jump made up of boards, and the correct height is determined by the size of your dog. Next he will jump over a broad jump, which consists of a maximum of four eight-inch boards laid flat and raised off the ground and telescoped in size from one to six inches. Again the number of boards and the length of the jump are determined by your dog's size.

In the Utility Class as in the Open Class, all the work is done off leash. You will need three white work gloves, a set of Scent Discrimination articles, a high jump which you will also use in the Open work, and a bar jump. The bar jump consists of two uprights which hold a wooden black and white bar. The high jump and the bar jump will be set at the same height, determined by the size of your dog. If you teach your dog to Track, he will need a tracking harness and a thirty-foot line.

When you buy a choke collar for your dog, be sure that it is the correct size. When it is pulled snug around the dog's neck, there should be no more than three and one-half inches left, including the ring. The chain links should be small for the small breeds, medium-sized for the large breeds. Don't make the mistake of getting a heavy collar with large links because you have a large or aggressive dog. The medium-sized links are strong enough, and when the leash is jerked the collar will tighten and then release itself immediately. The collars with the large links are too heavy on the dog's neck and often fail to release when jerked. The collar is designed so that when it is jerked it will tighten quickly and then release itself. This throws the dog off balance and reminds him to behave. The rest of the time when the dog is wearing a choke collar it should be comfortably loose. If your collar is too long, it will be useless and possibly dangerous, so take the trouble to get the right size.

I prefer to start all dogs, regardless of age or size, with thick, round nylon choke collars that are the right size. There is a proper way to put on the collar so that it will be most effective. The ring that can be drawn down from the stationary ring should point toward the dog's right shoulder. When the collar is worn in this manner (as shown in the photo on page 50), it can be jerked more easily and will release itself instantly. The collar can be made of leather, fabric, or chain, and nothing may hang from it.

This dog wears a choke chain collar that is too high on his neck and too tight. The nylon choke collar, lower down on his neck, is in the correct position and is the right size. It fits so perfectly that only the rings and a couple of inches of nylon are visible.

Some Obedience clubs and individuals recommend and use collars with clips on one end so that the dog is fitted with a tight collar that is kept high on his neck. Dogs are not permitted to compete in AKC Obedience Trials with these collars or prong collars. These collars are unnecessary. With the right training methods intelligent and humane trainers do not need them to train dogs.

The leash that I prefer myself is made of soft leather, one-quarter inch wide and five feet long. Any leash more than five feet in length is just a nuisance. I also prefer a small lightweight bolt clip. This leash is very soft and pliable but strong and durable. It is easy on your hands and will fit in your pocket. It is so light that your dog will be unaware that it is attached to his collar. Later, when this type of leash is removed for training off leash, it will make little difference to your dog because he has not experienced any pressure from a heavy leash. This is a subtle method I suggest you use to prepare your dog to Heel off Leash. If the dog begins his training with a light leash, it gives him the impression that he is free and on his own. By the time you advance to a point where you remove the leash, he will accept this next step without running away from you. There is no great change to attract his attention, such as removing a heavy leather lead which has been weighing him down.

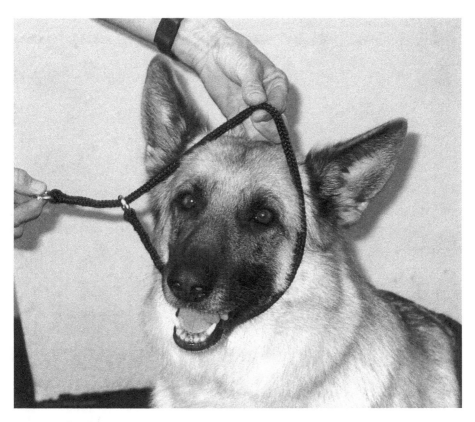

Putting the choke collar on the dog correctly.

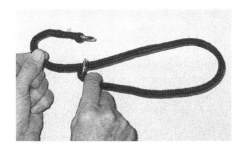

Pass the nylon cord through one of the rings to form a collar.

You will need a thirty-foot web tracking leash and a web harness. These items can be ordered through dog equipment catalogs.

You will need a dumbbell for the Open work, the small size for small dogs, the medium size for medium to large dogs. Great Danes and other breeds of their size will need the large size. Be sure that the centerpiece is high enough off the floor so that your dog can grasp it easily with his teeth. In picking up a dumbbell the dog thrusts his lower jaw under the centerpiece or uses one canine fang to lift it. The centerpiece should be wide enough

When you start competing in Obedience, you will be pleased to note that the rings are fully enclosed with gates. At one time just narrow rope was used. This made competition more difficult, because the people who sat along the ropes distracted the dogs. A few backward specialty clubs still use ropes, so you should practice with both. You can purchase ten-foot gate sections, like those shown here, at dog supply stores. I suggest you buy at least three sections. Teach your dog to Heel or Retrieve near the gates. They are invaluable in the Utility exercises. Practice sending your dog to the gates, and so on.

for your dog to grasp comfortably. The ends should be square so that it stops quickly when it lands. Paint the dumbbell white so your dog can see it easily. Many dogs fail to retrieve an unpainted dumbbell because the color blends in with the ground.

You will need three white work gloves for the Directed Retrieve exercise. You might as well buy three pairs so you will always have a clean set.

You will need a set of Scent Discrimination articles, five of leather and five of metal. If you are handy at making things, it is a simple matter to make the set yourself. Make five rectangular blocks of wood one by four inches for large dogs, or one-half by two inches for small dogs and cover them completely with leather, using small upholstery tacks or a stapler. For your metal articles, get some aluminum tubing and cut it the same size as the leather. Each set — leather and metal — should be numbered from one to five so they can be easily identified. If you make your own set, make one extra article of each kind so you can practice with them. Matched sets can be purchased at most shows holding Obedience Trials. The ready-made sets are available for any size dog, and come with twelve articles. Be sure to leave your two practice articles at home when you compete in a show.

The instructions and illustrations for making the high jump and the broad jump appear in Appendix B. The Working class hurdles that I designed are also described and illustrated. When I lived in New England, I had a carpenter make me a set of portable jumps from designs I had made. These jumps were three feet wide and very lightweight. It is imperative when training dogs for advanced work to practice in various locations with different distractions. These lightweight, portable jumps make this training much less tedious. Many people have copied my jumps, and they are now available across the country. Lightweight matched jump sets can be ordered at dog shows or through dog supply catalogs. They also sell nylon bags to hold them. This is a great convenience for handlers.

Try to assemble all your equipment before you begin formal training; you will need everything within a few months in any case. For instance, if your jumps are there when you need them, you can begin teaching your dog to jump whenever you feel he is ready. If they are not, you may lose two or three months' time waiting to have them built and painted.

My red tracking flags slip down snugly over steel rods. The other ends of the rods are pointed so they can easily be pushed into the ground.

My tracking poles are the same in size as broom handles, rounded on one end and pointed on the other. They are painted green except for the rounded end; this is red and is painted with fluorescent paint to make it visible to the tracklayer at a distance. Your poles should be numbered consecutively so that upon removing them the tracklayer will pick them up in the correct sequence.

Chapter 12

Formal Training

This and the following chapters will deal with all aspects of formal training (competitive training of a more serious nature), as a prelude to handling your dog in American Kennel Club licensed Obedience Trials.

Formal training may begin at any time after your puppy is fourteen weeks of age. It is both impractical and unwise to delay training until he is older. The longer you put off training him, the more bad habits he will acquire, and you will waste hours of training time trying to correct them. *However, it is imperative that you make the lessons fun and enjoyable.* You must always show the puppy what you want him to do. If you need to make a correction, your tone of voice should be enough. Where I say "jerk" your dog, I mean you should give a tug on the leash. And when I say "tap" your dog to make him Sit, it will be similar to a little push. I have trained hundreds of puppies, and it is such a joy to watch them respond to their training. My puppies and dogs love to be trained. They even love to watch their littermates being trained.

The Novice exercises are so simple that any puppy can learn them quite easily. Therefore, regardless of his temperament, start your formal training early, while your puppy is young and tractable. If you have followed my suggestions in chapter 8, "Preliminary Training," and chapter 9, "Practical Tricks," your puppy will be quite advanced.

Although it is best to start training early, dogs can learn these Obedience exercises at any age. I trained Champion Questor Maximian von Grossland, UDT, when he was six years old. He earned his Companion Dog Excellent and Utility Dog degrees with very high scores and passed Tracking with perfect form. This fine German Shepherd dog was always very young at heart.

My German import, Canadian Grand Victrix and Am. Ch. Fara von der Erikaklause, CDX, began her training when she was six years old. She earned her CD and CDX in three and a half months with four Firsts, one Second, and one Fourth, including a Highest Score in Show. She did this between having two litters. It is much more difficult training an older dog, particularly one who has lived with someone else and been abused by them.

A dog eight years of age should not be trained to jump. By the time he reaches eight he is beyond his prime, and jumping will do him more harm than good. He lacks the coordination, timing, and vigor of younger dogs, and cannot take the rigorous practice necessary to learn the advanced work. At eight, a dog has earned the right to take life easy.

Small dogs who are light on their feet are the exception to this. Many of these are still going strong when they are ten years old.

I never asked my dogs to jump after they were eight years old, but they still spent many happy hours doing simple errands and being generally useful. This satisfies their intrinsic need to be included in all family activities.

My method of training is to teach the dog advanced exercises as soon as he is ready to learn them. Novice work becomes very dull to a dog if it is repeated in a monotonous fashion week after week. One of the main reasons why handlers drop out of shows after obtaining their Novice degrees is because they have become bored and discouraged with the length of time it took them to master the basic work. For the same reason a high percentage of handlers drop out of Obedience Training Classes. If you follow the training program I have outlined at the end of this chapter, you will advance too rapidly for either you or your dog to get tired or discouraged.

Whether you are training to obtain titles for your dog, to enrich your life, or just for the fun of it, you can count on getting your CD, CDX, and UD titles within a year's time. It will be more interesting to give yourself a goal to shoot at, and an incentive is conducive to consistent practice. Any handler with a sound dog of any breed can accomplish this. In fact, you might do it in less than this. It is also possible to earn your Tracking title within the year if you enjoy working outdoors.

Once you have earned your Utility title, you can continue to compete in shows by entering the Open B and the Utility B classes. By qualifying in ten shows in both Open B and Utility B, you will be able to earn the AKC title UDX (Utility Dog Excellent). In all probability you will need no urging to continue; long before this you will have become an enthusiast.

This book has been written with the desire to show you how you can obtain high scores with precision handling and have fun doing it. A dog loves and respects a handler more for insisting upon perfection than for training him half-heartedly. Dogs have an enormous amount of pride and can appreciate a job well done as much as you can. It will require no more effort on your part to train your dog correctly from the beginning. By doing this you will avoid most of the pitfalls the casual trainer encounters. If you are shooting for the top, remember that no error is too small to correct. Dogs learn by correction.

I would suggest that you read each chapter through several times before going out to train your dog. The small details that will seem unimportant to you at first will make you an expert handler. When all these details are fitted together like a jigsaw puzzle, the result becomes training magic to the uninitiated.

The one question that I have been asked repeatedly over the years is, "How do you handle dogs so smoothly?" The answer is found in my training method which is an accumulation of a great number of training tips that I have perfected.

With this method your dog's spirit will improve. In fact you must continually strive to instill a feeling of fun in your training to keep your dog enthusiastic. In the normal process of training dogs I often improve their personalities and make gay, eager workers out of dullards. Improving a dog's character is the most difficult phase of training but definitely the most rewarding.

When I started training Margelen's Chieftain, UDT (Topper), I found that praise was as necessary to him as breathing. Throughout the years I have used praise as an incentive and as a reward in personally training hundreds of dogs. Knowing when and how to give praise is extremely important and an integral part of my training method. I have stressed the use of praise in my Obedience classes, clinics, lectures, and magazine articles and am glad to note that other trainers have gradually come to recognize its importance. It is gratifying to know that many thousands of dogs who are being trained in various parts of the country are now praised for their efforts because of my belief that this is a vital factor in training dogs.

Regardless of your dog's temperament, you should praise him for all good work and for every gallant effort; and praise should be used as an inducement to encourage better work. Do not be embarrassed if someone overhears you praising your dog. Be proud of it. You are setting a good example for him to follow.

Remember this while training. You are striving to perfect your dog's work every second you train; you want straight Sits, precision Turns, immediate response to commands, and you should always be watching to see that you get them. When your dog Sits straight, Turns, or Heels with precision, don't just make a mental note of it — tell him about it; praise him. You do not have to stop the work. If a Turn is good, keep right on heeling, but say to your dog, "That was good! Good boy!" Always watch for each opportunity, however small, to praise your dog for his efforts.

Another important phase of training is learning to correct your dog promptly. I have seen so many handlers look at their dogs as if they were stunned when a mistake was made, instead of applying correction immediately. Timing is important, and corrections and praise should be given instantly; always remember this important fact.

If you have read chapter 8 and practiced my training suggestions, you have discovered how quickly your puppy responded to this method. As we start formal training with your puppy, or with any new dog, I am going to suggest a reward system that will work. In training any dog it is important that you make it fun for your dog. You can accomplish this by using common sense. Use a happy, persuasive tone of voice, be exuberant and extravagant with praise and petting when he responds, and before you correct him, be certain you have shown him what you want.

Not every handler is able to use his voice to the utmost advantage to train his dog to respond quickly and willingly. To simplify matters I suggest you use a small treat advantageously. For instance, when you are teaching your dog the Recall, hold a treat up near your chest with both hands, where the dog can see it. This will induce him to hurry in and line himself up for a straight Sit. Tell him to Sit and once he Sits, and as you give him the treat, say "Good," then hold your hands down by your side. Use this reward often enough for him to form the habit of sitting straight. Then, every so often, just give him praise as a reward. You can't use food treats in the show ring, but you will notice people using an excessive number of them around the outside of the ring. It is unlikely the majority of these people could train their dogs with just a leash and collar.

At first, I would suggest that you train your puppy twenty minutes a day, five days a week. When he gets older, you could extend the time to thirty minutes a day.

The member of the family who is with the dog the most and who has the time to train him consistently should be his handler. When two people train the same dog, they do not handle him in exactly the same way, and the results are never satisfactory. Generally, when a dog is trained by more than one person, he becomes confused with the erratic handling. It is better to have one person train him completely; then he will work for anyone in the family.

It is entirely possible and practical for you to train your dog yourself without the help of a second person. I have done so repeatedly with success. In the Stand for Examination exercise, where a second person is involved, a member of your family or a friend can participate with excellent results.

If you train your dog by yourself, it is advisable to attend a few sanctioned matches to get his reaction to working with distractions. Unless your dog has a very steady disposition and is already acquainted with the world, he is apt to forget what he has learned momentarily until he becomes accustomed to the many distractions of show competition. Puppies especially need the experience of working among other dogs and people. Sanctioned matches offer a good opportunity to get this experience.

A sanctioned match can be entered on the day of the show; no points are given toward a dog's championship in Breed or legs toward his Obedience title. It is simply a practice run to get you and your dog used to show conditions.

Obedience Training Classes will not always afford the answer to Formal Training. Many classes are overcrowded, and advancement is pathetically slow. The result is that it takes many months to accomplish what you could have done at home in a few weeks. However, Obedience Classes provide the distractions and atmosphere your dog needs to become a steady worker.

I am wholeheartedly in favor of Obedience Training Classes, provided the type of training outlined in this book is maintained. If the classes are limited to twenty and show conditions are duplicated or exaggerated, the dogs will become very reliable. Many owners work better in groups and are not so easily discouraged when they see that other people have the same training problems. Group training can be fun if everyone is congenial. It is almost as enjoyable to see your friends make progress with their dogs as it is for you to progress with your own.

I have, in writing this book, stressed the best way to train and handle your dog so that your work will at all times be close to perfection. You will automatically become a good handler if you follow the instructions carefully.

Every July and August I used to give a five-day Obedience Training Clinic at my home for handlers and instructors. Every phase of Obedience training was covered thoroughly, and in great detail, for every handler wanted to learn my method so they could teach or practice it back home. Hundreds of people attended my clinics from this country, Canada, and South America, who wanted to share their vacation with their dogs and have the enjoyment of working with them in a congenial atmosphere.

Chapter 13

Regulations for Obedience Trials

When you have started formal training it is time to sit down and read the American Kennel Club Rules and Regulations for Obedience Trials. They are printed in booklet form, and the latest edition can be obtained without charge by writing for it (see Appendix A).

You cannot become a good handler, trainer, or judge unless you thoroughly understand the Regulations. Reread them occasionally: There may be minor points that you have overlooked. An expert handler should be as familiar with the Regulations as the judge.

Here are some typical questions that you may have in mind that are answered clearly and simply in the Obedience Regulations booklet.

> *Can a bitch in season be entered in an Obedience Trial?*
> No.
>
> *How old must a dog be before it can compete in Obedience Trials?*
> Six months old.
>
> *May a dog that has its CDX title continue to compete in the Open Classes?*
> Yes, in the Open B Class.
>
> *Could an exhibitor enter more than one dog in the Novice A Class?*
> Yes, a person may enter more than one dog in this class, but the same person who handled each dog in the first four exercises must handle that dog in the group exercises.
>
> *May an exhibitor enter more than one dog in the Novice B Class?*
> Yes, provided each dog has a separate handler for the Long Sit and the Long Down exercises.
>
> *If a dog failed an exercise, could the handler decide not to show him any further?*
> No, the dog must compete in all the exercises in his class.
>
> *Could a handler get to the show early and practice working his dog in the Obedience rings?*
> No, this is strictly forbidden.
>
> *Can the handler praise his dog at will?*
> No, praise is permitted only between exercises.

Is it permissible to jerk a dog in the ring if he isn't paying attention to his handler?
No, such action should be penalized by the judge, even between exercises, because the handler is disciplining his dog.

Is it permissible to shout at a dog in order to intimidate him into obeying?
No, this is another form of disciplining a dog by the handler and will be penalized.

Could a handler give a dog extra hand signals while heeling in order to keep the dog up with him?
No, any extra signals should be penalized by the judge. If the handler can't keep his hand in one position while he is heeling, he should be penalized for furtive signals.

Should a handler walk slowly so that his dog will be sure to keep up with him?
No, the rules specifically state that the handler should always walk briskly. Any handler that deliberately adapts a slow pace should be penalized.

If a dog is lagging, is it better for the handler to hop up and down on the fast instead of running?
No, this should be penalized by the judge. Every breed of dog can run fast; it is up to the handler to train the dog to stay with him before he goes to a show.

It will be to your advantage to understand the Regulations thoroughly. If you do, you may show your dog anywhere in the country with complete confidence.

Chapter 14

The Novice Exercises

HEELING ON LEASH

The Novice exercises consist of Heeling on Leash, Figure 8 on Leash, Stand for Examination off Leash, Heeling Free, Recall off Leash, Long Sit for One Minute, and Long Down for Three Minutes. To obtain your CD (Companion Dog) title you must earn some 179 points out of a possible 200 to qualify; and in doing so, you must earn more than half the points for each specific exercise. You will need to earn a qualifying score at three different shows under three different judges to gain your CD. This degree is equivalent to an elementary school diploma.

Heeling for your dog is your most important exercise; it will occur in Novice, Open, and Utility work. Heeling is not merely a routine where the dog walks at the handler's left side. It calls for perfect coordination between the handler and the dog, and the changes of pace, turns, and frequent halts must be so smoothly executed as to seem effortless. The perfect rhythm and complete harmony between a well-trained dog and an expert handler are beautiful to behold but, unfortunately, a rare sight. The dog must show his zest for the work by the rapt expression on his face and the proud manner in which he moves. After "Exercise finished," he should happily wag his tail. Many people think that because a dog wags his tail continuously he is an exceptionally happy worker. Actually this is often a nervous trait and not always a true indication of a dog's well-being. An expertly trained, intelligent dog knows as well as his trainer when he has done a good job; his eyes fairly sparkle with joy. The word of praise and the hand caress are nevertheless essential so that complete harmony exists between dog and handler.

You should practice in an area at least forty square feet, fairly smooth, with no trees or posts on it. You will progress faster and both you and your dog will concentrate better if you start your training in a quiet secluded area. A fenced-in area is ideal. When you have completed about eight weeks of training, start taking your dog to different surroundings to practice. At first it will be beginning all over again, but gradually your dog will become accustomed to working anywhere.

I have described the equipment you need, so assuming that you have the choke collar on your dog correctly and the leash attached, let us begin. Always start your practice sessions with your dog sitting at your left side, perfectly straight, as in the illustration. By

At the beginning, hold the leash in both hands for medium or large dogs. The leash should be tight enough for you to control the dog, but loose enough so there is no pressure on his neck.

If you have a smaller dog, hold the leash in your left hand, as shown, and control the dog with a wrist motion.

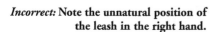

Incorrect: Note the unnatural position of the leash in the right hand.

"perfectly straight" that is just what I mean. It does not mean to have your dog's left foot ahead of the other or vice versa. Nor does it mean that the dog may slouch into a lazy Sit. Any dog of any breed can be taught to Sit straight if watched carefully and corrected. Nor may the dog lean his weight against you as many of the large breeds are prone to do. It is up to you to watch your dog constantly from the very beginning to see that all his Sits pass inspection.

I have always thought that dog training was fun. Because it is quite obvious to the dog I am training that I am enjoying myself, he or she takes the cue from me and looks forward to the lessons. Say your dog's name in a happy tone of voice, start walking briskly and reach down and pet your dog on his shoulder as you do so. After about ten feet, take a right turn, snap the leash if your dog isn't with you, laugh happily when he catches up, and pet him as you continue walking.

Let me explain here that your objective is to keep your dog by your left side regardless of the number of turns you make. If you did not teach him to Heel with you when he was younger, it will be new to him. This means you will be busy doing several things to keep him by your side. It is far, far more beneficial to the dog to make a great number of sharp turns during the first fifteen minutes of his daily lesson than it is to walk in a straight line or a circle. He will learn to Heel *much* faster if you do this.

Each time you make a turn, if your dog is not keeping up with you, you must snap, tug, or jerk the leash to remind him to stay with you. But, at the moment you do this you must call his name, remind him to Heel, laugh good-naturedly after the turn, and reach down to pet him as you tell him he is a good boy. Make about three or four turns and then have him Sit. Always pet and praise him. You should hold the leash short enough so that you can control the dog, but it should always be slack, never tight. He should feel *no* restrictions as he is walking along and there should be *no* pressure on his neck.

Practice heeling with your dog about fifteen minutes at a time. Make both right and left turns and frequently make about turns. In executing an about turn you simply slow down, pivot to the right on the soles of both feet, and reverse your direction. As you start to make the turn, remind your dog to Heel. In the beginning your dog will be forging ahead, so you will have to snap or jerk the leash to keep him with you. Later, when you become more confident, you can clap your hands on the turns to get your dog's attention instead of using your leash every time. You can also encourage him to stay up with you by calling his name as you tap your leg to keep him close to you. Keep showing him where you want him to be. Make any and all corrections quickly and guide him whenever necessary. *Use your voice effectively; let him know you love him.*

Try to practice every day and your dog will reward you by sitting automatically when you stop. If you have made his lessons enjoyable, he will start making the turns when you do. Test him to see if he will Heel with you when you hold him on a *very* slack leash. You will have to watch him very closely to be certain that he Sits perfectly straight each time he Sits. It will take him at least a couple of months to Heel with any degree of precision, even though you help him and show him what to do.

Give your dog the command, "Jack, Heel," and start walking forward on the Heel portion of the command. Always speak your dog's name first to get his attention, and give the command in a firm, well-modulated tone of voice; never use a loud voice. Remember — a dog's hearing is acute, and the high-pitched feminine shrieks are as unpleasant to him as the domineering masculine bellows. Learn to control the tone of your voice so that it sounds both pleasant and firm. Your voice is an important part of training, and it must carry authority.

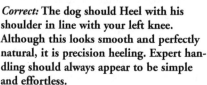

Correct: **The dog should Heel with his shoulder in line with your left knee. Although this looks smooth and perfectly natural, it is precision heeling. Expert handling should always appear to be simple and effortless.**

Incorrect: **Poor handling. The leash is held too tight.**

Regardless of the size of your dog, your pace should be brisk so the dog will not lose interest. This is the natural walking pace for most people, including myself, and the normal trotting pace for dogs. It is also the most invigorating. Be certain to walk in the direction you choose and do not let your dog take you where he wants to go. Remember during formal training that you are the trainer and you make all the decisions.

Walk along briskly and guide the dog back to you as often as is necessary to keep him by your side, and as you walk keep talking to him. When you snap him back with the leash, tell him to "Heel," and when he is by your side again, say "That's it. Good boy," or something similar. Encourage him frequently by reaching down to pet him while heeling. He may try to jump up on you when you pet him, so just say "No," and continue walking without breaking your pace.

After walking about twenty feet in one direction, make an about turn by pivoting to the right slowly on the soles of both feet and reverse your direction. As you make the about turn, say "Jack, Heel," and if he is not with you, give him a tug and then praise him when he is again by your side. Later, when you have mastered the turn, do not slow down but pivot and reverse at the same speed so the whole movement is smooth. By pivoting, you are giving your dog the time he needs to walk around you so that at the first step you take from the about turn, you will be together. The dog's shoulder should be on a line with your knee.

Make several right angle turns, snapping the leash if he is not up with you and praising him when he is. To execute a right angle turn, keep both your feet together and make a quarter-turn pivot to the right on the soles of your feet. Do not rise on your toes. This looks unnatural. Make your turns to both the right and left. If you catch your dog with your knee as you are making the left turn, he will soon learn not to bump into you or get in your way. If you have a small dog, check him on left turns by lifting your foot to block his path. He will then watch for these turns and will hesitate long enough so that you can turn together. Novice handlers quickly learn to negotiate the turns with ease if they use this method. Later, when they have become so proficient at turning that they do not think about it, they will automatically substitute shorter steps for the actual pivot. Be ready with a quick word of praise at all times.

Always watch your dog carefully and if he is not paying strict attention, make a quick turn. Always keep one eye on your dog so you can help him immediately. If you notice that your dog is heeling wide or lagging behind, slap your left leg and encourage him with your voice to Heel closely. When he moves up by your side, praise him. If your dog is heeling very close, this is excellent, for as you progress the dog will naturally move over slightly so that he will be heeling with precision. A dog that does this is eager to please, and as he becomes more confident of his work, he will realize it is not necessary to crowd

Incorrect: **Poor handling. Note the unnatural position of the left arm and the leash in the wrong hand.**

The advanced way to hold the leash when your dog is heeling nicely.

you. In extreme cases where a dog persists in crowding you after several weeks of training, you can correct him by lifting your knees high for a few steps. The dog will be bumped and thus discouraged from leaning against you.

From the very first week when you are teaching your dog to Heel, you should practice a change of pace. There is the normal pace, which is a natural brisk walk. There is the slow pace, where you move along slowly but not so slowly that your dog expects you to stop. Guide your dog back if he doesn't change to the slow pace, saying "Heel, easy." If he does change pace with you, praise him.

If you are changing from the slow pace to the normal pace, encourage your dog by saying, "Jack, Heel," in an excited tone of voice. Praise him when he responds. To change from the normal pace to the fast pace is a little more difficult. Your dog may not be alert enough at first to keep up with you. To execute a fast pace, you must run forward briskly. This does not mean you should run fast. Neither does it mean a fast walk or a pantomime where you go up and down and not forward. It is simply a natural running pace. Small dogs can run just as fast as you can, so insist that your dog keeps up with you. If you make a game of it, your dog will be eager to stay at Heel. By making a game of it, I mean touch your dog playfully, clap your hands, laugh a little, and encourage him with your voice so it is fun for him to keep up with you. Be sure to keep control of your dog. If he should start jumping when you start to run, say, "No, Heel," in a matter-of-fact tone of voice, but if he persists give him a quick jerk.

In a show the judge will tell you what to do, and you must keep moving at the pace he calls until he orders you to do otherwise.

When your dog is under control and will Heel reasonably well, it is time to concentrate on your own precision. Each time you start to Heel with your dog, take the first step with your left foot. Your dog will be aware of this because he lines himself up with your left leg. Later, when your dog is expertly trained, he will Heel with precision even though you start off with your right foot. This also applies to about turns and right turns. On either turn, take just enough small steps to negotiate the turn but immediately thereafter step out with your left foot. Don't bow, stop, nod your head, duck your shoulders, take one step backward, or leave one foot way in back of you on the turns, but do practice turns until you can execute them very smoothly and naturally.

As soon as your dog is heeling by your side satisfactorily, carry your leash in the advanced manner, as in the photograph on page 66. Hold the leash in your left hand and keep it in front of you, near your waist. Swing your right hand as you normally would when walking.

In training a dog, try to be as natural as possible. Avoid any exaggerated signals or poses. The primary purpose of this training is to teach a dog to be obedient under any conditions. If you are taking your dog for a walk on leash, the most natural and simple way is to hold the leash in your left hand. Your right hand is free to open doors, shake hands with friends you meet, or do a dozen other normal things. If you are carrying bundles with your right arm, your dog is completely under control close to your left side. Later, when you take your leash off to Heel Free, your dog is ready because he is now used to heeling without being aware of the leash. According to the AKC Regulations, you may hold the leash in either hand or both.

It is normal for your dog to stride out ahead of you, and he will be eager to do this. It is up to you to keep an eye on him at all times and prevent him from doing this. Keep your leash slack at all times and if you notice your dog trying to pull ahead, make a quick turn, call your dog's name in a happy voice, tap your leg to show him where he should be, and walk briskly in the opposite direction. Your dog will be eager to be with you, so take command of his training and keep him so busy with Turns and Sits that he will pay attention to you. This means you will not waste any time when you are training him. You will be moving continuously, keeping one step ahead of your dog.

Small dogs are very easy to train, and they enjoy the challenge of keeping pace with you. After fifteen minutes of heeling like this you will feel that you have really had a workout yourself. This is how I teach all of my dogs to Heel, and they get used to moving fast. All Heeling routines like this should, from the very beginning, incorporate changes of pace. In other words, try a normal pace, which is a brisk walk, then go slow for several steps and frequently try running a short distance. *Remember* that you *must keep a slack leash on your dog* at all times. Until you get used to working like this you might get winded. But it will be good for both of you and will build up your energy level.

During this Heeling lesson, you should be talking to your dog continuously, keeping him up with you, praising him, calling his name on turns to keep him alert, teaching him to Sit fast, petting him as you are walking, and keeping him so interested in the lesson that he will want to watch you to see what you do next.

Sitting at Heel is to be incorporated into the Heeling routine from the very first lesson, so the following instructions should be studied before you are ready to start teaching your dog to Heel.

TEACHING YOUR DOG TO SIT AT HEEL

This is comparatively simple and should be started with the first Heeling lesson. You should start the Heeling lesson by having your dog Sit straight by your left side. Have the dog Heel a short distance and then halt. When you halt, grasp the leash about a foot from the dog's collar with your right hand (holding him steady by your *left side* as illustrated), and very quickly reach down and give the dog a quick tap on his croup with your left hand. Do not move your feet out of position. *Immediately* pet the dog with your left hand and praise him. This should all be done with such speed that it will be almost one action. Repeat this until the dog Sits automatically.

At first, each time you halt and tap the dog, tell him to Sit. If you notice the dog about to Sit do not tap him but quickly praise him in a very pleased tone of voice. If your dog is not sitting automatically after a week, then you are not tapping him properly. A Novice handler is hesitant about tapping his dog and compromises by pushing him down with his left hand. If you do this, it will take you months to teach the dog to Sit automatically; and in the meantime, the dog will lose his respect for you as a trainer. When you tap your dog and praise him instantly, the dog's mind is on the praise. A dog respects authority when it is administered pleasantly. A correct tap is done with the fingers only, and you may practice on yourself by tapping your right hand with the fingers of your left hand. Think of the tap as a reminder. If you are right-handed, that fact will not lessen your ability to correct your dog with your left hand. After a day or so you will be able to use both hands with equal ease.

Tap your dog to make him Sit.

Immediately pet and praise your dog.

At first your dog may Sit wide; and if this is the case, it may be because he is heeling wide. Make the dog Heel in close, and his Sits will be straighter. When the dog stands straight in the Heel position, the tap should be on his croup just above his tail. Never step over to your dog as you stop in order to make him look good. You are fooling no one but yourself. Your dog must be taught to Sit straight wherever and whenever you stop, and he should be immediately corrected if he fails to do so.

If your dog is in close but swings his hindquarters wide to your left, tap him quickly on his left thigh as you halt. This will make him Sit quickly; at the same time it brings him in close and straight.

Do not tap your dog repeatedly to make him Sit. This sort of treatment is unnecessary. Your dog should be tapped just once, but it should be a sharp enough tap to make him Sit, and the praise should follow instantly. A dog will learn to Sit automatically in a few days if this method is used correctly.

If your dog forges ahead of you when you halt, this can be easily corrected. As you stop, grasp the leash about a foot from his collar with your right hand but *hold the leash steady by your left side.* This will prevent him from bolting ahead, and you can then easily tap his croup for a quick Sit. You must learn to be very fast on these corrections if you wish to get results. As soon as the dog Sits, *be sure the leash is slack,* and praise him. The dog should not be aware of the leash at all. As the dog begins to Sit automatically, you should gradually release all pressure on the leash until it is completely slack.

The common error that most beginners make is to permit the dog to walk out ahead of them when they stop. The dog is then out of reach, and they cannot control the Sit. You must hold the leash taut by your left side as you tap the dog to make him Sit quickly, and then praise him. Do not pull up or jerk on the leash to make the dog Sit. This will eventually cause him to back up a step or two to avoid the correction. It creates a bad habit.

If the dog leans against you when he Sits, step aside quickly so that he will fall over. Then ask him to Sit again, making sure that he Sits straight; and praise him. Sometimes if you give a slight nudge with your left knee, you can make him Sit straight.

To correct a dog that Sits with his hindquarters in back of your left foot, push him over into a straight Sit with the side of your right foot. If the dog has made this mistake once, you know it will happen again; so be prepared. Try to catch the dog just as he is sitting, as it is easier to direct the Sit with your foot. Another correction to try for this type of Sit or for the dog that Sits straight but a little too far back is to hold the fingers of the left hand out beyond the dog's nose and motion him to come up to your fingers. When he comes up by your side and Sits again, praise him.

If, when the dog Sits, he slouches over slightly on his hind leg, reach down and pull the offending leg out where it belongs. Or, if it is a very bad Sit, ask the dog to Sit over again.

Correct: **straight Sit.**

Incorrect: **sloppy Sit.**

Correct: **straight Sit.**　　　　　　*Incorrect:* **This Great Dane is not sitting up straight.**

Use the verbal command "Sit" each time you halt until you are sure your dog understands what it means. If, during the second week of training, your dog stands when he is supposed to Sit, command him to "Sit" in a quiet tone of voice. If he Sits, then he understands the Sit at Heel. He probably would not Sit anywhere else for you but at Heel position unless you have started his training with the tricks I explained in the section, "Teaching Your Dog to Come when Called," in Chapter 8.

THE FIGURE 8

In a show your dog will be asked to Heel in a Figure 8 pattern around two stewards acting as posts. You yourself will face the judge on the opposite side, in the center, in line with but not between the stewards. When beginning this exercise at home, use the posts from your bar jump. Place them about eight feet apart. Give your dog the command to Heel and go through the center and around the post to your left, then again through the center and around the post to your right. Then halt. This is the Figure 8. Practice starting off to the left, and then changing to the right to keep your dog alert.

Make this a game with your dog, talking to him, and coaxing him to stay up with you. If he lags at any point, you may need to jerk him at that spot the next time around. If he crowds against you on the inside turn, lift your knee. You should always keep close to both posts and encourage your dog to do the same. Practice your halts in various places around the Figure 8.

When practicing, always walk at a very brisk pace. Do not slow down to accommodate your dog on turns. If he lags, quicken your pace and encourage him to keep up with you. In shows, maintain a steady normal pace. Do not be discouraged if your dog lags on this exercise. It takes many hours of practice and many words of encouragement to do it perfectly.

When you compete in the Novice Class in a show you will do this exercise on leash. However, when you start Heeling off Leash, practice the Figure 8 each day both on and off leash. The Figure 8 off Leash is one of the exercises in the Open work, and you may just as well learn it early.

In keeping with my theory that Obedience should be a part of daily life, I teach my dogs to do the Figure 8 around other dogs as well as people. I want my dogs to get along together because I keep several dogs loose in the house. This teaches them to be friendly, to ignore other dogs, and to keep their minds on their work.

I have never had a dogfight in my home, although I have introduced dozens of dogs into the family circle over the years. The other male dogs accept the newcomer with friendly interest, and their attitude sets the behavior pattern for the new arrival.

The Figure 8 exercise has a very practical purpose. If your dog is heeling with you in a crowded area, you want him to stay close by your side as you pass people along the way. An untrained dog will very likely go to the left to avoid a pedestrian as you go to the right, and this tends to create an embarrassing entanglement. This is the reason why you should train your dog to stay close to the posts. Handlers who take a wide circle around the posts in the Figure 8 exercise have missed the point entirely. What good will this type of training be on a busy city street? If the handler tries to make a wide circle around every person he meets, he will be bumping into every other one. A dog that is expertly trained should be able to Heel on a busy street quite unobtrusively. He should unconsciously stick close by your side as you pass people, lampposts, or any other objects.

The author and her dog stand opposite the judge as they prepare to do the Figure 8 around her two German Shepherds, who are acting as stewards. *Left to right:* Wynthea's Roger, UD (DW); Wynthea's Donna II, CDX (DW), OTCH, OV; and Wynthea's Tony, UD (DW).

THE SHY, NERVOUS DOG

In teaching the high-strung dog to Heel and Sit you must never aggravate his temperament. Your manner must be one of assurance, your tone should be quiet and authoritative, and you should remember that this type of dog is very sensitive.

A shy dog will learn to Sit after two or three taps and can be encouraged to work by your voice. If he should Sit behind you, do not push him with your foot. Encourage him to Sit straight by your side by holding your fingers in front of his nose and asking him to step up into a straight Sit. Do not jerk him to make him Sit.

The shy dog is apt to lag behind because of his timidity. You must talk him up by your side continually, and slap your left leg occasionally to encourage him. Reach down and pet him gently as you Heel so he will be happy to be close to you. Don't be surprised if he ducks away from your hand as you reach to pet him, for he will be suspicious of everything. If necessary, hold him by the ruff while you pet him until he gets used to it.

The shy dog may be afraid of people, noises, strange places, storms, other dogs, or anything flapping in the wind. Whatever he fears must be overcome by working him in that environment.

You should always be calm and assured. A nervous dog is easily panicked. It takes the utmost patience and many hours of work to succeed, for you must first heal his mind before you can get through to him to train him. The dog must trust you completely, and if you make one harsh correction you may ruin your earlier work or add many more weeks of additional training before you regain his confidence.

Even when this type of dog is expertly trained he may someday be frightened into disobedience by an unexpected incident or an overwrought mind.

Praise, patience, understanding, and firmness compose the formula you will need.

I trained three dogs of this type (not Topper, Hussan, and Arry), and they each became top workers and won many firsts with very high scores. The judges and spectators admired their spirit and gaiety and never realized their true temperaments. It was a long, grueling process reshaping their personalities and giving them courage and fortitude. But I proved to myself that it could be done, and that satisfaction was reward enough.

However, there are shy, nervous dogs that never entirely overcome their fears. Despite the fact that they have been trained with kindness, praise, and understanding, there will be instances when they appear to be cowed. While the over-all improvement is about ninety-five percent, the true character of the dog will be evident when he shrinks away from being petted or approaches the handler timidly. To a judge this may look as if the dog has been harshly trained or overtrained. Nothing could be farther from the truth. A firm "No" given in a moderate tone of voice is the only correction necessary for this type of dog. The balance of the training is spent trying to encourage the dog to work, through patience and kindness.

THE ROUGH, AGGRESSIVE DOG

This dog, though rough and wild at first, can be a lot of fun once he starts to grasp his training. The method outlined below of bringing a very rough or tough dog under control is not to be tried on any other type. You must realize that what is good for one dog is entirely wrong for another of a different temperament.

If you have a large, strong dog over a year old that is very difficult to control, try this: Have the dog Sit in the Heel position. Take hold of his ruff in your left hand. If you grasp the skin below the dog's left ear, you can hold him steady while your right hand slides the choke collar under his chin and just in back of his ears. Next, Heel with the collar in this position and jerk the dog if he tries to bolt. In just one or two lessons the roughest dog can be brought under control with the choke collar up high. After this, leave the collar down in its normal position: The dog can now be trained like any other. If the dog should become obstreperous occasionally, move the collar up, and the dog will very likely quiet down without being jerked.

Once you have shown the roughneck who is master, he will respond quickly if you give your commands in a quiet tone of voice. This type of dog craves praise and can often be turned into a top worker by lavish praise when he is good and quick correction when he is bad. By correction, I mean a snap of the leash and a disapproving tone of voice.

The dog will not learn to respect you if you yell at him or speak sharply when you start to lose your temper. You must speak calmly, quietly, and with authority. It is amazing what you can do with these dogs with your voice alone. After a couple of weeks I have been able to take the leash off this type of dog and control him with my voice alone. Although I could tell from the dog's expression that he wanted to bolt, I could stop him from doing so by saying quite calmly, and in a matter-of-fact tone of voice, "No, Heel." The dog would meekly Heel along and I would praise him quietly. If the dog on an about turn would stand and look at me boldly, I would simply continue to Heel, beckon the dog with my left arm, slap my leg, and quietly tell him to Heel. This is appealing to the dog's finer instincts, and it works in 99 cases out of 100. If I had raised my voice or seemed the slightest bit unsure of myself, the dog would have bolted.

These dogs are so excitable that they keep jumping up once they have sat at Heel position. If the dog is beginning to get out of control, grasp his ruff and give him a sharp tap on the nose saying, "No, Sit, Stay," then hold him quietly for a second saying, "Easy," then praise him.

Dogs that are biters through lack of earlier discipline can be cured effectively. An older dog that has been allowed to run wild is going to resent any attempt to control him. If such a dog should try to bite you, quickly give him a sharp tap on the nose. If he snaps at you, give him a sharp tap under his chin. Don't do this slowly, or miss, or you may get bitten. This type of dog does not bite out of meanness, but only because he is fresh. You must tell him quickly that he is a bad dog and should be ashamed of himself. You should make it very clear to him that you are boss. Look him in the eye when you reprimand him. Be sure to praise him when he deserves it.

Friendly dogs that are somewhat rough and jump up biting the handler's hand while heeling should also receive a sharp tap on the nose. There is no excuse for such behavior, and it should be stopped. A habit of this kind can only go from bad to worse. Two or three corrections, properly administered, will correct this.

VICIOUS DOGS

There are some dogs that come under the above category, and no amount of training will make them trustworthy. You may teach them to go through the motions, but underneath the surface lies an evil disposition. If a dog bites without justification, you can tell by his expression whether he is mentally ill. Such a dog should never be bred, for he will pass his bad disposition along to his offspring. The wisest course is to have the dog put away before he injures an innocent human being or kills another dog.

Certain dogs do not respond to Obedience training because they are downright vicious. A woman stopped by one day and asked me to train her large male Boxer. She took the dog out of her car, and I proceeded to tell her how to teach him to Heel. She wasn't able to control him and asked me to demonstrate. She handed me the leash, and I walked forward a couple of steps as I told the dog to Heel. I was wearing a leather jacket at the time, and the Boxer suddenly lunged at me and ripped one side of my jacket, including the pocket, right off. I immediately held the dog away from me at arm's length. He was snapping and snarling, trying his best to bite me, but couldn't get close enough. I quickly jerked him up with the leash, and this made him Sit. This incident took all of my strength.

His owner had watched this without saying a word to the dog. Then I ordered the woman to take her dog and put him in her car. With the dog safely inside, I asked her why she didn't warn me that he was vicious. She related that he had bitten her husband and her neighbor quite badly. As a result, the authorities told her to have the dog trained or put down. Aware of this problem, she still didn't have enough sense to warn me. In her hands, the dog was a definite liability. I didn't think this dog would ever be trustworthy and advised her to tell her husband this fact.

THE RECALL EXERCISE

(You may start teaching your dog this exercise on the same day that you start teaching him to Heel.)

To start the Recall exercise, have your dog on leash at the Heel position. Now, with your leash taut in your left hand and held in back of your dog's head, step directly in front of him and face him. Continue to hold the leash taut in back of his head as you say "Stay" and give him the Stay signal with your right hand. Show your dog the palm of your right hand and have your fingers pointing down toward the ground. Hold pressure on the leash as you step back and, if your dog tries to follow you, hold the leash steady so he can't move toward you, and say "No, Stay." If the dog steps out of position before you can control him, say "No, Stay," and quickly put him back where he was originally. Put your right hand under his chin and push him into a Sit position. Next time, try to caution him to Stay before he actually gets up.

After the third or fourth attempt, you should be able to step back two or three steps. If he stays a few seconds, quickly call him to you, giving his name first and the word "Come." Don't worry about the leash at this point, but concentrate on gently putting your left hand under his chin to lift his head up when he comes to you, tapping him quickly on the croup with your right hand as you say "Sit," then petting him immediately with your right hand. Your left hand at this time should be scratching him under the chin. This should all be done very quickly and smoothly on your part, and after you have practiced it a few times it will become automatic.

When you have your part down pat, leave him again, give him the verbal command "Stay" and the Stay signal, and try to step back to the end of the leash. Do this gradually and, when you feel there is no pressure on the leash from the dog's trying to surge forward, call him. If he starts toward you, praise him and repeat the aforementioned procedure. If he doesn't move when you call him, give him a jerk toward you with the leash, then when he responds, praise him and let the leash go slack. You should practice Recalls like this until you can do it smoothly and correctly each time. If you do it right, your dog will Sit automatically in one or two lessons.

Hold the leash taut in back of your dog's head as you give him the Stay signal and the verbal command "Stay."

Be prepared to take your dog back to his original position many times before he really learns to Stay. It takes patience and persistence to teach a dog to Stay. When you have progressed to the point where the dog will do this nicely, you may go on to the next step.

Never give your dog's name when you order him to Stay.

If you have already taught your dog the preliminary training as outlined in Chapter 8, he will be so accustomed to responding to your commands that he will come to you willingly when he is called. If not, try this.

Put the tracking leash on your dog, give him the Sit-Stay command, and leave him. Walk away about twenty feet, and then turn around and face him. Call him to you and use the leash only if you find it necessary to guide him just as you did on the short leash. As your dog starts toward you, clap your hands and praise him. Try to get him to come in to your hands. As the dog learns to come in to your hands, you can eventually place them down by your sides quietly. Talk to the dog as he Sits so he will look up at your face. If the dog wanders, jerk the leash, order him to "Come," and praise him when he responds. Be sure he Sits straight. Repeat this until he responds nicely on the full length of the tracking leash. A straight Sit is often the difference between first and second place in a show. Insist upon straight Sits at all times.

The simplest way to teach a dog to Sit straight in front is this. If the dog swings his hindquarters out to your right, quickly push the side of your right foot against his hindquarter. It is easier to accomplish this if you catch the dog just as he is sitting. You can push him into a straight Sit. The same can be tried with the left foot. Do *not* kick the dog. Exert just enough pressure to make him Sit straight. If you push him too hard, you may make him Sit off-center. This method will save you from bending over every time to correct a crooked Sit. However, if you are training a shy dog, you will have to bend over and straighten him with your hand. A shy dog will become frightened if you use your foot. The temperament of your dog must be considered when giving corrections.

It is very important that you remember to be gentle with your dog when he comes to you. When you grasp his ruff or hold him under the chin, do so very gently, just enough to hold him steady. He should be aware of a tap to make him Sit, but the praise and petting should follow so quickly that the dog will remember to Sit next time.

When you are teaching your dog the Recall exercises, remember to use the reward system I mentioned earlier in Chapter 8. Your dog will be happy to hurry in to you and Sit if you give him a treat reward. Be sure to hold the treat up near your chest to encourage him to Sit straight. You will eliminate dozens of problems if you use this reward and praise wisely. Whenever you give your dog his dinner, ask him to Sit first. This way he will understand the word "sit" as well as his name.

Encourage your puppy to come in to your hands on a loose leash. Never pull your puppy in to you on a tight leash as if you were hauling in a fish.

Insist that your dog Sit perfectly straight in front of you each time he comes to you. Your hands must be placed down by your sides whenever the dog returns to you.

The tone of your voice is very important at this time. When you call your dog, raise your voice just loud enough for him to hear you and make it pleasant, but firm. Do not yell at your dog in a domineering tone or a high-pitched shriek, or he will want to go in the opposite direction. And do not say "Stay" in the form of a question. You are not asking him to Stay; you are ordering him to do so.

When your dog has mastered the Recall on the long tracking leash, you may go back to the short leash. Those of you who have done the preliminary training, or are training puppies, may find that this is your next step. Have your dog Sit at Heel position, give him the verbal command and the signal to Stay, and leave him and go to the end of the leash. Always precede the verbal command "Come" with your dog's name. Besides the fact that your dog should learn his own name, this will get his attention. Unless you have your dog's undivided attention, you are not going to be successful in training him. Call your dog, and when he is coming to you, run backward, throw the leash off to your left side, clap your hands, and encourage him to come directly in front of you by bringing your hands in close to your body. Gently guide him into a straight Sit. If he doesn't Sit automatically, tap him on his croup, then praise him and pet him.

If your dog has shown no tendency to run away when you call him, it is time to practice the Recalls off Leash. Continue to use treats as a reward for Recalls and straight Sits in front. This works so well that you might be tempted to overdo it. You will be able to use this reward when you do ten-, twenty-, or forty-foot Recalls, so do not use it every time. For an especially correct Recall and a straight Sit in front, give him the reward. However, if he has a sloppy or crooked Sit, correct him and make him do it right. He will soon realize that he will only get a reward when he has earned it. Dogs are quick to notice things like this. When your dog has learned to Sit straight most of the time, give him a sincere word of praise instead of the treat. The dog that prides himself for a straight Sit will appreciate your kind word just as much as a treat.

If your dog is doing twenty-foot Recalls off Leash, it is time to try the next step. When you call your dog at twenty feet, do not run backward when he is coming toward you. It is time that he learned that you are going to stand still, and he will have to Sit straight or be corrected. When you command your dog to Come, the dog should be taught that this means to Come and Sit straight in front of you. No other command should be used. Repeat "Come" if it is necessary.

Do not step over to your dog if he is coming in crooked. Stay where you are and make him come to you. Then, straighten his Sit before he Sits. You should notice if your dog is standing at an angle when he is in front of you; if so, quickly tap him on the hindquarter with your hand or push him over with the side of your foot so he will Sit straight. If he comes in too fast, tell him to Sit when he is about two yards away from you. This will slow him down so he will Sit directly in front of you. If he comes in too slowly, make it more fun; call to him encouragingly and clap your hands. Sound very gay and cheerful and laugh a little.

Up to now the different steps in teaching a dog the Recall have taken about three weeks. Any handler with a new dog who is following my method in its entirety can accomplish this very easily. However, if you have a dog who is being retrained, an older dog who has acquired bad habits through lack of training, a hard-headed dog who has inherited the inclination to be stubborn, a bright dog who has outwitted his inept handler who neither understood nor controlled him, or a dog who has been force trained with a cruel method, it will take about twice as long to train him because one must first gain the respect and trust of the dog and, through the correct training method, build a sound foundation for intelligent communication.

The same method should be employed to teach one of these dogs the Recall, but the handler must be very firm and insist that the dog obey the first command. If the dog is told to Stay and he disobeys the command, the handler should walk toward his dog, give him a tap on his nose as he calmly but firmly says "No, shame," and puts him back where he was. The correction should be given at the point where the handler meets the dog. The exercise should be repeated immediately. If the dog doesn't come the first time he is called, clap your hands and give him the treat reward when he responds. He will be willing to come the first time after that.

Sooner or later the dog you are training will run away from you. I always like this to happen in the early stage of training so the dog can get this normal phase out of his system and get back to the business of learning. In the very beginning if your dog runs away from you but returns after you have called him two or three times, you should praise him. Later if he runs away and refuses to come after you have called once, you should go after him. Follow him until you corner him, clip the leash on his collar, say "Come," jerk him toward you as you run backward a few steps, and repeat this four or five times. Then do a Recall and praise him if he responds. If he runs away more than once, keep your leash out of sight when you go after him or he will associate the leash with the correction. Seeing the leash might make him hesitate about coming to you. If you kneel down when you call your runaway dog it is more likely that he will come to you. The dog assumes that you are friendly if you are in this position.

About the second week of training your dog to do Recalls try a Finish every third Recall. Watch the dog carefully and insist upon a straight Sit in front and at Heel position.

Do not let your dog bump into you when he comes in. If he nudges you in a show he will be penalized. This method of gently holding his head up with your hand when he comes to you will teach him where he should Sit. Dogs are not permitted to Sit between their handlers' feet as small dogs are prone to do. Your dog must Sit close to you, in front of your feet, without touching you, and you should be able to reach his head easily. If he Sits straight in front of you but so far away that you cannot reach out and touch him without moving a foot or stretching forward, he will fail the exercise.

Now try thirty-foot Recalls and, as your dog improves, increase the distance to forty or fifty feet. By this time you should incorporate the Come signal with the verbal command. As you stand with your arms down by your sides, raise your right arm out shoulder high and then sweep your right hand in to your chest. Then drop your arm to its original position. Once your dog has learned this signal, which you will use later in Utility, return to the verbal command. Use the signal often enough to make sure the dog retains it.

It is about the sixth week in your training schedule, and you should be concentrating upon your dog's precision in coming and sitting in front of you. It is possible that he doesn't know what Come means, and just trots toward you when you called without realizing that he must Sit very straight in front of you. To help him learn where he should Sit you should now practice angle Recalls with him. After you leave him, take a position that is not directly opposite him, but at a slight angle. When you call him to you, motion him into position with your hands and repeat the command "Come" so he will associate the word with the straight Sit. Try this repeatedly at different angles and from different directions so he will become proficient at coming to you and positioning himself for a straight Sit in front of you. When he will straighten his Sit in front of you when you say "Come" or motion to him with your hand, then you know he understands what is expected of him. An expertly trained dog will execute the Recall even though his handler has his back to him. This dog will prove that he understands the command and is not merely ring trained. When you have reached the point in your training where you can control your dog with your voice or a slight motion, you will experience the thrill of working together as a team.

Each time you call your dog, remember to place your hands down by your sides. The rules require that you hold your hands in this position whenever your dog is returning to you. If you use my method of training to teach your dog the Recalls, you will find that he will be looking up at your face, and he will center himself in front of you as he does so. If your dog tries to nudge your hand as he is going to Heel position, just press your hand flat against your leg, and he will gradually stop this.

Practice your Recalls in various locations until you feel that your dog will obey you anywhere. If you do not trust him at first in a strange place, use the tracking leash, then let him drag the short leash, and finally try him off leash. Use both the signal and the verbal commands until the dog is responding with precision.

When he is close, guide him into a straight Sit with your hands and, as he looks up, encourage him with your voice saying "Good, Come."

Try angle Recalls. Stand facing away from your dog. Hold your hands out to guide the dog to you as you say "Come."

Try the same thing without using your hands. Control him with your voice.

Keep his attention on you as you talk to him.

Dog Sits straight and he and his handler smile happily.

TEACHING YOUR DOG TO GO TO THE HEEL POSITION

Once you have learned the following exercise, you will be able to use it to good advantage if your dog Sits crooked when heeling. The Finish exercise will be used many times throughout the Novice, Open, and Utility Classes. In every exercise where the dog comes and Sits in front of you, he will be asked to Finish (go to Heel). He should learn to do so smartly and with precision.

To begin this exercise, step directly in front of your dog and face him. Hold the leash in your left hand, palm down, about a foot from the dog's collar, as illustrated. Keep the right foot stationary while you take one step back with the left foot. As you step back, put most of your weight on your left foot, give the dog a sharp jerk, and say "Hussan, Heel." The jerk should propel the dog past your left side, at which point you give him another jerk, which makes him turn to his left toward you and brings him into the Heel position. Switch the leash to your right hand, but hold it taut by your left side. If the dog refuses to Sit, give him a quick tap on his croup with your left hand and then pet him with your left hand and praise him. He should now be sitting straight by your left side. If the dog Sits with his hindquarters out to the left, tap him on his left thigh; this will bring him in close.

The important thing to remember in teaching your dog this exercise is to give him a quick jerk past your left side. Do not pull him around on a tight leash or he will learn to hate the exercise. If you pull him or drag him around, he will balk and probably refuse to move. If you do get him to move, he will get into the habit of moving slowly and half-heartedly. The jerk will teach him to move fast and get him back far enough so he has room to turn, take three steps, and Sit next to you. Do not let your dog anticipate the finish by moving when you speak his name; he must wait for the "Heel" portion of the command.

When the above exercise is performed correctly, it takes about three seconds. Most dogs learn this exercise after six or seven attempts. When your dog begins to understand, you will find that he doesn't need the second jerk, for he will walk right into the Heel position. You must praise him extravagantly when he Sits so he will enjoy the exercise.

After the sixth attempt, see if your dog will do the exercise without being jerked. Try guiding him past your left side with the leash held in your left hand, help him turn toward you and walk up by your side, then have him Sit and praise him. If he stops before he is completely past your left side, quickly guide him all the way back telling him to "Heel." When a dog goes halfway back and makes a shallow turn, he Sits with his hindquarters out to the left. Only the toy breeds can turn in a small space. The larger breeds must, out of necessity, go past your left side in order to have room to turn completely around toward you, reversing their direction and taking the two or three steps that will bring them in line for a straight Sit at Heel position. If you insist upon the dog's going far enough back each time you try the exercise, he will soon get the idea.

You will soon find that you rarely ever need to snap him back with the leash. However, as he becomes proficient, do not step back but be sure that he goes past your left side, or he will turn too quickly and Sit crooked. Insist upon a straight Sit every time.

Teach your dog to respond to the signal or the verbal command. The signal is a quick sweep back with your left arm. Because the dog is already used to the downward sweep when you jerk him back on leash, he will readily understand what you mean. This is one of the signals you will use in the Utility work. Keep your right arm folded in front of you out of the way. If your right arm is hanging down by your side, it will attract the dog's attention, and he may start to the right.

Hold the leash taut in your left hand about a foot from your dog's collar.

When you say "Joll, Heel," jerk him back past your left side as you step back with your left foot.

Tap your dog to make him Sit.

He should turn in toward you and, as he does, bring your left foot back in line with your right. The leash should be slack at this point.

He Sits.

Immediately pet and praise your dog.

There are other methods of teaching a dog to go into the Heel position that are accepted in shows, but this is my preference, and it is the most natural. With the idea in mind that your dog will be your companion, this method is the most practical. If, for instance, you were shopping and had your arms full of bundles and the dog stepped out ahead, you could tell him to go Heel, and he would do so very simply and smoothly. If, on the other hand, the dog was trained to go to your right and get to the Heel position, he would get you entangled in the leash.

If you wish to retrain a dog who has been taught to go past his handler's right side to Finish, use the same method to keep your right arm folded in front of you until the dog is doing the exercise correctly. The dog will follow your hand signal. A dog can be retrained to do the left Finish in one lesson. However, it may take the handler several weeks to break his own habits.

Beginners will have difficulty with this exercise if they pull their dog back instead of jerking him. The leash should be slack as soon as the dog is jerked, but the jerk must land the dog past your left side. Then the dog will turn and walk up into Heel position and Sit. The dog should be praised the very instant he Sits. The important point to remember in teaching a dog to Finish is that it requires speed. The Jerk Back, the turn, the few steps to reach Heel position, the Quick Sit, and the praise should be accomplished with such alacrity that it is almost one motion.

Once the dog is trained, have him Finish from different positions. Have him Sit at Heel position and suddenly take a ninety-degree turn to the right as you tell him to Heel. Don't step out to do this, just move your feet in the same spot. Now try a ninety-degree turn to the left and stay in the same spot by pivoting on your right foot and stepping back slightly with your left. In both instances make the dog move swiftly. He will have to get up and go to Heel all over again. If you practice this now, your dog will be partially trained for the Directed Retrieve exercise in the Utility Class.

This exercise should not be practiced for too long a period of time, as it makes the dog start anticipating. Dogs who are trained to Finish every time they are called will anticipate the Finish and fail to Sit in front of the handler. This error can be avoided by doing three or four Recalls to every Finish at first. Later, when your dog is trained, you won't have this problem.

At Obedience Trials I always notice dogs who Sit slowly throughout the various exercises. This is caused by the handler who has inadvertently taught his dog to Sit slowly by pushing his rear end down. The dog forms the habit of sitting slowly, and later the handler places the blame on the dog when in reality, it is his own fault for training his dog incorrectly.

If you want your dog to Sit quickly, my method of switching hands on the leash, quickly tapping the dog's croup, and immediately petting him, will give you a fast-moving dog. This method is particularly effective when the dog is heeling or finishing.

STAND FOR EXAMINATION

(As soon as your dog will Sit automatically at Heel, and Stay upon command, he is ready to learn this exercise.)

The Stand for Examination exercise teaches your dog to accept the attention of strangers in a quiet, friendly manner. It is also of great benefit to the dog that is shown in the Conformation Classes. A well-behaved dog who will hold his pose is much more likely to attract the attention of the judge. Many people who show dogs in the Conformation Classes have objected to Obedience Training on the grounds that the dog automatically Sits when the handler stops. This may be true in some cases, but when the following method is used, there is no danger of that. You simply give your dog the Stand-Stay signal and walk him into the pose suitable for his particular breed. Now, your dog is set up for the judge to admire, and it has all been done very smoothly.

When I show my dogs in the Conformation Classes I find this training gives them a decided advantage over the untrained dogs. My dogs will not only walk into a Stand, but will hold the pose indefinitely.

To teach the dog to Stand, start heeling at a normal pace and then take two slow steps. At this point quickly bring your right hand down in front of the dog's nose with the fingers outstretched and pointing down, and tell the dog to "Stand, Stay" in a firm tone of voice. As you do this, quickly move out to the end of the leash, which you are holding in your left hand. Stay there for a few seconds. Then, as you move back to the Heel position, give the dog both the verbal and signal commands to Stay. Extend your left arm and hold the leash on the dog's right side as you walk around his left side then in back of him and so into the Heel position. Stay there a few seconds, praise him, and then ask the dog to Heel a few steps. With some dogs, it may be necessary at first to hold the leash taut in the left hand to prevent them from moving forward. This should be done as you give the hand signal to Stay. Be careful not to jerk up on the leash or you will make the dog Sit.

From the moment you tell your dog to Stay, he is not to move his legs or body out of position. If he should move at first, which is normal, tell him to "Stay." If he tries to move, say "No" firmly.

If your dog Sits as you leave him, you may be too slow in giving the hand signal and stepping away. This must be done quickly. If he still continues to Sit, try this: Reach down with your left hand if he is a large dog and hold his right hind leg as you tell him to "Stand, Stay." Then repeat the Stay command and move away. With a small dog, just place your foot under his stomach to prop him up. Do not kick him; hold your foot there while you command him to "Stand, Stay" again. Your dog may try to turn in a circle as

"Stay." Can. Ch. OTCH Joll von Summerland, UDT.

If you have a small dog, hold the leash taut in your left hand and place your left foot under your dog's stomach to prevent him from sitting as you give him the signal and verbal command "Stay." At first, bend over this far to give him the signal; later, when he is trained, it will not be necessary to bend over to give him the signal.

you return to him. If he does, bend over and hold his right hind leg with your left hand as you quickly walk back around him. If you hold your dog's hind leg, it will prevent him from walking or sitting.

If your dog should Sit when you return to the Heel position, make him stand again and walk in circles around him until he remains standing. If, when returning to your dog you will stand there for a few seconds, he will soon realize that he is not to move until you give him the command to Heel. Caution him to "Stay" if he tries to move.

If you are training a small dog, it is completely unnecessary to bend over to give him the Stay signal. Teach your dog to look up at you in the early stages of his training and later, when you start his advance work, it will be much easier. Give the signal as illustrated and, if your dog ignores it, quickly correct him. You may have to correct him several times in the beginning, but it will be well worth it to gain his attention. When a handler bends way down to give his dog a signal, it is a sign that the dog is not paying attention and an indication of inferior training and handling.

The shy dog must learn to accept the attention of strangers while he is sitting before he can go on to the aforementioned routine.

When your dog has reached the point where he will Stay in position until you return and tell him to Heel, you may go on to the next step. Now, when you go to the end of the leash, drop it on the ground and wait there a few seconds. Next, step up to your dog and, as you tell him to Stay, run your hand over his head, shoulders, back, and croup. Circle around the dog and go back to the leash and pick it up. Then return to the dog, as in the illustration. If the dog moves one leg at any time, say "No, Stay," and place his leg back in its original position.

When the dog has mastered this phase of the exercise, it is time for you to ask some-one strange to him to go over him as would an Obedience judge while you hold the leash. When the stranger has finished examining your dog, return to him by holding the leash in your left hand and walking around and in back of your dog's forelegs. If you return and stand ahead of your dog he may feel he should step forward to be with you. Stand there for five seconds before you tell your dog to "Heel." Praise him as you move forward. In a show, you are not supposed to move forward until the judge says, "Exercise finished," which is approximately five seconds. If the dog were to move when you returned to Heel position, he would be penalized. If your dog growls or shies away from a stranger, the correction should be given immediately to be effective. The dog that growls should receive a sharp tap on his nose as you say "No, shame." The dog that shies away should be put back in position quickly and cautioned "No, Stay." You will probably have to repeat this exercise many, many times before the dog will stand quietly and let a stranger examine him, but he will gradually reach the point of perfection.

When your dog is very steady on leash and will stand quietly every time a stranger examines him, you may remove the leash. This exercise will be performed off leash at shows. Give your dog the command "Heel," and walk forward a few steps. Notice when he puts his weight on his right front foot, for his left foreleg will be raised off the ground at this time. Quickly give him the Stay signal and say "Stay," and he will place his left foot in line with his right. Practice this until you both do it smoothly. After you have told him to Stay, walk out at least six feet from him and turn to face him. The judge will examine your dog and then ask you to return; you will do so by walking around and in back of your dog and into Heel position. After the judge says "Exercise finished," you may praise and pat your dog.

It is permissible to pose your dog by hand, but I think this encourages poor handling. Why fuss over your dog, adjusting each leg, etc., when you can walk him into a Stand very smoothly and expertly? You will be way ahead of the game if you teach your dog to Stand this way. Beside the fact that this method of handling is far superior to any other, it is also the quickest and most practical. By teaching your dog the Novice Stand this way, you have also taught him the Stand-Stay signal you will use later in the Utility exercises. This is another instance where expert training improves your handling.

As you walk forward slowly, quickly hold the leash taut and give your dog the Stay signal and the verbal command "Stay."

At first, when you return to your dog, hold your dog's right hind leg so that he won't move or circle.

Give the Stay signal as your dog is bringing his left foot up in line with his right. This method looks smoother than any other. It is perfect teamwork and expert handling.

In the Novice Class, the judge is expected to touch only the dog's head, body, and hindquarters. In the Utility Class, the judge is expected to examine the dog as in the Conformation Classes. This means he will approach the dog from the front and go over him with his hands. He is not supposed to examine his teeth or testicles.

If you plan to show your dog in the Conformation Classes, I believe you should teach your dog to stand quietly while you examine his teeth, and you can learn to do so without putting your fingers in his mouth. Wait until your dog can perform the Stand for Examination very well; then when you start to go over him, open his mouth to examine his teeth. Place your right hand over your dog's nose, lift his lip up on one side with your fingers, and on the other with your thumb to expose the teeth. Then draw the lips back to show the front teeth and bite. This should all be done quietly and gently as you talk calmly to the dog. If the lips are drawn back correctly, you will find you do not have to put your fingers in the dog's mouth to examine his teeth.

HEEL FREE

If you have been precise about following my instructions for the Heeling on Leash, this phase of heeling will develop quite smoothly.

You are ready to try Heeling off Leash when your dog is doing very nicely on leash, which should be about the fourth week of training. At this time he should Heel quite close to you and take turns and changes of pace reasonably well. The Sits at this point should be automatic.

First, do the Heeling on Leash, the Figure 8, the Stand for Examination, and the Recall exercise. If you are somewhat uncertain of your ability to keep your dog under control off leash, try the following method first. Tuck the end of the leash in your belt, or throw it over your shoulder and try heeling by controlling the dog with your voice and hands. Use the leash if the dog tries to bolt. On turns, clap your hands to alert your dog and remind him to Heel. If he is not paying attention, call his name. If he lags behind, tap your left leg and tell him to Heel in a pleasant voice. Correct poor Sits by commanding him to "Heel" both verbally and by signal. If he Sits slightly back, signal him to come up by your side by motioning to him with your fingers. If he goes wide, slap your leg, and motion him to Heel close to you. If he does not respond to your voice or signal when he forges ahead or goes wide, jerk him back with the leash. Praise the dog sensibly for everything he does well. Train him to move forward on the Heel portion of the command and not on his name.

When you are confident that you can control your dog quietly, remove the leash and fold it in half. Hold the fold in your left hand and let the ends dangle. The dog, seeing the leash, will think he is still attached to it. Continue to Heel as above. Do not panic if the dog runs out from you. Simply command him to "Heel" in a calm tone of voice as you continue to walk forward. Praise the dog if he starts to respond.

You should give your dog the impression that you trust him. Be very calm and assured, and your dog will sense this and be calm himself. Many times a handler feels sure that if he takes his dog off leash he will run away; and when he summons up enough courage to try it, he handles the dog in an entirely different manner. He keeps looking at his dog

Heeling off Leash. This stance is incorrect: Hold your left arm folded in front of you, out of your dog's way, and swing your right arm down by your side in a natural manner.

nervously and his handling becomes jumpy and erratic. If the dog forges ahead or goes wide, the handler panics; he raises his voice to give commands and wildly waves his arms in exaggerated signals. The dog confronted with this peculiar handling takes advantage of the situation and runs away.

If you have used a loose leash consistently, its removal will make little difference to your dog. Holding the unattached leash in your left hand will give you a feeling of security, and you will be able to control the dog in a normal manner. Once you realize that the dog will stay with you, you will be confident enough to try the next step.

Do not Heel Free too long the first time. Make the occasion a pleasant one. Try to avoid any errors by outguessing your dog. At this point you know your dog's weak points, so be prepared to meet them smoothly. One place to watch is when you go from normal pace to fast. The dog may spurt ahead of you. If this happens, gradually assume a normal pace as you say matter-of-factly, "No, Heel," and slap your leg to get the dog back by your side. If you treat this capriciousness lightly, the dog will resume heeling. If you make a wild grab for your dog, you will panic him, and he will dash away. To control a dog off leash, you must let him think that you trust him; if you don't, he will outwit you.

If you think that your dog is going wide too often, reach out quietly as you are heeling, grasp the choke collar and jerk him toward you saying "Heel" in a firm tone of voice. Then continue heeling and, if the dog is with you, reach down, pet him, and praise him. If the dog Sits slowly, be sure to tap him for a quick Sit, but be ready to hold him by the ruff in case he moves.

If you have started the training with a mature, obstreperous dog, you should start the Heeling off Leash by using a tracking leash for a few days to get the dog's reaction. A light line such as a Venetian blind cord is ideal for small dogs. If the dog dashes off after you have corrected him several times, your only recourse is to go up to him by walking on the leash and jerk him toward you a couple of times saying, "No, Heel." Some dogs are below average in intelligence and only respect and understand this form of correction. When the dog begins to respond, use the short leash in the same way and then continue as mentioned in the beginning. Whenever this type of dog acts up, put him back on the tracking leash for some practice work where you can reach him quickly to correct every error.

While you are practicing the Heeling off Leash, do the Figure 8. Keep your dog close by talking to him, clapping your hands or speaking his name to get his attention. Make this fun and watch your dog carefully so you can correct him the instant he makes a mistake. Be careful about Sits and insist that each one is perfect. I have found that the most common error incurred in the Figure 8 exercise is that the dog will lag. An occasional jerk will help correct this, but talking to your dog and making the whole exercise seem like fun will make him eager to keep up with you.

If he should crowd you on the inside turn, bump into him with your knee. When he steps back into Heel position speak to him in an encouraging tone of voice as you continue heeling. I have observed in shows that the majority of dogs lag on the outside turn, so practice this exercise until you can do it perfectly. Encourage your dog repeatedly with your voice to keep him from lagging. Be careful to Heel fairly close to the posts.

When your dog is Heeling off Leash nicely, add a Heeling signal to your routine. As you say "Hussan, Heel," remembering to alert your dog by calling him first by name, give him the signal to Heel. This signal, which is a forward scooping motion with your left hand and arm, should be given in front of the dog's head where he can see it. You do not need to bend down to give the signal to small dogs. They will notice the same signal given with your left arm held down lower. This signal will be used in the Utility work, and it is practical to teach it at this time. As soon as your dog understands the signal, go back to using the verbal command only.

The judge will examine your dog off leash at a show.

THE LONG SIT — NOVICE

The Long Sit in the Novice Class is for a duration of one minute; but when you practice each day, gradually increase the time to three minutes.

You may start this exercise the first week of formal training and practice it with your dog every single day that you train.

To start this exercise, have your dog Sit in the Heel position on leash. Give him the verbal command to "Sit, Stay," and the hand signal; then walk out to the end of the leash and drop it on the ground as you turn and face your dog. I would suggest that you assume the same position each time that you leave your dog on a Long Sit or Long Down. I think you will find the most comfortable position to maintain is to fold your arms across your chest. If you hold them down by your sides, it will become tiresome; and if you change your position, the steward in a show, or your dog, may interpret it as a signal.

If your dog moves toward you, say "No, Stay," and take him back to the exact spot where you left him. Again, say "Sit, Stay," and leave him. Repeat this until the dog will remain in position. When the one minute is up, pick up the leash and return to the Heel Position by walking around the dog's left side and in back of him. Stand by your dog for a few seconds quietly and then praise him. You may have to caution him to Stay as you return to him. He is not supposed to move until you speak to him.

When the dog is doing well, gradually increase the distance between you to forty feet.

Some dogs will bolt and take the leash with them. If your dog should do this, quietly tie the leash to a post or fence, and the next time he tries to run he will jerk himself back. One or two experiences of this kind will convince him that he should Stay.

Dogs taught to Sit this closely in class will be very reliable in a show.

If your dog will Stay on a three-minute Sit on Leash at a distance of forty feet, it is safe to remove the leash entirely and try it. At this time it is not necessary to give the dog the Stay signal. When you remove your leash, place it on the ground about two feet behind the dog. In a show you would tuck the leash into your armband, making sure that the judge can see the number on the band. The judge enlists the help of his stewards to watch the dogs and handlers for the duration of the Long Sit and the Long Down exercises. If the dogs move, or if the handlers signal to their dogs, such action will be noted on the individual's score sheet, and points will be deducted.

When you give your dog the command to "Stay," your tone of voice should be low but firm. Do not raise your voice. Nothing sounds more crude than the handler who yells at the dog sitting by his side. If you have attended Obedience Trials, you have probably noted that many handlers are guilty of this offense, especially on the Long Sit and the Long Down exercises. They are trying to intimidate their dogs into submission by shouting at them. They have evidently never tried the gentle approach.

If you are training a dog that simply refuses to Stay after you have repeatedly taken him back to his Sit-Stay position, try this: When the dog follows you, turn around and grasp him by the ruff and give him a quick tap on his nose, saying, "Shame, bad dog." Put him back in position, look him in the eye and say "Sit, Stay." The dog will quickly decide it is wiser to Stay if you use this correction. There is no point in being squeamish about this; a dog has no respect for someone he suspects of being weak. Sometimes a dog will lie down when he has been told to Sit. The quickest way to correct this is to take his collar and lift him into a Sitting position, command him to "Sit," and leave him without further comment.

THE LONG SIT — OPEN

The Long Sit out of sight in the Open Class is for three minutes, but in practicing, gradually increase your time to five minutes. It is time to try this exercise when the dog has done the Long Sit with you in sight consistently, even in different locations.

Leave your dog as before, but this time disappear out of sight around the corner of a building. Watch your dog without showing yourself to be sure he is Staying. By doing so you can catch him the second that he either moves out of position or lies down. If this happens, quickly walk back and correct him. Do not try to correct him from a distance, but go right back to him every time. Gradually build the time up to five minutes and try a variety of locations.

Sometimes a handler will have a problem he cannot solve. I have never yet come across a training problem I could not solve, so I have been able to help many people with theirs. Several people have had dogs that would do the Long Sit everywhere but at a show, and there the dog would eventually leave the ring to look for his handler or lie down.

You cannot correct the dog in the ring, but you can correct him before you go in the ring. Tell your dog to "Sit, Stay," and have a friend sit nearby to watch him, but do not let the dog be aware of this. Because a dog at a show must be on a leash at all times except when he is working in the ring, spread your leash on the ground quietly near your friend so that he may grab it instantly if the dog breaks. It is easy to fool a dog this way if you use a lightweight leash. As you spread it on the ground with one hand, pet the dog with the other and talk to him to distract his attention. If the dog breaks, your friend should hold the dog until you return. Walk away from your dog and hide. Keep an eye on your dog so you can return the instant he breaks. When he does, return quickly, hold him by the choke collar with the left hand, take him back, and make him Sit exactly where you left him. Continue to hold the collar in your left hand and shake your right finger in the dog's face saying "Shame, bad dog. I told you to Stay. Shame on you." Then leave him again, pointing your finger at him and looking him in the eye and saying "Now you Sit, Stay." By this time the dog will feel humiliated from the scolding and the finger wagging, and he will Stay.

THE LONG DOWN — NOVICE

The Long Down in the Novice Class is for a period of three minutes; but when you practice each day, gradually increase the time to five minutes.

Practice this exercise directly after you have done the Long Sit each time you train your dog.

You would think that a dog would be glad to perform this exercise after he has been practicing, but a Novice can be quite contrary about it.

If you have followed my directions for preliminary training, your dog will already know how to lie down by voice or signal. If not, go back and reread the section, "Teaching Your Dog to Lie Down," in chapter 8.

Some Novice handlers experience difficulty in making their dogs lie down. Have your dog Sit next to you, and give him the Down signal and the verbal command "Down." If your dog doesn't Drop, quickly pull him down by his collar and place a treat between his feet. Say, "Good, good down." Try this three or four times in succession. He should Drop on command and/or signal the fourth time (maybe sooner.) At first, bend over to give him the signal where he can see it. Later, teach him to go down when you stand in front of him. You must praise and pet him each time.

This is the signal you will use in the Open and Utility work, so insist upon a quick Drop without allowing the dog to move out of position. If he tries to crawl aside, hold him and tell him to Stay. Next time you give the signal, hold the leash in your left hand about a foot from the dog's collar. If the dog tries to crawl, hold him back with the leash as you command him to "Stay."

Do not permit the dog to roll over on his back or lie flat on his side. Correct him immediately if he does this by pushing him into a relaxed Down position.

If your dog becomes playful and refuses to lie down quietly, have the dog Sit, then repeat the Down signal and command. When he Drops, say "Stay," and move away from him. As soon as you leave him, the dog will lie down properly. If you stay near him, fussing over him, he will only become more excited. Be calm and firm with a playful dog. If you laugh at him or fuss over him, you will get nowhere. If you experience any difficulty, reread the instructions to be sure you are following them correctly.

When you have reached the point where the dog will Drop on command and signal, which will be the first lesson, you may leave him and take your stance at the end of the leash. If the dog gets up, take him back to his original position and put him down again. Gradually increase the time to three minutes, don't pick up your leash, return to the Heel position as in the Long Sit, and praise your dog. At first you may have to caution him to Stay. He is not supposed to move in a show until the judge says "Exercise finished," or until, in practice, you speak to him.

Do not get into the habit of asking your dog to Sit as soon as you return or he may anticipate this and do it without command. Stand beside him for ten seconds before you reach down and before you praise him. You may then have him Sit.

Give your dog the Down signal without bending over. Teach him to watch you.

When your dog fully understands the Down signal and verbal command, start practicing the Long Down the inconspicuous way you will do it in a show. Have your dog Sit at Heel position and give him the Down signal and verbal command "Down" without bending over. Just use your right hand and arm for the signal and, if he doesn't Drop immediately, reach down and remind him by pointing to the ground. If he did Drop, be sure to praise him.

When you are practicing the Long Down in both Novice and Open, try two false returns. In other words, return to your dog, stand there for two seconds, and then leave him. Repeat this again. The third time you return, stand there for thirty seconds and then praise your dog. This is done when you practice so that he will remain on a Down Stay when he is in competition. (Many dogs are so happy to see their owners return that they get up before the judge says, "Exercise finished.")

In shows, a handler is permitted to bend as far as necessary to bring his hand on a level with the dog's eyes in giving a signal, but I believe this encourages both poor training and

Handlers should stand about twenty feet from their dogs. Later the distance should be increased to forty feet.

poor handling. If you train your dog expertly from the beginning, these excessive body signals will never be necessary, and your handling will be smooth and natural.

In a show, you will wait for the judge to tell you to Down your dogs before you do so. The handler that touches his dog or his dog's collar to make him go down will be penalized.

THE LONG DOWN — OPEN

In the Open work, the Long Down out of sight is for a period of five minutes, but in your practice sessions, increase it to seven minutes.

When you leave your dog on a Long Down and disappear from sight, he will be eager to see where you are going and may Sit up to do so. Watch him constantly from a hiding place so you can hurry back to put him Down if he moves. If he sniffs the area near him or if he creeps forward, go back immediately and correct him, saying "No, Stay." Be firm with him from the beginning and insist that he obey your command to stay Down. If you can make your dog realize that you will not tolerate any nonsense from him, even though he cannot see you, he will decide to be good. You can control a dog at a distance or out of sight if you are quick with corrections and impress upon the dog that you are watching him every second.

Be sure that your voice is low and firm when you tell him to Stay. Later, you may wish to put your dog Down by quietly giving him just the voice command. This is an excellent way to do it.

The dog that whines or barks during the Long Sit or Long Down exercises should be corrected early in his training before this becomes a serious problem. This is easy to correct in the beginning with either a little tap under his chin or by putting your hands over his muzzle and saying, "Now you stop that and be a good boy," in a very serious, low tone of voice. I have always found that dogs will pay attention when I lower my voice and speak in a serious tone.

These corrections may not work on the dog who is spoiled. The dog who is genuinely upset because he thinks his handler is leaving him can be taught to Stay quietly if the handler will just teach him the exercise gradually. Remain in sight of the dog and gradually increase the distance between you, if he stays quietly, until you are fifty or sixty feet from him. If a correction is necessary because your dog has moved, whined, or barked, administer it swiftly.

When you are ready to try a Long Sit or Long Down out of sight, leave your dog and walk about fifty feet from him and hide behind a tree or corner of a building. Be sure to let the dog see you peeking at him. If he knows you are just around a corner or bush, he will feel secure and gradually accept your disappearance as just another lesson. The exercises should be practiced once or twice a day in different locations.

If your dog tries to follow, you should return and correct him where you meet him. If he moves a little, Sits, or Stands when he should Lie Down, Lies Down or Stands when he should Sit, you should return to him quickly and correct him. Later, when your dog is obedient about staying but makes an occasional mistake, you can correct him at a distance with a verbal command or signal. However, don't correct your dog this way in the beginning or make a habit of correcting him at a distance. It is better to go right back to the dog and give the necessary correction.

Handlers who have permitted their dogs to develop bad habits such as whining should try this method of leaving their dogs. If the dog will Stay but persists in whining, an assistant should be employed. The dog should be on a fifteen-foot leash, and it should be spread out directly in back of him. The assistant, who is stationed at the end of the leash, should quietly jerk the dog out of position when he wines, then his handler should run back quickly and correct the dog. The timing should be perfect, and the exercise should be repeated until the dog has learned to Stay quietly. If the dog becomes suspicious of a person sitting a few yards in back of him, the leash should be placed under, or behind, a tree or object so the dog cannot see the assistant. Later, the same method should be employed in a practice class where several dogs are lined up for the Long Sit and Long Down exercises.

A dog should be able to learn the Long Sit and Long Down exercises out of sight in about a week. However, the exercises should be practiced every time the rest of the Open exercises are taught. This daily practice will make your dog steady and eliminate any costly failures when you are in show competition.

The basic training you give your dog is the most important training he will ever receive. In this chapter I have stressed the correct way to teach your dog to Heel with precision. This means your dog should keep his shoulder by your left leg regardless of the pace you adapt or the type of turns you make. He should Heel by your side without crowding, going wide, forging ahead, or lagging behind.

When you leave your dog he should Stay on one command. When you call him he should respond willingly and immediately, and his attitude should reflect the kind of training he is receiving. Your dog should be trained to Sit straight in front of you and at Heel position. He should thoroughly understand the word "Come."

Every dog who is destined to become a top working dog will have to master these fundamentals. The formula for success is contained in this chapter, and any breed of dog can be an Obedience Champion if this method is applied correctly.

Once your dog has mastered the basic work, the Open and Utility exercises are relatively simple. The dogs who repeatedly fail the advanced exercises are doing so because they have never actually learned to be obedient. The handlers in Utility have a rude awakening when they find their dogs are failing not because of a new exercise, but because they are basically disobedient and lack even elementary precision.

I suggest that you continue to strive for perfection as you start your Open training. You will not experience any failures tomorrow if you give your dog a sound foundation today.

Chapter 15

Handling

Handling is an art that can be acquired only through experience. It is not anything you will pick up in several months. It is the culmination of all the knowledge that you have attained through different sources such as reading, studying the different breeds of dogs, digesting the Obedience Regulations, conducting frequent practice sessions, observing top handlers in competition, and developing your own style for Obedience competition. Of course the first requisite is a genuine love for dogs, and if you have that it should follow that you will have the patience and understanding to cope with them. The second requisite is perseverance, for without it you will not get very far. And last but not least you must have a sense of humor, for in Obedience Trial competition anything can happen.

The following is a true incident that happened when I was showing Joll. He is a dog who thinks and acts more like a human being than any dog I have owned. I generally take him everywhere with me, for he is extremely well behaved and very good company. He is an American and Canadian Utility Dog and in gaining these titles had many near-perfect scores as well as perfect scores. He is a dog that is expertly trained and can work with flawless precision; however, after he won his Utility titles he decided it was all too boring at shows and he would add a little spice to his routine. He had done a commendable job one day in the Open exercises, and we were doing the Long Sit and Long Down out of sight. He did the Long Sit exercise perfectly. The handlers left their dogs on the Long Down, and we filed out of the ring and went walking off and disappeared out of sight behind a tent. As soon as I was out of sight, Joll got up and stood for a while, then he crossed the ring and stood quietly, minding his own business, and just looked around at the large crowd watching at ringside. The judge didn't touch him, for he wasn't disturbing anyone. When the five-minute period was nearly up, he walked back to his original position and lay down exactly as I had left him. It was just as if he were thinking, and I'm sure he was, "I'd better go back before Wynne gets back." I filed back into the ring with the other handlers and noticed the smiles and chuckles at ringside but didn't realize Joll was the cause of all the hilarity. He looked so angelic that I praised him for being a good boy, and then the judge came over and explained what he had done. Joll at this point was sitting there smugly, thinking he had pulled a fast one, so I turned to him and said, "Oh, you were a bad dog, were you?" A guilty look swept over his face as he realized I knew. He has never done this since. I think it is very funny, as did the people who witnessed it.

It has long been my contention that if you want to learn something you should go to the person who is most qualified to teach it. By qualified I mean he is at the top of his profession because of what he has accomplished personally. The teacher who has made a fine record himself in Obedience is the one who can help you. There are hundreds of Obedience trainers in the country, but most are passing on bits of training advice they have picked up willy-nilly. With coaching like this you can expect very little consistency and much confusion.

I feel qualified to teach you how to train and handle your dog because my record shows that all the dogs that I have trained and handled myself over the past forty years have been in the ribbons 99 percent of the time. The training advice that I give you in this book will help you to become a top handler, and the observations I make on handling in this chapter and throughout the book will acquaint you with the proper techniques.

The first thing you will notice when you watch a top handler is the relaxed, easy manner in which he controls his dog and the rapport that is evident between the two. The dog will be attentive and responsive to the handler's firm but soft-spoken commands, the signals will be given with just one hand and arm, and the exercises will be performed very smoothly and skillfully. The first time you witness this type of handling you will be more impressed with how easy it looks than by anything else. If you haven't started training you will be quite certain that you could do it yourself — it looked so easy.

The first step to becoming a good handler is to train your dog correctly. Good handling is synonymous with expert training. Your voice is important — give the commands in a firm, well-modulated tone and praise your dog in a very pleased tone that rings with sincerity. When the dog is close to you teach him to respond to commands that are given to him softly. When working away from you, teach him to execute the commands that are given crisply but just loud enough for him to hear. Don't keep repeating commands, rather correct him for not paying attention. I do not believe in giving a command twice — I haven't got that much time to waste. If the dog doesn't respond to the first command I immediately show him what I expect him to do. This teaches the dog to be attentive. Remember, you can't teach a dog anything if you don't have his attention.

Signals should be given with one hand and arm only. In the earliest stages you may exaggerate the signals to gain the dog's attention, but in the final analysis all signals must be given smoothly and swiftly without any excess body motion. The size of your dog is not a factor here, for you can train any dog to pay attention, and if he is paying attention to you he will see your signals. The people who would disagree with this theory are those who have yet to learn how to make their dogs pay attention to them. You will have to watch yourself very carefully to avoid giving unintentional body signals to your dog. It is natural for a beginner to nod his head, lean forward, or move his hands when he calls his dog. He is so intent in watching his dog that he is unaware of his own actions. Have someone watch you so he can tell you when he notices you doing this.

Be consistent — never scold a dog for a misdemeanor one day and praise him the next for the same act. You cannot expect your dog to understand an exercise if you keep changing your training methods each time you try it. Dogs learn the basic work by repetition, and the entire training program should proceed smoothly and consistently. For instance, the techniques that you will use in the Novice training will be repeated in the Advanced exercises, and your handling will be just the same.

You should study your dog so you can foresee his reaction to any situation. You should become attuned to your dog's sensitivities. If you have a gentle, quiet dog, do not antagonize him by rough treatment. He will become very alert and responsive if you train him in a calm and gentle manner with consideration for his feelings. Aggressive or overly playful dogs need a more forceful approach. While your voice should remain moderate in tone, your correction should be fast and to the point. Dogs of this type should always be aware that you are the master. If you neglect to be firm, the dog will try to take advantage of you. You will have to learn to outguess him throughout the whole training period. Dogs, like people, have different temperaments and personalities. Your training methods must vary according to the temperament of the dog. As you become adept at handling, this fact will become very apparent to you.

Be careful of your turns, for many points are lost on these deceivingly simple moves. On the left turn your dog should turn precisely when you do without touching you. Small dogs are afraid of being stepped on, so they will watch out for you. Be ready to jerk a small dog closer to you after a turn, for they have a tendency to veer off to the left. The larger dogs can be taught to take a left turn with precision if you lift your left knee or bump them or tap them over lightly with your right hand.

On the right turn and about turn don't stop to wait for your dog. Teach him to keep his shoulder in line with your left knee at all times. Keep your feet close together on the turns by taking short steps, and get your dog in the habit of moving fast. If you make a military about turn and leave one foot out behind you, your poor dog will have to walk all the way around it in order to make the turn; he will lag and you will be penalized for a poor turn. Any bending over, nodding your head, wiggling your fingers, or making any overt motion with your body or arm will be construed as an extra signal to your dog and will be penalized.

When the judge orders you to Halt, take one or two steps to bring your feet in line, no more. Do not keep turning around to look at your dog when heeling, and do not turn to look at him when he is going to the Heel position. Keep your shoulders straight, your head up high, your left arm tucked in close to your waist, and your left eye on your dog. Your attention should be focused on the judge so you can follow his commands swiftly, and you should proceed in a straight line when heeling until ordered to do otherwise.

When your dog is heeling he should do so with precision. Besides keeping up with you he should remain an equal distance from your side at all times. He should not weave in and out as you are walking. This precision can only be acquired by practicing with him consistently and in different environments. If you keep your left eye riveted on your dog while you are practicing, you can correct him the second he gets careless.

Your commands should be given crisply. The command should not be drawn out until it is as lengthy as a sentence. For instance, if you use the verbal command to Drop, it should be "Down," not "Dow-w-w-w-w-wn-n-n." The verbal command to jump should be "Hup," or "Over," not "O-o-o-o-o-o-ver-r-r-r-r." Of course, shouting commands at your dog is another indication of poor handling, for it shows that he has been improperly trained and you neither trust nor control him.

Talking to your dog, snapping your fingers, clapping your hands, swinging your arms too fast to create the illusion that you are going fast, or adapting your pace to that of your dog in an attempt to hide his faults will be penalized by the competent judge.

I say "competent" because not all judges are capable of judging good work or recognizing good handling. Generally speaking, judges have trained one or more dogs before they decide to try their hand at judging. If they have not been very successful at training their own dogs it is unlikely that they will appreciate the finer points of handling when they see them. It will take considerable judging experience for them to develop an "eye" for good work. Some judges are considered "tough" because they deduct more points than others for a specific error, such as a poor Sit. Yet they haven't the ability to distinguish top handling from that which is mediocre.

Although some judges are competent in scoring the dogs in their classes, they completely lack the correct ring posture. They follow the handler and his dog so closely, even running next to and bending over to watch the handler and his dog on the fast pace, that they actually interfere with the dog's work. When they give the halt command they run around the handler and his dog to observe the dog's Sit from all angles. This sort of freakish behavior makes both the handler and his dog wonder about his capabilities. A judge should be able to observe the handler and his dog when he is ten or more feet from them and see every possible error that they can make.

Some judges do well in every respect but forget to keep an eye on their stewards or their rings. Children might be playing on the ropes that form the ring, spectators and their dogs might be crowding too close, or under the ropes, and trash might be blowing inside the ring. Stewards might be standing gossiping, unaware that they are in the dog's way when he is retrieving or finishing an exercise. Some stewards even walk directly in a dog's path when he is about to jump the broad jump or some other exercise. The judge is blissfully unaware of anything that goes on in his ring and penalizes the handler for infractions caused by his own incompetence.

Do not pick your dog up and carry him in an Obedience ring. In the Novice Classes you will be permitted to guide your dog gently by the collar between exercises, but this will not be allowed in the Open and Utility exercises.

Everyone competing in Obedience likes to get high scores, but I believe they should be earned fairly. Both handlers and judges alike should understand what constitutes good work. Both should carry a mental picture of the theoretically perfect performance and score the dog against this standard of perfection. A Novice handler is happy at first to get a leg toward his title, but after he has been in a few shows he wants more than that — he wants to place in the ribbons. This is natural. It is the American way — to want to excel in what you are doing, and in my book it denotes character. You can do well if you are particular with your handling. I don't believe in taking the "easy way out" or the "path of least resistance" in training a dog or handling one. It is just as easy to train and handle your dog properly from the first lesson and the first show as it is to train him halfheartedly and then try to cover the dog's errors in the ring by cheating. It is certainly more fun for you and the dog when he is trained so well that you can enter the ring with confidence, knowing that, whatever transpires, your handling was above reproach. A well-trained dog may one day goof a particular exercise, but it should not disturb you. Remember that you are working with an animal, not a machine. I expect a dog to fault once in a while. This is perfectly normal even for the most brilliantly trained dog, but the balance of the work should be nearly perfect. What I cannot condone is sloppy handling or poor basic work, for this shows that the handler is unfamiliar with the regulations, has not trained his dog properly, and is too complacent to care. A good handler who has trained his dog expertly doesn't have to resort to various and sundry cover-up maneuvers to win: He relies solely upon his knowledge of the Obedience Regulations and his faith in his dog's ability to remember his training.

My training method produces consistently high scores and superior handling; by following it carefully, with close attention to details, you will automatically become a good handler. Dogs trained with this type of handling become happy, alert workers. It gives the handler a great sense of achievement when he can handle his dog faultlessly.

If something is worth doing, it is worth doing well.

Chapter 16

The Open Exercises

HEEL FREE (FIGURE 8)

The Open exercises consist of Heel Free, Figure 8 off Leash, Drop on Recall, Retrieve on the Flat, Retrieve over a High Jump, Jump over a Broad Jump, a Long Sit out of sight for three minutes, and a Long Down out of sight for five minutes.

By qualifying in these exercises in three shows, under three different judges, you may earn your CDX (Companion Dog Excellent) degree. This is equivalent to a high school diploma.

The Heel Free exercise has already been described in the chapter 14, "The Novice Exercises," so at this point all you will require is practice to keep your dog perfect. The Figure 8 is done off leash and has also been described, so we do not need to discuss these exercises further.

DROP ON RECALL

There is a preliminary exercise you should teach your dog before you try the Drop on Recall exercise. Stand in front of your dog and give him the Down signal. If he doesn't Drop immediately follow the instructions in the "Teaching Your Dog to Lie Down" section of chapter 8, "Preliminary Training." If you give your dog the Down signal and he lies down immediately without moving forward or sideways, it is called a fast Drop. When your dog does this it is time to try dropping him at a distance. Because a dog can be taught to Drop fast in just one lesson, you should be ready for the next step in just two or three lessons.

Have your dog Sit and Stay and try the Down signal at five feet. If he Drops go back to him and pet and praise him. If he doesn't Drop go up and tap him on the nose as you quietly say, "Down." Then as you continue to practice the Down signal, increase the distance between you five feet at a time. Always insist upon a very fast Drop. It is important to praise him exuberantly when he does it correctly and equally important to tap him if he tries to ignore your signal.

Once your dog has mastered the Down signal at a distance of forty feet and responds quickly and consistently, you are ready for the next step. I have found that dogs who learn the Down signal this way have no trouble when given the signal during a Recall. At this

103

point they understand the signal, and there is no doubt in their minds what it means. Your dog may be surprised the very first time you give him the Down signal when he is coming to you, but he will Drop. You should quickly say, "Stay, good," and go to him and praise and pet him.

The first time that you try a Drop on Recall with your dog, try to have the right attitude. If you have a negative attitude your dog will sense it, and you will probably show it when you give him the signal. I always expect my dog, no matter which one I am training, to do the work correctly. As I train each individual dog I learn to read him so I can determine what his reactions will be to a given situation. For instance, a very sensitive dog will probably Drop fast the first time you give him the Down signal on a Recall, but he will turn so that he faces away from you. By giving this dog quick praise in a happy tone of voice, you will soon have him dropping fast and looking at you. By communicating with your dog you will have a fast, happy, reliable, accurate worker.

The handler who doesn't teach his dog this preliminary exercise before he trains his dog to Drop, either verbally or by signal, has to correct his dog dozens and dozens of time when he is responding to his call. This has a crushing effect on the dog, and his Recalls become slower and slower as he half-heartedly responds to his handler's call and anticipates being corrected on his way in. So, go back and repeat the preliminary training "Teaching Your Dog to Lie Down," outlined in chapter 8.

I prefer to use a signal for the Drop because it teaches the dog to be more alert and attentive, and it is one more signal that the dog will use in the Utility work. The majority of people who shout "Down" at their dogs do so in a very loud, unpleasant tone of voice. If you decide to use your voice, make it firm but pleasant and just loud enough for the dog to hear you. A loud, intimidating tone of voice is as much an error as a hand signal held too long.

When your dog has mastered the first step have him Sit at Heel and give him the command to Stay. Go back about forty feet, turn and face your dog, wait a few seconds, and then call your dog to you saying, "Hussan, come." Remember to use your dog's name first in giving all commands except the Stay command. When he has covered two-thirds of the distance, give him the Drop signal and say "Down." The dog will Drop. Command him to Stay while you go up to him and praise him in a very pleased tone of voice. Again tell him to Stay, and leave him; go back to your first position, wait a few seconds, then call him in to you and have him Sit. Praise him, and then have him go to the Heel position and praise him again. If you do not intend to Drop him with the verbal command, just use the signal.

If the dog does not Drop, take a heavy step toward him and repeat the signal. Quickly walk up to him and pet and praise him if he Drops. A dog that stubbornly ignores the signal needs a different approach. Go up to the dog and stand in front of him. Give him the verbal command "Down" and the signal. He will obey you because you are standing in front of him, so have him Sit and Down twice in succession, and say "Good" each time he Drops. Now continue with his lesson. He should be left in a Down position, and the handler should go back forty feet, call her dog and Drop him when he is halfway in. If the dog Drops, the handler should quickly pet and praise him. This routine should be practiced by doing three or four straight Recalls, then practicing a Drop on Recall. When your dog becomes proficient at dropping fast, a word of praise should be given instead of going up to the dog each time and petting and praising him. Even when he is fully trained, a word of praise for a good Drop will let your dog know that you appreciate his good work.

Raise your right hand quickly as your dog is coming to you.   **Place your hands down by your sides after giving the Down signal when your dog is coming to you.**

When you give the Down signal, your right hand and arm should be raised quickly. Show your dog the palm of your right hand with your arm just about shoulder high. Many handlers give their dogs poor signals and wonder why their dogs fail to respond. Don't bend your wrist backward over your shoulder, as the dog will ignore this type of signal. Get your hand in plain view where your dog can see it.

Usually in the Open Class at a show, the judge will instruct the handler to Drop his dog opposite the jump or himself. This means that the dog will cover about half the distance before he is Dropped. Very few dogs ever Drop opposite the specified object. Study your dog thoroughly, and practice with him until you can Drop him exactly where you want him. To get your dog to Drop at a certain point, you will have to run up to him quickly the second he takes that extra step. As he does, say "No," and repeat the Down signal. If the dog ignores you, go stand in front of him, have him Down, and Sit, four times in succession. He will get the message and behave himself. Be sure to praise him in a happy tone of voice. Although the regulations say the most important part of the exercise is the fast Drop, it follows that if you can Drop your dog at any specific point during a Recall, it proves that he is fast and accurate.

Your dog will learn this exercise very quickly, so be sure not to overdo it. If you practice it too frequently, he will start to slow down, anticipating the Drop. When this happens, call him in quickly without dropping him. Do not practice the exercise every day. Practice dropping your dog in different locations, and increase or decrease the distance between you to vary the routine. If after the Drop the dog starts to walk in slowly in response to your call, go up to him, put your finger in the ring of his collar and give him a quick pull toward you as you say "Come" and run backwards. You might have to repeat this two or three times, but it is a very effective way to get a dog to move fast.

RETRIEVE ON FLAT

The Retrieve on Flat must be learned step by step.

First, you should teach your dog to take the dumbbell and hold it. Even though a handler has never tried this with his dog he should be able to accomplish it in one lesson. If you are training a dog who refused to retrieve when some other method was used, and he has become stubborn or frightened, it might take two or three lessons. The length of time it takes will depend upon your skill in using your voice as you tighten his collar. Scores of handlers who have spent many, many futile months and tried various cruel methods on their dogs have taught them to retrieve quite willingly during one of our five-day clinics.

My method of teaching a dog to retrieve is one of persuasion, and your voice is your most important asset here. You must use your dog's name repeatedly before each command and do so in a most persuasive tone of voice. Your voice should be kept low, firm, and pleasant, and you should talk to the dog continually as you urge him to take the dumbbell. When your dog takes it, you should immediately sound very pleased and praise him happily and excitedly as you pet him. Never raise your voice in anger or impatience; if the dog appears to be stubborn, never shove the dumbbell in your dog's mouth or against his gums, never jerk your dog's collar, and don't hit him over the head with the dumbbell. Be gentle but firm with him at all times.

Start your dog in a quiet corner and keep him on a leash for the first three steps. Stand by your dog's right side, or kneel down if you have a small dog, and hold one end of the dumbbell in your right hand. Always keep your fingers off the middle piece (the dowel). Place the dumbbell under, in front of, and close to, your dog's upper lip, and as you tell him to "Get it," put your third finger behind his canine tooth. This will open his mouth slightly and you can gently slide the dumbbell into his mouth. If you can't use your right hand to open his mouth, use the index finger of your left hand. Quickly tell your dog to "Hold it," as you stroke his nose on top, in one direction away from his nose, with your right hand, and you stroke him under the chin with your left hand. By stroking him this way you will keep the dumbbell in his mouth. You should be praising him as you do this. Keep the dumbbell in your dog's mouth for two or three seconds at first so he can get the feel of it.

Most dogs accept the dumbbell gracefully and hold it firmly the first time. This is especially true of puppies who will actually reach out to take it and hold it for you. However, some dogs will put up a struggle, and you will have to hold their jaws closed gently with both hands around their muzzles as you command them firmly, but quietly, to "Hold it." Generally speaking, the majority of dogs will hold the dumbbell if you are gentle with them and talk to them reassuringly. Be careful not to bang the dog's teeth with the

dumbbell. Once in a great while you will find a dog who becomes hysterical if something is placed in his mouth. If gentle handling and verbal control don't work, a good slap on his nose will calm him down. This type of dog is not any fun to train, but he can learn the exercise.

After placing the dumbbell in your dog's mouth two or three times to get his reaction to it, teach him to take it by himself. Slide your dog's medium link chain or heavy nylon choke collar up high on his neck, behind his ears and high under his chin, and hold it in your left hand. Your right hand will be holding the dumbbell. By pushing against the dead ring with your thumb you will be able to draw the collar into the palm of your hand very steadily and smoothly. Do not jerk the collar, just tighten it smoothly and quickly. When the dog takes the dumbbell you should let go of his collar immediately and praise him.

It is very important that you talk to your dog at the same time you are tightening his collar. Say, "Hussan, get it," and keep repeating the command, your dog's name, and a few words of encouragement, until he takes the dumbbell. I find that most dogs will reach for the dumbbell the second time that I tighten the collar and encourage them in a very

"Get it," as you lift one end of the dumbbell.

persuasive tone of voice to "Get it." It is not necessary to tighten the collar after this, but if it is kept high on your dog's neck, it will act as a reminder. Be sure to let go of the collar when your dog takes the dumbbell, and praise and pet him. The type of verbal praise you give your dog after you take the dumbbell from him is very important; you must let your dog feel that he did something very special and wonderful.

If your dog doesn't reach out to grasp the dumbbell, it is because you either stopped tightening his collar, didn't tighten it smoothly and continually, or didn't notice that he wanted to take it and you failed to keep the dumbbell close to his mouth. Remember to keep the dumbbell directly in front and next to his upper lip all the time, even when he turns his head.

The second step is to teach your dog to reach out and take the dumbbell when he is standing, turn and carry it to you as you run backward, and Sit and hold the dumbbell in front of you. Your dog should be ready for this step the third or fourth day. Walk forward slowly, reach down to the level of your dog's head, and hand the dumbbell to your dog with the command "Get it." When your dog reaches out and takes the dumbbell,

"Get it," as you walk forward slowly and hand the dumbbell to your dog at his level.

swing around quickly and as you turn backward and say, "Come." The dog will hold the dumbbell because he is coming to you briskly, but you should command him to Sit as you place one hand under his chin to prevent him from dropping it. Practice this, and the first step, for several days. Your dog should learn this step easily if you praise him excitedly as he is coming to you. It is normal for a dog to drop the dumbbell at first, either when he is coming in, or when he is sitting, so be forewarned to prevent this by placing your hand under his chin as you command him to "Hold it."

If your dog doesn't take the dumbbell, you might be making one of the following errors. You could be walking too fast (stop and give your dog a chance to take it); you are making the routine too dull (sound excited when you encourage your dog to take it); or you may be holding the dumbbell too high, too low, or too far away from his mouth (position the dumbbell correctly, and your dog will be willing to take it).

The third step is to throw the dumbbell about six feet from you, and as you give your dog the command "Get it," run out with him. There could be several different reactions at this point as not all dogs respond the same way. A young dog or a puppy will pick it up immediately and carry it to you. Praise this fellow vociferously. Another dog might run out with you and lower his head but refuse to pick it up. Wiggle the dumbbell and hold it a few inches off the ground. If you encourage him to take it, he will do so. If you run out fast and lift the dumbbell a little lower each time you practice, you can get this dog to take it. Very soon you will be able to run out with him and just place your hand over the end of the dumbbell. The dog will pick it up off the ground if your hand is there. Just be sure to run backward quickly and make a fuss over him when he follows you and Sits. Then there is the dog who runs out with you and balks completely. Put the collar high on this dog's neck and as you hold his head over the dumbbell tighten his collar and command him to "Get it." If you do this when he gets stubborn, he will be willing to pick it up for you.

Your dog can learn this third step very quickly if you will just time your praise correctly. In other words, just as the dog is reaching down for the dumbbell you should say "Good, that's it," and run backward. By failing to praise the dog at the right time he could easily lose interest and refuse to cooperate.

Your dog should have been working on leash up to this point. If you find that he is coming along nicely and retrieving the dumbbell on leash, it is time to practice the same work off leash.

In the beginning when you trained your dog to take the dumbbell from your hand, you taught him to hold it quietly until you took it from him. At this time you did this so that he would learn not to chew or mouth it. This point should be emphasized not only in the beginning, but every step you go through in teaching him to retrieve. When your dog carries the dumbbell to you and Sits, you should watch him carefully and be ready to caution him to hold it if he tries to chew it. You can stop this from becoming a bad habit by either tapping the dog on the nose or by gently holding his jaws closed over the dumbbell. When he is still on leash and retrieving the dumbbell from the ground be ready to correct him if he mouths or chews it. You should also watch him carefully through each step to be sure that he holds the dumbbell by the middle piece and never by the end. It is normal for a dog to try this occasionally, but he should be corrected immediately. Either

Throw the dumbbell six feet away, run up to it with your dog and encourage him to retrieve it as you say, "Good, get it."

When the dog takes the dumbbell, quickly run backward as you say, "Come, hold it."

make him pick it up off the ground while you hold one end or hand it to him so that he must grab the middle piece. If necessary, take it out of his mouth and hand it to him so that he holds it correctly. As you progress from one step to the next, these are two of the errors you can avoid by anticipating them and correcting the dog before either one of them becomes a bad habit.

The handler who has failed to correct the chewer or mouther will find either one a very difficult habit to break. Have your dog practice retrieving a dumbbell with a middle piece he will not want to chew, such as heavy metal, or studded metal. Save the solid wooden dumbbell for shows.

You are now ready for the fourth or last step.

The first few times you try the Retrieve off Leash, run up with your dog, command him to "Get it," then run backward as you say "Come," and have him Sit. Take the dumbbell, praise him, and then have him Finish.

Increase the distance that you throw the dumbbell as your dog responds. Then, as he starts to run after it, stop, and let him continue alone. If he stops halfway, run up and send him on again toward the dumbbell. You will have to repeat this until he is willing to go all the way alone.

Gradually drop the command "Hold it" as he progresses. However, if at any time he chews or mouths the dumbbell, caution him to "Hold it."

Now, when you take the dumbbell from him, tell him to go to Heel. Check the Finish each time to be sure that he Sits straight. If he refuses to go out, take his collar and scoot or throw him out.

As soon as your dog starts retrieving the dumbbell at a distance of fifteen feet or more, precede the command with your dog's name. He should start forward on the command "Get it." Many dogs enjoy retrieving so much that they go dashing out after the dumbbell as soon as you throw it and before they are ordered to do so. If your dog anticipates your command and retrieves the dumbbell before you have a chance to tell him or stop him, try this.

Put your left index finger in the ring of his collar, and as you do so scratch his neck so he will not realize you are holding him, and give him the verbal command "Stay." If he darts out before you command him to "Get it," guide him back, saying "No, Stay." If you have a small breed, attach a two-foot nylon cord to his collar; you can hold this in your left hand and let go of it when you say, "Get it." This short grab lead will save your back when you are training the smaller breeds. Make your dog Sit there for ten seconds before you send him out after the dumbbell. Try this every time he anticipates, and he will soon be waiting for your command. It is a sign of superior handling if you can control your dog with a quiet verbal command "Stay," and eliminate the signal. However, if you prefer to give your dog both a verbal command and a signal, do not give the signal with the hand that is holding the dumbbell.

Your dog should return the dumbbell to you without touching you, and he should be close enough so that you do not have to step forward or lean over to take it. This can be accomplished in training by holding him gently when he comes in, either by the ruff or under his chin. It is simply a matter of showing him where you want him to Sit.

Encourage him to go out fast each time, to pick up the dumbbell without hesitating, and to return at a trot. Some dogs naturally run when they retrieve, but it is not necessary. The dog that trots back and forth at a brisk pace deserves as much credit, for he is using his natural gait. If your dog should anticipate any of your commands, call him back to you, repeat the exercise, and make sure that he waits the next time.

When your dog is retrieving consistently at a distance, the exercise should look like this. Your dog should Sit straight in the Heel position while you tell him to "Stay" and you throw the dumbbell. When you give the command "Get it," he should move forward briskly and pick up the dumbbell and return it to you at a brisk trot. (If he runs, that is also correct.) He should then Sit straight in front of you and hold the dumbbell in his mouth without chewing or mouthing it until you take it. Once you have taken the dumbbell, he must remain stationary until you tell him to "Heel," whereupon he will Finish in a smart manner and Sit straight.

If it is a hot day when you are practicing retrieving, and the dog is panting, you will notice that the dumbbell will move up and down in the dog's mouth. This is neither chewing nor mouthing, and points should not be deducted from your score in a show for a similar incident. The dumbbell is merely moving in rhythm as the dog breathes hard or pants.

TEACHING YOUR DOG TO JUMP

(As soon as your dog is Heeling off Leash, you may begin the following exercises.)

When you are ready to teach your dog to jump, check the latest AKC Obedience Regulations to determine the height he should jump. (Up to the 1990s the AKC jump heights were physically hard on dogs. Fortunately, today the regulations are more realistic, and the dogs are far less likely to injure themselves by being forced to jump too high.)

Before your dog can learn to retrieve the dumbbell over the high or solid jump, he must first learn how to jump. Not all dogs are natural jumpers, and many of them must be taught to jump smoothly and with coordination. Two of the main problems are dogs who jump too close to the jump, almost from a standstill, and those who start too far back. Any dog can be taught to jump smoothly if he is started correctly and if he is physically sound. Even in cases where a dog is not sound physically you can make jumping much easier for him by teaching him to jump with rhythm and coordination.

If you have started with the preliminary training and tricks, you are well ahead at this point. Your dog will take to formal jumping with very little effort. A puppy that I am training as I write this book has learned to jump the three jumps at three-quarters of the desired height and retrieve over the high jump — all within three days. This puppy has mastered all the tricks I have explained, and so has found formal jumping easy.

If you are just starting, I suggest that you follow this procedure. Set up the solid jump and the bar jump on opposite sides of a square about twenty-five feet apart, with the broad jump laid out on a third side. The solid and bar jumps should be set at about one-third the height that your dog will be required to jump in a show; the broad jump should be about one-half as long. Use three boards on the broad jump and turn two of them over on their edges. After your dog has jumped in this way two or three times, lay the boards of the broad jump flat.

As soon as your dog realizes that he is to jump, walk around the jump instead of jumping with him. Keep close to the jump, even move toward it, but take a detour around it at the last second holding the leash in your left hand over the jump so that your dog will continue straight on and over. (You will note as you advance with your training how natural and practical it is to hold the leash consistently in your left hand as you train your dog.)

Lift your dog with the leash as you run toward the high jump and take a detour around it at the last second.

When the dog will do all three jumps on a loose leash, combine the three by running around in a circle and having him jump each one as you come to it. Try not to stop, but have him jump the three jumps before you pause to pet him. Words of praise can be given on the way.

Watch your dog closely, and when he is in the most advantageous position for a smooth jump, command him to "Hup." Repeat this until your dog has acquired the rhythm on leash.

The next stage is to repeat this off leash, being careful that your dog jumps smoothly. An athlete with the correct rhythm and coordination will perform smoothly, and the same is true of a dog.

As the dog's jumping ability improves, gradually increase the height of the bar and the high jump. Also gradually increase the length of the broad jump.

Large breeds of dogs, such as German Shepherds, should not be asked to jump the full height until they are over eleven months old.

Further instructions on jumping will follow in the ensuing chapters.

RETRIEVING OVER THE HIGH JUMP

When your dog has mastered the Retrieve over the High Jump, the exercise should go smoothly. Your dog is sitting attentively at Heel position. You give the command "Stay" in a quiet tone of voice and throw the dumbbell. Then, with the command "Get it," the dog runs forward, jumps gracefully, retrieves the dumbbell, jumps cleanly on his way back with the dumbbell, and Sits straight in front of you holding the dumbbell patiently. You take it and tell him to "Heel." He goes to the Heel position smartly and Sits straight. When the judge says, "Exercise finished," you praise your dog.

Now that your dog knows how to jump, you will find this exercise quite easy.

Adjust the jump so that the dog will jump one-half the required height.

Stand about fifteen feet from the jump with your dog in Heel position. Give the command "Stay," and throw the dumbbell, being careful to have it land about fifteen feet beyond the jump if you have a medium- or large-sized dog. If your dog is small, throw the dumbbell about ten feet beyond the jump. As you give your dog the command "Get it," run up to the jump with him saying "Hup." As soon as the dog jumps, again command him to "Get it," and point to the dumbbell. When the dog reaches for the dumbbell, praise him, saying, "Good. Come," and as the dog starts back say, "Hup. Hold it." If it is necessary, touch the top of the jump with your hands to direct your dog over. As the dog jumps, step back quickly and stand in your original position. Have your dog Sit in front of you holding the dumbbell for a few seconds; then take it and praise him warmly. Next, command him to "Heel," and praise him again.

The AKC Obedience Regulations state that the handler must stand at least eight feet or any reasonable distance beyond eight feet, from the jump but must remain in the same spot throughout the exercise.

If your dog starts to wander after he jumps, call him back and make him pick up the dumbbell, jump again, and Finish as I have described.

If your dog tries to come back around the jump, quickly block his path, take him back several feet, and insist that he jump. You will probably have to hold his collar as you run up to the jump with him and, if necessary, give him a lift to get him over.

Remember that this is new to the dog, and for this reason be patient. It is more difficult for him to jump with a dumbbell in his mouth. If he should drop it a few times at first, tell him to "Get it" again, and resume the lesson. Be particularly exuberant by clapping your hands and encouraging him with praise when you see he is trying hard.

Eventually, if not at first, the dog will drop the dumbbell when he comes back to you. This is where the step-by-step method of retrieving will be of great value. When you tell your dog to "Get it," he will understand that the command is to reach down and pick it up again. Do not move out of position yourself. When the dog picks it up, caution him to "Hold it." The next couple of times, caution him to "Hold it" as he approaches you. This command will come in handy many times in the future when you want your dog to hold some object firmly. Never permit your dog to chew, mouth, or play with the dumbbell when he is retrieving.

If your dog is working too slowly, inspire him by running up to the jump with him, repeating the command "Get it" in an excited tone of voice, and clapping your hands when you say "Hup." Praise will also work magic. It is up to you to convince your dog that retrieving is fun.

Call your dog to you as you place your hands just above the high jump.

When your dog retrieves the dumbbell and starts toward you, quickly raise your hands in the air to encourage him to jump as you say, "Hup."

There is a knack to throwing the dumbbell that you can learn after practicing. If you take the trouble to become expert at throwing, you can always place it in the best position for your dog. Contrast this with the handler who, when he throws, hits the jump, lands the dumbbell too far away, or tosses it to the left or right, thereby making the retrieve unnecessarily difficult.

To throw the dumbbell correctly, grasp one end in your right hand and hold it down by your side. As you throw it, flip it up in the air, spinning it toward the spot where you wish it to land. The dumbbell should stop dead on landing.

Stand back far enough from the jump so that your dog can jump gracefully and come up to you in just a few steps.

Increase the height of the jump until your dog is jumping the required height he will jump in a show. Be careful that he works smoothly. Whenever he veers from a graceful, coordinated jump, help him by calling "Hup" at the right moment.

In recent years I have used my four-foot practice jumps for training purposes. They are plywood jumps four feet wide. I have been able to correct any type of jumping problem by calling "Hup" at the right moment.

Once you teach your dog the rhythm of jumping, he will retain it. To do this properly, you must study your dog while he is in the act of jumping to determine the correct distance from the hurdle that he should leap to jump clear. This varies with the size of the dog or the way he jumps. If you are consistently correct in your judgment, your dog will trust you and jump at your command. When he has learned to coordinate his movements and has the rhythm down perfectly, it will not be necessary for you to cadence his jump.

Be sure that your dog is sitting straight, and then tell him to Stay.

Look at the spot where you want the dumbbell to land, then throw it.

Oversensitive dogs will sometimes develop a mental block about jumping if they had an unpleasant experience like knocking the jump over accidentally. Even though they are physically able to jump, they become afraid of it. The only way to conquer this is to pace them carefully and call "Hup" at the precise moment. It will be necessary to start on leash with the jumps set low. As the dog improves you can gradually reach the required height.

If you force a dog to jump higher than he is able to, you may cause him to strain himself needlessly. A sensitive dog who strains to clear a jump will become afraid to jump. When asked to jump he will approach the jump and stand there, hesitating nervously. Then when he attempts to jump, he will fling himself into the jump striking the top. Do not ask your dog to jump more than the required height unless he is a natural jumper like a Doberman. Do not let him anticipate your command.

If your dog refuses to release the dumbbell when you reach for it, grasp the end of the dumbbell in your right hand, say "Out," and give him a quick tap under the chin with your left hand. The tap will surprise him into releasing his hold on it, and you can then take it from him. After he has been corrected in this manner once or twice he will be willing to release the dumbbell as soon as he sees you reaching for it. It should not be necessary to use the command "Out" after this.

Insist upon perfect Sits in front and at Heel position.

You should practice the retrieving and jumping in different locations until the dog will work consistently anywhere.

Your dog jumps when you tell him, "Get it."

He retrieves it.

He returns over the high jump with the dumbbell.

He Sits straight in front of you, holding the dumbbell patiently. Then you take it.

Your dog goes to the Heel position and Sits straight. You praise him.

THE BROAD JUMP

The Broad Jump consists of four flat boards or hurdles, so designed that they are raised from one to six inches off the ground to telescope for convenience. To execute this exercise the handler should have his dog sitting at Heel position ten feet from the Broad Jump. He should command his dog to "Stay," and take a position two feet out from the sides of the jump opposite the space between the third and fourth hurdles. Upon the handler's command "Hussan, Hup," his dog should jump straight ahead and clear all the hurdles without touching them, turn, and Sit straight in front of his handler. At the command "Hussan, Heel," the dog should go to Heel smartly.

If you have read the suggestions on Jumping, you are ready for this chapter. Your dog will enjoy this exercise if you start it at the same time you teach him to jump the high and bar jumps. Dogs that learn the three jumps at one time rarely have difficulty with the broad jump.

Lift your dog over the broad jump with the leash as you run around it.

As you stand near the hurdle, be prepared to lift your dog over with the leash as you say "Hup" and run alongside the broad jump.

To start, use three hurdles; the first and third should be lying upright on their edges, and the middle hurdle should be flat in its normal position. The first few times, jump over the hurdles yourself with your dog as you say "Hup." Then, with the dog still on leash, run up to the jump and as you say "Hup," help him over with the leash as you swerve around the jump. Next, as you approach the jump, say "Hup," and hold him on a loose leash. The leash, of course, is held in your left hand.

When your dog has mastered this exercise, lay the hurdles flat in their normal position, about eight inches apart, as shown in the photo on page 122. If the dog steps on a hurdle, lay the fourth hurdle on its edge in front of him, run up to the jump with your dog on leash, and lift him over as you say "Hup." Try this two or three times before you repeat the procedure on a loose leash. Then try it with all the hurdles laid flat in their normal position.

When this point has been reached successfully, try this. Have your dog Sit in the center and face the broad jump six feet away. Tell him to "Stay," walk over to the first hurdle, and stand there. Call your dog's name; as he responds, say "Hup," and assist him over the jump with your left arm and leash. Repeat this several times until he does it well. The next step is to stand in the same position and try this off leash. When you give the command "Hup," wave your dog over the jump with your left arm. If you run alongside the hurdles as your dog approaches, it will give him the incentive to jump them. Be sure to praise him every time he clears the hurdles and also to pet him. If he steps on one of the hurdles or in between them, say "No," and quickly put your left index finger in the ring of his collar, run up to the jump with him and lift him over. As soon as he starts to jump, let go of the collar.

If you have a stubborn dog who persists in stepping on or in between the hurdles and this method does not work, try this: Have someone hold the bar from the bar jump down on the ground between the first and second hurdles. As you run up to the jump with your dog, the bar should be raised about four inches above the hurdles. Your dog will have to clear the hurdles or crash into the bar. If he does, he will soon learn to pick up his feet and jump clear. This should be tried on leash first.

Sooner or later your dog will run around the jump instead of jumping over the hurdles. When this happens, say "No," quickly take his collar, run him up to the jump, and assist him over it. Help him this way twice before you let him try it again by himself.

The hurdles should be spaced so as to cover a distance equal to twice the height of the high jump. As the dog learns to jump on command, gradually lengthen the jump to the desired number of feet. When your dog stands in the Heel position, you should be at least eight feet from the jump; and when you leave him, you should stand facing the right side of the jump two feet from it and between the first and last hurdles. I have found through experience that the ideal place to stand is between the last two hurdles.

Call your dog's name first and then give the command "Hup." He should move forward on the "Hup" portion of the command. When he is in mid-air over the jump, take a quarter turn to the right in the same spot. You will then be facing your dog after he turns and comes in to you. If he goes too wide, it may be necessary to call him in to you after he jumps. As your dog lands, tell him "Come," and have him sit straight in front of you. Always make him return to you promptly, go smartly to Heel and Sit straight. Never permit him to anticipate your commands.

At this point in your training you should concentrate upon straight Sits in front of you. Almost any dog will come in to his handler and Sit straight if the handler is in a direct line with him. This is simple enough for him to learn, but it is not enough. A dog should come to his handler and Sit straight in front of him even though the handler is facing away from his dog. Try calling your dog to you from various angles. Even turn your back on him and call him to you. Once he has mastered this he will come in for a straight Sit regardless of the direction in which he had to approach you. This will be of value to you in the broad jump exercise in case the dog takes a wide turn.

Look at your dog to be sure he is sitting straight, tell him "Stay" and leave him.

Stand two feet from the broad jump, between the first and fourth hurdles, as you give your command, "Hup."

When your dog is in mid-air, pivot a quarter turn.

When your dog lands, he should turn toward you.

He should Sit straight in front of you.

And finish with a perfect Sit.

I am again emphasizing the point here that you can obtain top results in your training only if you strive for perfection. I have taught all my dogs to come in to me from any direction, and they have rewarded me with dozens of perfect scores or near-perfect performances.

The dog that I am training as I write is so delighted with his ability to Sit straight in front of me that he beams like a ray of sunshine each time he does it. I have made quite a fuss over him for his efforts, and he is very eager to do it correctly.

This is still not a guarantee that he will have a perfect Sit each time in a show, but it is the next thing to it.

A fast way to teach a dog to jump the broad jump. Use fifteen-inch tent stakes with white nylon string. Taut nylon string will remind the dog not to touch the jumps.

This works for all dogs.

If, when the jump is fully extended, your dog should absent-mindedly step on or in between a hurdle, do not allow him to Finish, but quickly say "No" and run him over the jump twice. Then ask him to jump in the formal manner.

There is one problem that may crop up later. Your dog may start cutting the right corner of the jump, jumping diagonally instead of straight. If he does, try this. As he leaps over the jump, hold your right leg out straight: he will veer to the left to avoid it. If you time this correction properly, your dog will soon remember to jump straight.

Throughout this exercise praise should be spontaneous whenever the dog is responding to your commands. Always give praise quickly and naturally.

THE LONG SIT (3 MINUTES) AND THE LONG DOWN (5 MINUTES)

These exercises have already been explained in chapter 14.

A handler has the choice throughout these exercises, with the exception of the Utility Signal exercise, of using either a verbal command or a signal. Throughout this book I have recommended a verbal command simply for the psychological effect it has upon your dog. Have you noticed how a dog becomes alive at the sound of his master's voice? One minute asleep and the next fully alert, on his feet, eyes sparkling, tail wagging, his whole being trembling with joyful anticipation. Don't deny him the joy of listening to it.

Chapter 17

Small Dogs

Use the same training technique for training your small dog. Hold the leash in your left hand, and use a wrist motion to jerk him back if he forges or goes wide. Start out on your left foot and *never* step on him. Don't adapt your pace to his, and do walk briskly. Don't let him sit between your feet.

Be firm and patient, but don't baby him. *Do not carry him when he is being trained.*

A small dog should Sit in front of your toes.

Let your dog sight down your arm at his level for the Directed Retrieve.

Chapter 18

The Utility Exercises

The Utility exercises consist of the Signal Exercise, Scent Discrimination Article No. 1, Scent Discrimination Article No. 2, Directed Retrieve, Moving Stand and Examination, and Directed Jumping. It will be necessary for you to qualify at three shows, under three different judges, in order to obtain your UD (Utility Dog). This is comparable to a college degree.

In order to train your dog for the Utility work, you will need the high jump that you used in the Open work and a bar jump that consists of a square, wooden horizontal bar resting on pegs that fit into two uprights. This bar is between two and two-and-a-half square inches and can be adjusted to the height that your dog should jump. You will need three white work gloves for the Directed Retrieve exercises. The Scent Discrimination exercise calls for ten articles, two sets of five each, of leather and metal, already fully described in chapter 11, "Equipment."

All work in this class is done off leash. When you enter the Utility ring with your dog on leash, you tell the steward what height your dog will jump. Then, hand her your leash and your case that contains your Scent Discrimination articles and white gloves.

THE SIGNAL EXERCISE

This exercise can be taught at any time after the dog has learned to retrieve. It is done entirely by hand signal, and no verbal commands may be given at any time. During the first part of the exercise, the Heel Free routine is used and a Left Turn, Right Turn, Slow, About Turn, Fast, and Halt are included in the judge's commands. Then, when the handler and his dog are at one end of the ring, the judge will order the handler to "Stand his dog" and "Leave him." The handler will carry out these orders by signaling his dog to Stand and then to Stay. Then he will leave his dog and walk to the far end of the ring, turn, and face him. The judge will signal the handler to Drop his dog, Sit his dog, Call him in, and then Finish, in that order. The dog should be alert and respond to his handler's signals willingly and quickly.

Your dog has been learning all the signals except the Sit signal since you started your Novice work, and now all you have to do is put them together.

With your dog sitting at Heel position, give him the Heel signal (scoop your left hand forward over his head), and walk along briskly. Try a few Halts to be sure he will respond instantly to the Heel signal. Do a short Heeling routine, and then give your dog the Stand signal (quickly bring your right hand down in front of the dog's nose, fingers outstretched and pointing down), and return your hand to your right side. After a second, give your dog the Stay signal with your left hand (the same signal as the Stand signal but with the left hand). Walk about five feet from your dog, turn around and face him, and place your hands down by your sides as in the Recall exercise. Give your dog the Down signal (raise your right arm quickly over your head and hold it there until the dog starts to Drop). Later when the dog responds, hold the Down signal for just an instant. Praise him. Next, give your dog the Sit signal (raise your left arm quickly from your side in a lifting motion), reach forward, and lift the dog to a Sitting position with his collar, saying "Sit," and praise him. Tell him to "Stay," and step back a few paces. Give the dog the Come signal (sweep your hand out sideways and then into your chest), and praise him when he Sits in front of you. Then give your dog the Finish signal (sweep your left hand down by your side and back, then place it down by your side), and praise him again.

You should start the series of signals with your hands down by your sides, and after each signal you should return your hands to the same position. If you follow this same procedure in all the exercises, your whole performance will be smooth and integrated. Notice that this same routine is used consistently throughout the Novice, Open, and Utility exercises; and at this point you are probably doing it so smoothly that you are not even thinking about it.

"Stand."

"Stay."

"Down."   **"Sit."**

In the beginning, it may be necessary to give your dog the verbal commands along with the signals in order to make him respond more quickly.

If you have not taught your dog any signals, you will need to keep him on leash until he has learned all of them. He will learn the signals more easily if you guide him with the leash. Be especially patient with him when teaching him the Sit signal; it generally takes a dog longer to learn this signal than the others. If he seems a little slow to grasp the idea, put him on leash, and as you give the signal lift him up with the leash. Praise him each time he does it for you. If you have him off leash and he fails to respond to the Sit signal, say "Sit" as you run up and lift him into a Sitting position with his collar. Encourage him by praising him as he carries out the signal.

Your dog will learn the signals by constant repetition. Gradually increase the distance between you as your dog responds. When you have progressed to the point where you have left him on the Stay signal and walked about twenty feet away, you may have a problem. Many dogs purposely look away as you are about the give the signals. If this is the case, do not repeat the signal more than once, but run up to your dog and make him carry out the command. This will force him to be alert and watch for the signals.

Gradually increase the distance between you to fifty feet. Praise your dog after each signal when he responds correctly. Teach him to respond to each signal quickly but wait a few seconds before giving each signal so that he won't perform automatically.

"Come."

Place hands down by sides after each signal.

Sooner or later when you give your dog the Stay signal, leave him standing, and walk to the other end of the ring; he will anticipate the Down signal and drop before you give him the signal. This is a normal reaction you can expect, and it is easily corrected. Try returning to your dog every other time you leave him instead of dropping him. Walk around your dog one or twice, then stop in the Heel position and signal him to Heel. If he should go down before you have a chance to do anything, say "No, Stand," and run up to him and lift him into a stance.

In the beginning vary your routine so that your dog will learn to wait for your signals. Once he understands the routine you should hesitate before each signal. Try practicing the signals where there are distractions so that your dog will make mistakes and you can correct him. He will soon become reliable as he gains more experience.

A straight Sit in front.   **"Heel."**

SCENT DISCRIMINATION

The judge will take two articles (one from each set) from your box and place them on his table. He will then tell you where to stand with your dog at Heel position while he or his steward handles and places the remaining articles on the ground. You will be facing him, and your dog should be watching the procedure. The articles should be placed about six inches apart, and you should be standing about twenty feet from them. The judge will ask you to take an article from his table, and upon doing so you should show both the judge and his steward the number and type of article so that they can make a note of it. Some dogs dash up to the pile of articles and scatter them around so much that it is difficult to keep track of the correct article. When a record is kept of the number there is no question whether the dog retrieves the correct article. You then turn around so that both you and your dog have your backs to the articles. The judge will then ask, "What method will you be using to send your dog?" The handler must respond with either "After a Sit," or "Send directly." The judge will then ask "Are you ready?" At this time you place your hand

Dog turns toward you into Heel position.   **Dog Sits straight, and he and his handler smile happily.**

scent upon the article by rubbing it. After several seconds the judge takes it and places it in the pile. Then he orders you to "Send your dog," and you command your dog, "Hussan, get it," as you turn around and face the articles. Your dog should trot out briskly and search continuously for the scented article until he finds it. Then he should pick it up and return it to you briskly, without mouthing it, and Sit straight in front of you, holding it patiently. Upon order from the judge, you take the article. Your dog should relinquish it willingly. The judge will say "Finish," and you will tell your dog, "Hussan, Heel," which he should do quickly and with precision. The judge and his steward will then check the article that your dog retrieved to be sure it is the correct one. You will follow this same procedure for the remaining article.

You are ready to teach your dog the Scent Discrimination exercise when he is proficient at retrieving the dumbbell. You will not have any difficulty in teaching your dog Scent Discrimination if you do so in easy stages.

The following method has proven to be so fast and easy to teach that I use it exclusively. Any breed of dog will learn this exercise very quickly if you use this method. The length of time it takes varies with the individual dog — some will learn in one week and others will take three. However, even when your dog has learned the exercise and is doing it correctly, you should practice it every time you put him through the other Utility exercises.

A week before you decide to start practicing, put one leather and one metal article in your pocket. Carry them around with you and rub your hand scent on them occasionally so they will be impregnated with your scent.

First of all, you should set up a Utility ring about forty by fifty feet long. Occasionally you should work in a ring larger than this, because many breed specialty clubs make their rings far too large. Your dog should have the experience of working in both of these rings.

Place the jumps about eighteen feet apart in the center of the ring, one on each side, and about six feet in from the side of the ring. Be sure that the jumps are in line with each other by sighting them both as you stand on the ring side of one jump.

The easiest articles for a dog to retrieve are the two- or three-bar dumbbells as one bar is always high enough for the dog to grasp. The single-bar dumbbell is also easy for the dog to retrieve, but the ends will eventually loosen and become a nuisance. I have used both in the illustrations.

Cut the ends off six metal coat hangers and make them three inches long. This will give you twelve wire ends shaped like Us. Before you take your dog into the ring, take two clean, unscented metal articles and hammer each one into the grass with a U wire. Use a corner of the ring. Do not touch the articles; place them on the ground with tongs, and space them ten inches apart.

Have a small stool or chair in the ring and place your articles and gloves on it. The chair should be centered at one end of the ring. Have your dog sitting at Heel position, hand him the heavily scented metal article and tell him to "Get it." When he takes it, praise him. Now tell him to Stay and go place the scented article about ten inches from the other two articles. Let your dog see you do this. Return to your dog and command him "Get mine," or whatever you want to say. You will find that your dog will do one of several things. He may trot up to the articles and pick up the first article he comes to which could be the scented one. Praise him if he does this. If he goes to the unscented article first, he may try to pick it up, but if he is unable to do so he will go on to the scented article and retrieve it. Praise him. Or he may reach the unscented article first, try unsuccessfully to

Hammer each article into the ground with a U wire.

Your dog sniffs the article.   **As he starts to pick it up, praise him.**

pick it up, and then stand there wondering what to do next. In this case repeat your command to get it, and if necessary go up to him, take him over to the scented article and encourage him to get it. When he does pick it up, praise him.

You will find that your dog will be sniffing for the scented article the first day that you try this. The next day try the same procedure. If your dog does well, add two more articles. Be sure to encourage him with well-timed praise.

When your dog is sniffing carefully and choosing the heavily scented article each day from five articles you may now add one clean leather article to the group. When your dog sniffs the scented leather article encourage him to pick it up. After this first attempt do not praise him until he has the article in his mouth. Encourage your dog to return to you quickly and Sit straight in front of you. Then insist upon a straight Sit at Heel position.

If your dog doesn't seem to understand what you want, take him up to the articles on leash, push his head down so that his nose is close to an unscented article, and ask, "Is that it?" If he tries to pick it up say, "No." Then you would do the same thing to two other clean articles. And last of all you would hold his head over the heavily scented article and say, "Is that it?" and if he tried to pick it up you would say, "Yes, yes, that's it," and make a fuss over him. If you are patient and don't lose your temper, you will have this dog sniffing for the scented article by the second lesson. It would be wise to keep him on leash for a few days.

Gradually add the rest of the unscented leather articles to the group and be sure to secure each one by hammering it to the ground with a U wire. Follow this procedure for at least a week and try practicing this exercise in different parts of your yard and your ring with various distractions.

Now it is time to start working with the clean, unscented articles but continue to tie the others down with the U wires. Wash your practice articles that were heavily scented and air them for at least three days before you use them again. Practice each day with two different articles. The first few times you use all clean articles be sure to rub them well to give them a strong scent. As your dog becomes proficient, reduce the time you rub your hand scent on the articles to about ten seconds.

When you feel that your dog is quite reliable and consistent in choosing the scented articles, gradually reduce the number of articles that you tie down until you are working without the U wires. If you have followed the aforementioned method carefully, your dog will have no difficulty retrieving the correct articles.

Now practice the exercise with your backs to the articles. You may give your dog the command "Get mine," as you pivot to the right and your dog turns with you and moves out briskly to the articles. Or you may command your dog to "Heel" as you turn. Then the dog may stop and sit at Heel position, and upon your command "Get mine," move forward briskly to retrieve the article.

While the handler and his dog have their backs to the articles, the handler may give his dog his hand scent by pressing his palm against his dog's nose. This must be done gently or he will be penalized. While this is permitted, it is quite unnecessary. Any dog who has been working with his handler will be fully aware of his scent in a day. Since it takes most people weeks, months, or years to reach the Utility work, their dogs will have catalogued their scents long before this. While we remember people by their names or their appearances,

Your dog turns with you as you pivot. You should not move more than one step toward the articles as you do this. Send your dog after the article with the command or signal to retrieve.

Without stopping, your dog hurries out to retrieve the scented article.

Your dog picks the correct article from the pile.

dogs remember by scent. A person can change his appearance to try to fool his dog, but once the dog has gotten a whiff of his scent, the mystery is over.

If you haven't followed the above method, you may find that your dog is making a wide swing before he gets to the articles. To correct this you should have him Sit after you turn. Then when you send him, he will probably go straight to the articles. Other handlers who have used the above method will find it faster to pivot and send the dog at the same time.

It is important to practice this exercise by sending your dog in a different direction each time you practice. If you place the articles between the jumps each time you practice, your dog will head for that spot in a show even though the judge has placed the articles in a corner of the ring while your dog was watching. Dogs are creatures of habit and will fail an exercise if you don't anticipate their reactions and practice accordingly. This is one reason why I earn so many Obedience titles in the shortest possible time. I have learned to read my dogs' reactions when I practice with them. By watching dogs work I can tell how they will react in a given situation. I can also tell handlers what method they used to train their dogs when I see them making mistakes. The errors are a direct result of improper training and handling, and although they can be corrected, it takes a considerable amount of time to retrain the dogs and teach them to work consistently, precisely, and happily.

It is quite possible to practice this exercise by yourself, but if there is a second person present, ask him to place the articles in the pile for you. Practice this exercise in different locations; a dog will often miss an article where the ground scent is heavy, for instance in thick grass after a rainstorm, until he is experienced.

Be consistent and extravagant with your praise so your dog will work quickly and willingly. If he starts to slow down, it is either because you are making it tedious or you are not encouraging him enough. It is better to take three weeks to teach him this exercise than to dampen his spirits by long, tedious lessons. Make the lessons short but pleasant and to the point.

People who live in apartments, or those who live in areas where the winters are cold and the ground freezes, might want to practice the Scent Discrimination exercise indoors. Use the exact same method but instead of hammering the articles into the ground, use a piece of carpet. Buy an inexpensive four-by-six-foot washable shag rug. It should be at least this size so the dog can walk on it as he approaches the articles. An inexpensive carpet will be loosely woven, so it will be easy to poke the wires through it to tie the articles down. You will have to use a lightweight wire that is easy to twist.

You should place the articles in different positions every other day. The articles should be washed if there is any scent on them even though it is your dog's scent when he mouthed or tried to pick up an article. The rug should be washed after the second week when the dog knows the work. The practice sessions should then be on various types of flooring.

THE DIRECTED RETRIEVE

Start this exercise the way you would any new Retrieve exercise: Hand your dog the glove and say "Get it," and when he does this, say "Hold it." If he doesn't take it readily, place it in his mouth and make him hold it for a few seconds. Repeat this until your dog does it correctly.

Next, have your dog sit at Heel position with your backs to the glove, give him the Stay command, and go place the glove on the ground twenty feet away from you. Return to your dog and tell him to Heel as you turn toward the glove. Be sure he Sits straight, and then give him the Directed Signal to Retrieve as you say "Get it." The Directed Retrieve signal is given with your left hand and arm, and you may bend your knees and body if you wish. At first, exaggerate the signal by swishing your hand and arm down alongside your dog's head and out toward the glove. Take one or two steps toward the glove as you do this.

Your dog watched you place the glove down, and he knows how to retrieve, so he will no doubt trot out after the glove. If he doesn't, repeat the signal. If he still doesn't move, take him by the collar with your left hand and run him out toward the glove a few steps as you tell him to "Get it."

Directed Retrieve: **After you turn with your dog to face the glove, signal the direction with your left hand and arm, so your dog can sight down your arm toward the glove. Give the verbal command "Get it" either simultaneously with the signal, or directly after it.**

Retrieving the glove after the handler has pivoted to the left to face it.

Now place the other two gloves in line with the one you are using and place them about twenty feet apart. Keep sending your dog for a different glove each time.

If you practiced changing your position when you were teaching your dog to go to the Heel position, you are all ready. If not, go back and read the instructions at the end of the section "Teaching Your Dog to Go to the Heel Position," which will be found in the chapter 14, "The Novice Exercises." Your dog should change his position when you command him to Heel, and you should not touch him at this time. It is extremely important that you practice these turns so that your dog will turn and Sit straight when he faces the glove. If he doesn't Sit straight, he will probably go to the wrong glove. When your dog is fairly consistent about going out in the right direction, give the signal without stepping forward.

Practice the retrieve at a distance of twenty feet until your dog is doing it perfectly. Now place the gloves twenty feet apart and send your dog from a distance of thirty feet. You will have to move your jumps back to be centered between them. Your dog will probably continue to do it correctly, but if he doesn't, help him. If he doesn't go in a straight line toward the selected glove, bring him back and make him do it over again. Don't ever let him pick up the wrong glove; be quick to correct him if he attempts to do this. If he seems confused when you send him out, repeat and hold the signal as you run up to the glove with him. You may have to do this a good number of times before he gets the habit of going out straight. Whenever your dog veers from a straight line to the glove, prop up the glove you want him to retrieve by placing a clump of grass or a rock under it. If your dog can see it easily, he is more likely to head straight for it.

By teaching your dog to go out straight to retrieve the glove at a distance of thirty, then forty feet, you are also teaching him the Send Out in the Directed Jumping exercise. It will make it considerably easier for your dog when you start this exercise.

When you turn and face the gloves, Number One is on your left, Number Two is in the center, and Number Three is on your right. When retrieving gloves One and Two, I suggest you turn to the right. When retrieving glove Three, it is better to turn to the left. The distance to the gloves from where you are standing should be about twenty-two feet. The distance between the gloves should vary during practice sessions and be from fourteen to twenty feet. Every once in a while have your dog retrieve the center glove, with the jumps in the center of the ring, from a distance of forty feet.

In a show, with your backs to the gloves you would stand in the center, between, and in line with, the High Jump and the Bar Jump. On command of the judge who would call either "One," "Two," or "Three," you would turn to face the designated glove. As you turned, you would tell your dog to Heel by giving him a verbal command, and he should quickly go to Heel position and Sit straight. You may not touch your dog, but you should pivot toward the specified glove while you remain in the same spot. Then you should give your dog the Directed Retrieve signal as you say "Get it." Your dog should trot out briskly in the direction of the designated glove and return it to you at a brisk trot without mouthing or playing with it. He should Sit straight in front of you without touching you and close enough so that you do not have to step forward or stretch out to take the glove from him. Upon order from the judge to "Take it," you do so. Then upon order from the judge to "Finish," you send your dog to the Heel position for a straight Sit.

DIRECTED JUMPING

The exercise should look like this: Have your dog Sit at the Heel position about twenty feet from the jumps and centered between them. Give him the signal and the command "Go." The dog should trot out briskly until he is about twenty feet beyond the jumps. Then call his name and tell him to "Sit." After he has sat for a few seconds, give him the command "Hup," and signal him toward the jump. The dog should clear the jump without touching it, and while he is in mid-air you should turn in the direction in which he will come in to you. He should Sit straight in front of you, and then he should be sent to Heel for another straight Sit, and be praised. You should repeat the exercise again using the other jump.

Wait until your dog knows the Directed Retrieve exercise before you teach him the Send-out portion of this exercise.

A dog can become quite confused by this exercise if he is not taught properly. It should be done in two stages, and your dog should be rested when you teach him. Begin your practice session with this exercise so your dog will be alert and responsive.

At first, bend way down to give your dog the signal to go out.

When your dog understands the verbal command "Go" and the signal, give the signal without bending down.

Your dog will go out fast and straight if you place a piece of meat on a rock at the far end of the ring.

The first stage is to teach your dog to respond to a directed signal and the verbal command "Hup." Stand with your dog in Heel position twenty feet back from the jumps and centered between them. Give your dog the command "Go" and run with him down to the end of the ring, or about forty-five feet, and give him the command "Hussan, Sit," and as he turns toward you, step back and stand there as he Sits. If he Sits, praise him. If he doesn't Sit, or if he Sits crooked, go up to him and push him into a straight Sit as you repeat the verbal command "Sit." Then praise him.

At this time you are not actually teaching the Send-out, but because your dog must be at the far end of the ring, you might as well get him used to trotting out in a straight line. At this stage, he will be learning to turn and Sit on command, so teach him to Sit straight. A dog does not have to Sit straight in a show when he is sent out, but it is wise to practice straight Sits. If this is neglected in the beginning, the dog will become careless and might Sit with his back to a jump. This would make it harder for him to respond to your signal to jump the hurdle in back of him. Try to avoid such pitfalls during your training sessions.

Follow behind him quietly.

And help him Sit straight.

So that you will be close enough to help him turn.

Tell your dog to Stay and go stand about ten feet from the high jump and about five feet back. Give your dog the command "Hussan, Hup," as you signal in the direction of the high jump. Repeat the command (signal if necessary) and step toward the jump. The first time you might even have to touch the top of the jump as you stand beside (or behind) it, as you again repeat the signal and verbal command. Praise the dog happily as he responds.

Try the bar jump in the same way, but in the beginning have both jumps set low. Later, when the dog is jumping consistently, you should gradually raise them to the height he is required to jump in a show. During the first two lessons when you are teaching your dog the Directed Jumping signals, it won't be necessary to have him Sit in front of you after he jumps. Quickly take him back and repeat the exercise. He will probably progress very quickly, as most dogs learn the signals within a week.

Remember to call cadence at the right moment as your dog approaches either the high jump or the bar jump; this will teach him to jump gracefully. In a show, if he climbs the high jump or knocks off the bar, he will be disqualified.

Gradually increase the distance between you until you are twenty feet from the jumps and at least forty feet from your dog. If he should start in the wrong direction, say "No," and walk toward the correct jump. Give the signal again and say "Hup." Never let him jump the wrong jump even if you have to run up to it and block his path. Now, when your dog jumps, have him come all the way in to you and Sit straight in front of you, and praise him. Send him to Heel, and praise him again. As he is leaping over the jump, turn in that direction.

When you feel that your dog understands the Directed Jumping signals and works fast, willingly, and precisely, it is time to make the exercise more difficult. Because you have been practicing with your dog sitting in the center of the ring, next try the signals with

At first, stand close to the hurdle as you give the signal and verbal command, "Hup."

Finally, have him Sit forty-five feet away from you.

your dog way off center. Eventually try placing him behind the bar jump and give him the signal to jump the high jump, or vice versa. At first encourage him by repeating the signal and verbal command. Later he should obey the signal promptly without any extra commands. If he doesn't obey immediately, a verbal reprimand or a jerk on his collar might be necessary. Of course, when you place the dog off center, do so after he has trotted down the center of the ring and sat straight.

The second stage is to teach your dog to Go Out. If you have used my method to teach your dog the Directed Retrieve, you will find it a decided advantage now. Have your solid and bar jumps in line on opposite sides of your ring about eighteen feet apart and about twenty-five feet from the end of the ring. Stand with your dog at Heel position, in the center, about twenty feet back from the jumps. Place a white rock at the far end of the ring about twenty-five feet beyond the jumps and centered between them. Be sure your dog sees you do this. Now give your dog the exaggerated Directed Retrieve signal as you say "Go" and point straight ahead. When he is one-third of the way there, follow along behind him very quietly. Let him proceed to the rock, and when he reaches it, tell him to Sit, and give your dog's name first. If he Sits, praise him. If he doesn't Sit, quickly make him do so. If your dog doesn't go far enough, send him out again by repeating the signal and verbal command.

Give him the signal and/or the verbal command, "Hup."

Repeat the exercise for the bar jump.

He should clear the hurdle without touching the bar.

When the dog is in mid-air over the jump, turn in his direction so he will Sit straight in front of you.

Have him finish for a straight Sit.

If your dog works fast, and if you have control of him, you might find it wise to omit his name when you tell him to Sit. Generally speaking, it is better to use a dog's name before the command to get his attention.

There are some dogs who haven't started the Directed Retrieve exercise, so these dogs could use the following method for the Send Out. Have your dog sitting at one end of the ring. He should be in the center, about three feet in from the rope. Show your dog a small can that contains pieces of cooked dry liver. Open the can and give your dog a piece. Then command him to Stay while you walk down to the end of the ring and place the can on the ground near the ring rope directly opposite him. Be sure you draw your dog's attention to the can and the piece of liver that you place on top of it. Now return to your dog.

Call your dog's name and give the command "Go." When he runs down to eat the liver, follow behind him quickly. As soon as he has eaten the meat, order him to "Sit," then praise him. If he does not respond, make him Sit quickly. After a few times, you will find your dog will race down to get the meat. However, you must insist that he not only Sits quickly, but that he also turns toward the other end of the ring.

Because he has already learned how to do the directed jumping, you may now combine it with the Send Out. As the dog becomes proficient, use the meat every second or third time until he will go out on command, turn, and Sit straight.

A good square stance.   **The wrong stance — feet not together.**

MOVING STAND AND EXAMINATION

This exercise takes the place of the old Group Stand. It was a happy day for Obedience handlers and their dogs when this change was made.

Your dog will enjoy learning this new exercise. It is similar to the Stand for Examination exercise in the Novice Class. Have your dog in Heel position, give him the command to Heel, and walk forward about ten feet. Now give your dog the signal to Stand as you say "Stay," and walk forward about ten feet, turn around and face your dog. Your dog must be commanded to Stay without the handler slowing down, pausing, or stopping. And he must not move when you go back and examine him by running your hands down his back, sides, and tail. Then return to your position and give your dog the command and signal to Heel. He should always have a straight Sit.

The judge will give you the commands, "Stand and leave your dog," and after he examines him, "Call your dog to Heel." Your dog should stand quietly while being examined. Then, when you say his name and give the command and signal to Heel, he should quickly return to the Heel position and Sit straight. Ask your friends to go over your dog so he will learn to be quiet when examined. He must also remember to Stay without moving his feet until you call him.

Georg is given the signal and verbal command to Stay.

The handler walks ten feet from him and turns and waits while the judge examines him.

Georg quickly returns to the Heel position.

Chapter 19

Brace Competition

This competition is open to any brace of dogs or bitches, or combination of both, of the same breed. It is not a regular class, and no credit toward any Obedience title will be given. This class is generally found at Obedience Trials sponsored by a training club.

The Novice routine is employed, and a tandem chain may be used to clip the two dogs together. This is a short chain, about ten inches long, with a clip at both ends. You can make it yourself or buy one.

The dog that works the fastest, or the one that Heels the closest, should be on the outside because he will have to hurry on the turns. The other dog will work the inside position next to you. The first exercise is Heeling on Leash with the Slow, Fast, Halt, Normal, About Turn, Left Turn and Right Turn commands given at different intervals. The Figure 8 is employed, but the stewards will stand farther apart because two dogs will require more room to turn.

During the Stand for Examination exercise the judge will examine each dog individually by touching his head, back, and croup. This is done off leash.

Heeling off Leash should be done with the same precision as the Heeling on Leash.

The Recall exercise is next, and the dogs are expected to come in at a trot and Sit straight in front of the handler. Upon command they should go to Heel smartly.

The Long Sit for one minute, and the Long Down for three minutes will be executed with the braces lined up together in a row on one side of the ring. At the judge's command the handlers will leave their dogs, cross the ring, turn, and face them, and stand there for the allotted time. When the judge orders the handlers to "Return to your dogs," they will do so.

The brace that works with the most precision stands the best chance of winning. It is desirable that the dogs work as if they were one, keeping in step at all times while heeling, making turns, and sitting.

Brace work is very interesting and a great deal of fun. If you have trained two dogs that work equally well, you have good material for a brace. Each dog should understand the Novice work perfectly before you try the brace work. They should work at about the same speed and should Sit quietly. Their response to commands should be identical. This type of Obedience work is not worth watching unless it is nearly perfect. Precision and teamwork must be in evidence.

The Stay signal and verbal command as the dogs walk into a perfect stance.

I have used the name "Boys" for brace work commands since my first brace competition in the spring of 1952. Because they were used to being called "good boys," they readily understood the name. Of course you may choose any name you wish, but it should have character.

HEELING ON LEASH

Use just one leash and clip it to the collar of the dog nearest you. Practice the regular Novice heeling, and on your turns call the name of the dog that lags and tell him to Heel. If one dog forges ahead, reach down and jerk him back by using the tandem chain. Do not jerk the good dog — praise him. If both dogs are perfectly trained, your only problem will be to keep them in step and see that they Sit together. If one Sits more slowly than the other, tap him for a faster Sit. Praise them at every opportunity so they will think it is fun and enjoy working together.

Heeling on Leash — a beautiful brace. The leash should be attached to collar of the dog nearest the handler.

FIGURE 8

You will have to watch the outside dog on the Figure 8 and make him hurry around the outside turn. When working the inside turn, caution the dogs with the word "Easy." Your posts will have to be slightly farther apart than in the Novice Class.

STAND FOR EXAMINATION

You may pose the dogs singly or walk them into the pose. It looks smooth and impressive to walk both dogs into a pose and Stand them with a hand signal. It is a sign of expert handling. If the dogs are heeling with precision, they will stop in step with each other. Practice this until you have it down perfectly.

HEELING OFF LEASH

The dogs are still attached with the tandem chain or not, as you wish. I prefer to use it. This exercise is not very difficult for trained dogs. You must watch carefully to see that every change of pace, every turn, and every Sit is performed with perfect precision. Too often in brace work you will see a handler doing a fast pantomime instead of really running. If you practice, you can teach your dogs to do the fast pace with as much precision as the normal pace.

Be careful that your dogs do not weave in and out as they are heeling. They should not be wide one minute and crowd you the next. Practice to attain precision, and be quick to correct the dog that is making the mistake. Be equally fast with a word of praise when it is earned.

THE RECALL EXERCISE

You may remove the tandem chain in this exercise if you wish. When working off leash you must either keep the tandem chain on for all the exercises off leash or leave it off. When you call your dogs, say "Boys, come," using the name first. If one lags behind, urge him to come in faster. As they come in, be sure that they Sit directly in front of you. Practice the Finish that they know, and repeat it until they can do it smoothly together. One dog will learn to wait for the other, and they will become adjusted to working shoulder to shoulder.

THE LONG SIT AND THE LONG DOWN

These exercises are exactly the same as in the Novice Class except that the dogs are close together. They may or may not be connected with the tandem chain depending upon your choice in the Heel Free exercise.

If you are lucky enough to own two dogs, you will find this training most helpful. If you can handle both dogs at the same time, it will be no problem to take them places together. By teaching them the brace work you will gain even more control over them, and they will be better behaved. The training will teach them to get along well together, to give a thought to each other, and to learn the technique of keeping in step.

It is very heart-warming to handle a brace of dogs that has been precision trained. The pleasure you get from watching them respond is worth all the work you put into it.

Perfectly straight Sits in Front after a Recall.

A remarkable example of obedience training! The author trained and showed Wynthea's
Elissa, UD, and her sister, Wynthea's Elsie, UD. They were shown in ten shows. Competing
against one another, they each won their CD, CDX, and UD in eleven months with fifteen
Firsts, two Seconds, two Thirds, Dog World, Highest Single, and Highest Combined
Awards. Each had a litter between her CD and UD titles. These dogs were later highly
successful working as a brace.

Chapter 20

Graduate Novice

The Graduate Novice Class is one of several nonregular classes and is open to any dog or bitch that has not gained a leg toward the CDX title. This class is not provided at every Obedience Trial. It is generally included at Obedience Specialty Shows sponsored by training clubs. No credit is given toward any Obedience title.

In the Graduate Novice Class the Novice routine is used, except that the Figure 8 will be performed off leash, the Drop on Recall will be substituted for the straight Recall, and the Long Sit and the Long Down exercises will be as conducted in the Open Class work.

If your dog has already competed in the Novice Class, you should have no problem. Heeling on Leash, Standing for Examination, and Heeling off Leash, including the Figure 8 exercise, should be simple for your dog. The Drop on Recall should be practiced a week before the show, but do not repeat this so often that it slows down your dog's Recall. The Long Sit and Long Down exercises should be practiced about three weeks prior to the show to get your dog used to seeing you disappear out of sight. These exercises should be practiced in different locations during this period.

This is just a fun class, and if you enjoy showing your dog in Obedience Trials, this will appeal to you.

Roger and Randy enjoy a quiet moment with Wynn.

Chapter 21

The Working Class

There are many, many people who have won Utility titles for their dogs who would like to continue from there and teach their dogs something new.

I am one of those people who enjoy training, and I find it fun to teach my dogs different things that make them more interesting and better companions. I am introducing a set of exercise in this chapter that is not beyond the reach of an intelligent Utility dog. Not only will you have fun teaching these exercises, but you will find that they will develop your dog's mind.

I have devised these exercises exclusively for Obedience enthusiasts. They are new and exciting, and a challenge to every handler and every dog. All the dogs I have trained love this new work. Spectators find every exercise fascinating to watch. Your dog needs just his nylon or chain choke collar and a leash. You can train your dog successfully by using this method, a little patience, and a great deal of praise. It is not uncommon in the other fields of dog training for trainers to use shock collars, spike collars, and shock sticks. Such equipment will be completely unnecessary in teaching your dog these Obedience exercises.

The new jumps can be homemade, or you can have them made to order for about $70. The jumps I have designed are simple in principle and safe to use. Your dog will not be required to clear more than a three-foot-high jump, so he will not acquire the habit of climbing these jumps. For instance, if you have a German Shepherd whom you want to continue showing in both Open B and Utility but would love to try this new class, rest assured that this work will improve the other. The High Jump, Bar Jump, and Window Jump are three feet high and will have to be cleared. The Barrier is entirely different and must be climbed, so your dog will learn to differentiate between them. I designed the Barrier so that Breed Champions could compete without the danger of injuring themselves. The platform on the back will break their jump to the ground and make it reasonably safe. The largest dogs will be jumping down from a height of four feet, which is not difficult for a physically sound dog. The Long Jump is designed to improve a dog's jumping ability. The individual hurdles will fall over if a dog does not clear them, and this is a good reminder to him to pick his feet up.

These new exercises are listed below.

1. Search Exercise — A practical exercise that will teach your dog to recover your lost articles and that is a useful form of Scent Discrimination.

2. Vocabulary Exercise — If your dog understands everything you say, this will be a cinch. If not, this will teach him to listen to you.

3. Control Exercise — Devised to give you even better control of your dog — combining new and old with the "new look."

4. The Long Jump — A Long Jump that is a challenge to every handler and every dog.

5. Agility Exercise — A series of hurdles that will develop your dog's agility.

Not every dog will be able to do these exercises. Only the most intelligent and most agile will succeed. Not every dog could earn a Tracking title and fewer still could earn an Advanced Tracking title (if there was one), for many would be handicapped either mentally or physically. But for those who meet the mental and physical requirements, here is a new challenge. And to you handlers who are looking for new fields to conquer, I say "Try it."

SEARCH EXERCISE

The handler will stand with his dog in the Heel position and, on order from the judge, will execute such portions of the Heel Free exercise as the judge may direct. Upon order from the judge the handler will surreptitiously drop a small key case that is dark brown in color and about two by three inches in size. The judge will have the handler and his dog continue heeling until they are at the opposite end of the ring and will give them an order to "Halt." While the handler and his dog have their backs turned the judge will now place his own key case about two feet from that the handler dropped. The judge's case will be the same size and color. The judge will then direct the handler to "About Turn and Halt." On order from the judge to "Send your dog," the handler will give his dog the command or signal to "Seek Back." If the handler elects to use a signal it will be with one hand and arm only; body signals will be penalized. The handler must remain in the same spot and may not turn toward the key case.

The dog may check the judge's case by sniffing it but will be marked Failed if he picks it up. He should trot out briskly, find his handler's key case, and return at a brisk trot. He should return the case to his handler without mouthing or playing with it and should relinquish it immediately without any command. His Sit in Front should be perfectly straight, and his Finish should be as precise.

The first step in teaching this exercise is to have all of your jumps set up in the practice area. The High Jump, Bar Jump, Window Jump, and Barrier should be placed in that order eighteen feet apart in readiness for your dog to jump them in succession. They will be erected parallel to the left side of the ring fifteen feet in from the rope. The Long Jump will be placed parallel to the right side of the ring and fifteen feet in from the rope.

Have your dog Sit at Heel and offer him the key case saying "Get it." When he takes it tell him "Hold it," and after a few seconds take it from him. If your dog does not take the case when you command him to do so, open his mouth and put the case in it. Tell him "Hold it," and praise him. He will probably take it the next time you ask him. Now throw the case on the ground in front of you and tell your dog to "Get it, Seek Back." Discourage him from mouthing or playing with it when he gets it by saying "No, hold it."

Next have your dog Heel in a straight line out beyond the jumps and, as you turn around, drop the case, allowing the dog to see you do so. Walk back to your original position, turn around, and be sure your dog Sits. Then command your dog to "Get it, Seek Back." When he reaches for the case, say, "Good, come." Do not let him play with the case. Clap your hands and praise him to make him return to you quickly. Have him Sit

Joll finds a key case and sniffs it to be sure it belongs to his handler.

straight in front of you and hold the case, without mouthing it, for a few seconds. Take the case away from him and praise him. Have him go to Heel and praise him if he Sits straight. Repeat this procedure several times. Now drop the "Get it," and just say "Seek Back."

Now you can drop the case surreptitiously in various places to accustom him to search for it. Drop it behind the jumps occasionally so he will get used to looking for it anywhere. Keep him searching for the case. If he stops because he cannot find it, run out immediately and encourage him to keep working. Show him the case, if necessary, and repeat the exercise until he learns to keep searching for it until he finds it. It is only a matter of repetition, and he will learn if you are patient.

When a dog is learning this exercise he may become discouraged if he doesn't see the case after glancing around once or twice, and he may then lie down. When this happens run out to him and take him by the collar for a few steps as you take him over to the case. If you let him go out in front of you, he will see the case and think that he found it himself, so praise him. Then run back, telling him to "Come," and praise him if he responds. If he drops the case, say "No, get it," and when he picks it up again, caution him to "Hold it."

As soon as you feel your dog understands this exercise, it is time to drop a strange key case near yours. Because the strange key case must carry a stranger's scent, try this. Buy a key case similar to your own, give it to a friend, and ask him to keep it in his pocket for a week and occasionally rub it between his hands. At the end of that time have him place the case in a glass jar that has a cover you can screw down (like a peanut butter jar). Now you can use the case whenever you like, and it will carry a foreign scent. Just be careful you don't touch it yourself. You can always pick it up with the jar cover. Keep the strange case in an airtight glass jar when you are not using it. If both of these cases are identical in size and color, be sure to put your initial on the one you want your dog to retrieve.

At first, work the dog near you so you can correct him immediately if he tries to pick up the strange case. Because he is familiar with Scent Discrimination, he will catch on very quickly. The dog that will fail to do this exercise is the one who has searched diligently for the case, spots one of them, and picks it up quickly without checking. With a case this small, and an area this large, plus the Scent Discrimination factor, a dog will have to be working and thinking in order to do the exercise correctly. It is not easy, for there are many hiding places. The dog will be using his eyes and his nose to aid him in his search.

The important thing is to keep your dog working fast by encouraging him and, as he improves, keep making it harder to find the case. If you make a game of it, he will be eager to learn.

VOCABULARY EXERCISE

How many times have you heard people say "My dog understands every word I say to him." When you try this exercise the first time, you will be in for a surprise. Your dog will be more interested in retrieving the first thing he comes to than he will be in obeying your specific command. No matter how familiar he is with these articles, he will likely draw a blank when he is called upon to get one of them.

The articles you will need for this exercise are a dumbbell, a leather leash, a leather glove, and a basket with a rigid handle that is the correct size for your dog, not too small or too large.

You will be standing with your dog at Heel position while the judge places your four articles on the ground eight inches apart and twenty feet in front of you. The judge will tell you to Send your dog. Your dog will make four separate retrieves in this order: the basket, the dumbbell, the glove, and the leash. You will give your dog the verbal command for each article by naming the article, then ordering him to get it. It will be like this, "Basket, get the basket." Your tone of voice must be moderate, as any loud tones will be penalized. Your dog should trot out briskly, choose the correct article, return it to you at a brisk pace, and Sit straight in front of you without mouthing or playing with it. When the judge orders you to "Finish," your dog should do so in the proper manner. Then your dog must retrieve the remaining three articles in the aforementioned order.

Joll correctly selects the basket after his handler has given him the verbal command to do so.

To train your dog to designate between these articles, the first step is to start with just two articles. For instance, if you use the glove and the basket at first, keep working on these until he will retrieve either one without any difficulty. When he reaches this point, take one of the articles, such as the basket, which he can now retrieve by name, and add a new one, such as the leash, and work on these two. He will understand that if you do not say "Basket," you must want him to retrieve the other object. When he has this down, try the leash with the dumbbell. Never work with more than two articles at the same time until he is proficient at retrieving any one of the four articles in a set of two.

Now you may work with any three articles trying different combinations, but always including the four articles at one time or another. If he makes a mistake and selects the wrong article, such as a glove when he has been sent for a leash, say "No, get the leash," and put your hand on the leash. Praise him immediately when he gets the leash.

When your dog has reached the point where he will retrieve a specific object each time you give him the verbal command and you are practicing with three articles, you may add the fourth article.

If you have followed this method of instruction carefully, the addition of the fourth article will not make any difference.

CONTROL EXERCISE

The handler will stand with his dog in the Heel position, and upon order from the judge to "Start," the handler will give his dog the following commands, which the dog will execute at a smart pace. "Go — Sit — Come — Down — Crawl — Stand — Come — Heel." The handler may give his dog verbal commands or signals each time but not a combination of both. The dog that misses one command or signal fails the whole exercise. The dog must Go out about sixty feet, Crawl at least ten feet, Sit or Down quickly, and Sit straight in front of the handler and at Heel position.

Your dog already knows some of these commands and signals so we will work on the new ones and then combine all of them.

To teach your dog to Crawl, have him on leash and give him the Down signal. Call him to you and pull a little on the leash as you hold the Down signal, and control him by saying "Down, Crawl." Make him Crawl about ten feet, then have him Stand as you praise and pet him. When you say "Stand" to your dog, give him the Stand Signal. Start with your hands down by your sides, then swing your hand up toward your dog, bending your elbow to do so, and finish by swinging your hand out to your right side waist high, showing the dog the palm of your right hand all the while. Do this in a sweeping motion.

As soon as it is feasible, combine the Crawl signal with the verbal command Crawl, even though you still have to use the Down command and signal to keep him down. To execute the Crawl signal, hold your right hand down by your side with the back of your hand toward your dog and flick your hand back and forth twice by bending your wrist, then return your hand to its original position.

Be patient but firm; don't let your dog get up and walk one step when you tell him to Crawl. A verbal correction should be all that is necessary to teach him this exercise. Your dog may be taken off leash when you feel you have sufficient control over him to guide him with the verbal command "Crawl" or the Crawl signal.

Now you can combine the whole exercise in the proper sequence. On command or signal your dog should Go out about sixty feet, Sit promptly, Come toward you half the distance, Down quickly, Crawl about ten feet, and Stand. He should be at least fifteen feet

Pull your dog toward you as you give the Down signal and say "Down, Crawl."

Give your dog the Crawl signal as you say, "Crawl."

from you when he is standing. Then he should Come to you and Sit straight and Finish by sitting straight at Heel position. A dog that disobeys one of these commands will fail, and a dog that does not stay down while he is crawling will fail.

This is an interesting exercise to teach or watch, and the handler who succeeds in teaching his dog this exercise will gain more control over his dog. You may alternate the verbal commands and signals.

THE LONG JUMP

The Long Jump will be executed the same way as the Open Class Broad Jump except that the jump will be seven feet long for dogs twenty-two inches or over at the withers, six feet long for dogs sixteen through twenty-one inches at the withers, and a five-foot jump for all other dogs. The jump will be three feet wide, two feet high for all dogs over fifteen inches high, and one foot high for all other dogs.

Your dog already knows how to jump the Open Broad Jump, and this knowledge will be a help to him when you start to teach him this Long Jump. I designed this jump with the intention of improving a dog's jumping ability and this is exactly what it does. Any dog that masters this type of jump will find it much easier to jump any other type of hurdle or obstacle.

This is a difficult hurdle to jump, but it can be mastered if you teach your dog to do it in simple stages. There are three reasons why this hurdle is difficult and why it is a challenge. First, it is a long jump. Second, although it is two feet high (or one foot high depending upon the size of your dog), your dog must jump considerably higher than that in order to clear the full length. Third, it is what I call a blind jump because your dog will be able to see only a quarter of it until he is in the air. This means he must learn to gauge his distance by your position.

The first lesson will be an introduction to this type of jump. Have your dog jump over one hurdle, then two, and then three. Stretch them out until your dog is jumping half of the required length. Run up to the jump with your dog and say "Hup" as he approaches the jump. Try this several times and praise your dog every time he does it. Build up his confidence at this time; let him think this new jump is easy and great fun. A Utility dog should be able to do this easily off leash, but if your dog balks, try him on leash. Your dog should be jumping half the required distance off leash before you try the next step.

Now add another hurdle and leave your dog sitting about twenty feet from the jump. Tell him to Stay and go stand about two feet beyond the Long Jump. Call your dog by name and, when he gets to the most advantageous position for a takeoff, say "Hup." If he clears the jump, add another hurdle and space them an equal distance apart so your dog

Joll clears the Long Jump.

This is a practice jump the author designed to improve Joll's jumping ability. The jump is eight feet long and three feet three inches high. In this practice jump Joll actually cleared thirteen and one-half feet at a height of three and one-half feet. The handler must stand three feet beyond the jump so her dog can gauge the distance correctly.

will now be jumping three-quarters of the required jump. Work on this length for two or three lessons.

Now you will try a longer jump, and this type of hurdle should be taken with the dog going at a fast trot or gallop. It is a running jump, and the dog should build up enough momentum in his dash to the jump and his subsequent leap into the air to clear the hurdles. The principle is the same as that employed by an athlete or a pole vaulter taking a fast sprint to clear a jump. You should leave your dog thirty feet back but in a direct line with the jump. For two or three weeks start your dog at three-quarters of the required length and work up to the full length each day. Continue this practice until you are quite certain that your dog can clear the full length on his first attempt. Don't rush your dog into this, but play it safe and give your dog the chance to build up his confidence in his jumping ability. Above all, remember this is a difficult jump that will require considerable practice and patience. Do not practice this jump unless your dog has dry, firm footing for the takeoff and landing. Never practice when there is any danger of your dog's slipping. The ideal place to practice is a level stretch of lawn as the grass will cushion your dog's landing.

Have your dog Sit at Heel position thirty feet from the Long Jump and in a direct line with it. Tell him to "Stay" and go stand three feet beyond the hurdle and two feet out from it and face it. Say, "Joll, ready," giving your dog's name. You may give the Hup portion of the command when the dog is near the jump. When your dog is in mid-air make a right-angle turn. Your dog should come in to you and Sit straight, and upon command, he should Sit straight at Heel position.

AGILITY EXERCISE

This exercise will consist of four hurdles that are placed ahead of each other but directly in line so that by running and jumping, the dog will be able to clear all four hurdles in succession. The hurdles will be set up in this order — the High Jump, the Bar Jump, the Window Jump, and the Barrier. The jumps will be placed a distance of eighteen feet apart, and they will be painted a flat white. The width of each jump is four feet, with the exception of the Window Jump, which is twenty-eight inches wide. The inside measurement of the window is twenty by twenty inches.

The height of the High Jump, Bar Jump, and Window Jump will be three feet, and the Barrier will be six feet high for all dogs twenty-two inches or over at the withers. The first three jumps will be set at thirty inches and the Barrier at five feet for all dogs fifteen through twenty-one inches at the withers. For all other dogs, the first three jumps will be set at two feet, and the Barrier will be four feet high.

The first two jumps must be jumped clear. The dog must then jump through the window portion of the third jump without touching the hurdle with his feet. The Barrier must be climbed on the dog's first attempt.

The handler will be standing with his dog at Heel, and the judge will instruct the handler to leave his dog. The handler will take a position between the first and last jumps, about five feet out from them and facing them. Upon order from the judge to "Send your dog," the handler may give his dog a verbal command or signal. When the dog has jumped three hurdles, the handler will take a right-angle turn but remain in the same spot. After the dog has jumped all the hurdles, he will Sit straight in front of the handler and then Finish smartly upon command or signal.

Your dog already knows how to jump the High Jump and the Bar Jump, so the first lesson will be to teach him the Window Jump. Stand behind the jump so that you can place your hand on the bottom section of the window when you ask your dog to jump. By

Joll jumps through the window hurdle without touching it.

Joll scales the six-foot barrier with the jump in the Number Two position.

placing your hand there he will understand that you want him to jump through the opening. Simply repeat this until your dog jumps smoothly without touching the lower portion of the window with his feet.

When he has accomplished this, stand off to the side, give him the command "Hup," and praise him when he jumps. Don't let him go around this jump at any time; be fast with your corrections if he doesn't jump or if he tries to climb it.

As soon as you think he understands this hurdle and is jumping smoothly, combine the first three hurdles. Practice on just these three hurdles until your dog will take all three jumps on one command. At first you will have to give several commands and signals to accomplish this, but your dog will soon do it on his own.

The next step is to teach your dog to climb the Barrier. This can best be done in two stages. Set your jump up apart from the other hurdles and adjust the side brackets so the jump is more slanted and about two feet lower than normal. Have your dog on leash and run up to the jump with him as you say "Hup, Climb." When you encourage your dog with your voice and lift him a little with the leash, he will realize that he is expected to climb the Barrier. Quickly move over in back of the jump so you can teach him to step onto the platform before he jumps to the ground. This will have to be repeated a few times before he is ready for the next step.

When you have reached the final stage, set the jump to its full height, which is just five degrees short of being vertical, and make certain that it is strong and steady. Your dog

Wynn is encouraging four-month-old Jet to try the Dog Walk, the A-Frame, and the See-Saw. These are simplified Agility exercises that any puppy can learn. It teaches them to be unafraid of trying something new. It also gives them a sense of balance and accomplishment. Once learned, they love the exercises so much that they will go off and practice by themselves. Jet is learning these exercises as Wynn uses only verbal commands, encouragement, and praise.

Now that he has learned to jump all four hurdles, they are combined. The Barrier is in the succession, Sits straight in front of the author, then goes to Heel upon command. Everyone

realizes at this point that he must climb the Barrier, so run him up to the jump as you say "Climb." If he balks, try it again, encouraging him with your voice. Most dogs will attempt the high Barrier once they have learned to do it at a lower level. For stubborn dogs, you may have to keep lowering the Barrier until they get up enough courage to try it. A few dogs will stop at the jump and refuse to try. If this happens, put your dog on leash and throw the leash over the top of the Barrier. As you pull your dog up, another person should be giving him a boost by pushing him (not lifting him) so he can get the idea of scrambling up himself. It will take only one or two such experiences, and he will understand what to do. If you persevere, your dog will climb it quite swiftly. The more you praise him, the more eager he will be to climb.

Once your dog has acquired the knack of climbing this jump Barrier, you may combine all four jumps. At first when you give the command "Hup," run alongside the hurdles as he is jumping and encourage him to take each one. Be sure to praise him after each jump. Eventually you will be able to stand alongside the jumps, and when you call "Hup," he will jump all four hurdles.

If you want to set up a ring for these exercises, you will need a level piece of ground ninety by sixty feet. This new class is best suited for outdoor dog shows run by specialty clubs.

Number One, or Vertical position. On one command or signal Joll takes the four hurdles in seems to enjoy this exercise more than any other.

When you have taught your dog these exercises you will get a great deal of satisfaction and pleasure watching him do them. The people who have watched my dogs do this work claim it is the most interesting and enjoyable Obedience work they have ever seen. It is certainly exciting and thrilling to watch, often amusing as well as fascinating, but above all else, it unquestionably displays your dog's intelligence.

You might like to think of it as getting your dog's master's degree. I daresay the number of dogs capable of earning such a degree would be equivalent to the number of students earning a similar degree.

Chapter 22

Competing in Shows

I list a few suggestions that may be helpful to you in preparing for show competition.

When your dog works perfectly for you at home and in several other locations, he is ready for show competition. If you have tried him out at a Sanction Match, you know how he will react to show conditions. Your dog, at this time, should work very well for you with just a few words of praise and some gentle patting between exercises. The time will never arrive for you to stop praising your dog, but occasionally you should try working him without this because this is what you will have to do at a show.

Feed your dog early in the morning on the day of the show so he will not have his mind on dinner. Some shows last all day, and the dog that normally eats in the afternoon will become impatient to be fed.

Groom your dog carefully before leaving for the show so his appearance will be a credit to you. Spray an insecticide all over his coat to discourage insects from bothering him. Hold your hand over his eyes and face to avoid the chance of getting any spray there. A dog that has been sprayed in this way is less likely to pick up fleas from another dog.

Carry an extra leash and collar, a bench chain, and a water dish with you. Provide your dog with fresh water several times a day; they get very thirsty at dog shows. Often a change of water will have an adverse effect upon a dog, so it is wise to carry a gallon jug of water from home. Take a folding chair for yourself.

Be certain that your dog is protected against distemper and hepatitis by having your doctor give him a booster inoculation each year.

Stay with your dog at the show to keep him content. If you have trained him by my methods, he will not be tired with your company, but will be eager to please you.

Exercise your dog about twenty minutes before you are scheduled to go into the ring so he may relieve himself.

When it is time for your Class to be judged, report to your ring steward and obtain your armband, and ascertain the approximate time you will be judged. Later, when you have been judged, ask the steward when they are going to do the Long Sit and Down exercises. Then be at ringside at the proper time so the steward will not have to go looking for you. It is a source of annoyance to everyone concerned when the judging of the Long Sit and Long Down exercises are delayed because one inconsiderate handler has disappeared. If you are showing your dog in the Conformation Classes, be sure to let the steward know where you will be. As your turn approaches, watch the judging procedures so you will be familiar with the judge's routine.

While the person ahead of you is handling his dog in the ring, give your dog a warm-up, heeling him, so he will be alert.

At practically all Obedience Trials there is a long waiting period before it will be your turn to take your dog into the ring. While you are waiting, your dog will probably lie down and go to sleep. Don't expect him to do his best if you wake him up and march him right into the ring. It takes a dog a few minutes to become fully awake and alert, just as a human being requires a certain amount of time after he wakes up to become fully conscious.

Some Obedience people feel that this warm-up is unnecessary, but these people do not compete in shows with their dogs. They think a dog should be obedient at all times. This is true, but in Obedience Trials today, obedience alone is not enough to win. The dog must be fully alert and awake in order to work with precision, and this state can only be gained by a short warm-up period.

Dogs are creatures of varying mood, and different show conditions can affect them. I like to put my dogs through a short routine, not for the sake of practicing, but to understand the dog's mood on that particular day and be prepared to handle him wisely. A slight variation in your method of handling, in compliance with your dog's mood, is often the difference between winning and losing. This is one of the finer points to acquire in training, and one that will come to you in time if you make it a habit to study your dog's reactions to places, weather, other animals, and so forth. Do not let your thoughts dwell on winning when you should be concentrating upon your dog and your handling.

Whether you win or lose, try to rectify your errors at home and resolve to do it better next time. Remember that it is by trial and error that you will become an expert handler; it will not come to you overnight. You might just as well relax and have fun getting there.

Chapter 23

Tracking

If you enjoy working outside with your dog and love to take long walks in all kinds of weather, you will enjoy Tracking. It is fascinating to watch a trained dog follow a track that is invisible to your eyes, making turns after checking each direction and gaily discovering the article at the end of the trail. It is exciting and invigorating to pursue a dog working swiftly and surely at the end of a forty-foot Tracking leash as you try to keep your footing up hills, down hills, through puddles and briar patches. But it is worth every breathless moment when your dog triumphantly snatches the object of the search from its hidden place and proudly carries it back to your outstretched arms. Until you have experienced the exultation of that precious moment, you cannot imagine the enchantment that is Tracking.

The Tracking title, TD, is bestowed upon your dog by the American Kennel Club when he has successfully passed a Tracking Test.

A Tracking Test is conducted by an accredited Obedience Training Club, and there are very few tests in one area in the course of a year. Each month the Tracking Tests are listed in the leading dog publications. Not many handlers train their dogs to Track because it is time-consuming work, and there are very few qualified trainers who can help them.

Several large fields are required for a Tracking Test. Each contestant will work a track that is no less than 440 yards or no more than 500 yards long. It is easy to see why Tracking Tests are not held at dog shows. The scent left by the tracklayer should not be less than half an hour old or more than two hours old. The length of the leash used in Tracking must be 20 to 40 feet, and the dog must work at this length with no help from the handler.

Two judges will judge the Tracking Test and keep duplicate charts of each track showing the length in yards of each leg, major landmarks, and boundaries. The course the dog pursues is to be marked on the charts, and both judges will forward a signed copy to the American Kennel Club with a notation "Passed" or "Failed" on each copy.

If the dog is not Tracking and taking the turns correctly, he will not be marked "Passed," even though he may come upon the article while he is wandering around. The object of the test is for the dog to follow the tracklayer's scent as closely as weather conditions permit.

I believe it is best to start a dog Tracking after he has learned to retrieve, but it isn't absolutely necessary. Even if a dog has had no Obedience training at all, he should be able to comprehend the Tracking lessons and go on to earn his Tracking title. Tracking may be started during the sixth month of training, which should give you sufficient time to earn your Tracking degree within the year. It will take considerable time and practice to accomplish this. Check the dates of the Tracking Test scheduled in your area so you may plan to have your dog ready. To enter a Tracking Test, your entry must be accompanied by a certificate signed by a qualified Tracking judge stating that the dog is considered ready for such a test. The AKC can give you the names of the Tracking judges in your area. The judge will want to see your dog work an actual Track to determine if he is ready for a test.

Tracking is not the great mystery that many people claim it to be. The dog is simply following a scent that has been left by someone walking over the ground. Most of this scent clings to the ground, but some of it is wafted away on the wind and adheres to anything in its path. The scent is carried on air currents, and if you study these, you will have a good idea how the scent is carried along. You don't have to be a meteorologist or have any special scientific knowledge in order to teach a dog to track. All it requires is a little common sense.

When I go walking in the woods after a rainstorm, the scent all around me is very strong and pungent, which is a sharp contrast to the light fragrance I enjoy on a sunny day. My common sense tells me when I am Tracking that the scent is stronger on wet grass, low boggy areas, shady spots, sheltered valleys, or the leeward side of the hills. These, then, will be the easiest places for the dog to pick up the scent.

If you have ever noticed how the air currents carry along the smoke from the rubbish you are burning, it will give you an idea what it could do with scent. When the wind changes capriciously the smoke is tossed around helplessly. It is no wonder a dog will work off the track on a windy day, and it is a matter of common sense to train the dog to work as close to the actual track as you can determine. It is wiser to keep bringing him back on it by guiding him with the leash than to let him follow the scent which is being scattered by the wind. If you do this the first month or so, you will get him in the habit of sticking close to the track.

The training method I used in 1952 to earn my first two Tracking titles is basically the same one I use today. By observing and studying my dogs I have concluded that this method is a sound one. Any opinions I have on Tracking have been formed as a result of watching my dogs; I'm sure if anyone were to observe his own dog he would reach the same conclusions.

It is perfectly natural for a dog to use his nose in the same manner in which humans use their eyes. A person is never satisfied to have something described to him; he must see for himself. A dog is never satisfied to look at something; he wants to sniff it. A dog sees with his nose. Dogs do not accept what they see; they believe what they smell. They use their noses throughout their lives to help them make decisions. A dog will catalogue a person's scent in his mind for years and, eventually when he meets this old friend or foe, he will recognize him by scent alone.

Dogs differentiate between members of a family by scent alone. Even when one tries to fool a dog by having two members of a family exchange clothes, the dog finds it a very elementary test to distinguish between them. Everyone has a different scent just as everyone has a different set of fingerprints.

When following a trail, a dog is following a total scent. In other words, the scent of crushed vegetation and the tracklayer's clothing, personal articles, body odor, hair, and breath are mingling together. The dog will follow this scent in two ways: by finding it on the ground and by sniffing it in the air.

With a no-wind condition, scent will remain in the air for hours at a time. I have noticed this many times, and the following incident is just one example. One morning when my dog and I were visiting my mother, I called a friend and asked him to stop by my home at noontime and pick up some papers I needed. That evening when I returned and opened the door, my dog dashed through the house barking angrily. It gave me a start at first until I realized he had picked up the scent of my friend who had stopped in earlier. The person was a stranger to the dog, and his scent was that of an intruder. No one had been in the house all day, so the scent remained undisturbed.

I believe that scent flies off a person whether he is sitting or walking. I have seen a dog go up to a chair where a friend of his was sitting an hour earlier and start wagging his tail. He hadn't known that his friend was visiting us until he came in the house later and smelled the chair.

When a person is walking, scent particles fly out from him in all directions. The heaviest of these particles fall close to him, and those that are of medium weight fly out from him and settle to the ground a little farther away. The lightweight scent particles are airborne for different lengths of time depending upon the weather conditions at the time. It is my opinion that the scent a dog picks up on the ground is a combination of the total scent that I mentioned earlier and not just a shoe or foot odor scent. It has never seemed to make any difference to a good Tracking dog what kind of footwear, if any, the tracklayer wore. I found a dog would follow a scent even if the tracklayer wore plastic bags over his shoes. The dog appeared to be following the total scent which was present both on the ground and in the air.

The scent that is in the air is the same as that on the ground. To believe this, one must realize that a moving body is enveloped by an air current and, as one strides along, the body, arms, and legs create a certain amount of turbulence. I believe that the body creates small parallel shoulder vortices that are agitated by the arms swinging back and forth. The amount of turbulence caused by every stride forces the scent particles that are flying out from the body and up from the ground to be tumbled around in the air. The scent is therefore scattered along a track that could be twenty or more feet wide. Wind currents play a part here in depositing the scent particles on anything in their path. The scent that lasts the longest is the one that falls to the ground or adheres to some stationary object. The lightweight scent particles never reach the ground but remain airborne until they fade away or are dispersed by wind currents or weather conditions. It is my opinion that different kinds of vegetation absorb the heavy scent particles in different ways. Dogs very often will take more time to sniff certain weeds as if the scent is stronger on them than on others.

The older the track, the harder it is for the dog to find it. This might be for several reasons. Heavy rain will wash out a track, but a light drizzle, humidity, or early morning fog will preserve it. Direct sunlight seems to dry up the scent just as an exposed drop of perfume will fade away quickly in the sun. A strong wind seems to eradicate the air scent in a short time.

Years ago I used to do all the preliminary Tracking work myself. This included laying all the different kinds of tracks until I had reached the point where the tracks had been laid (aged) twenty minutes. Then I would have a stranger lay the tracks for me. You can do it yourself if you have no one around to help you, but it will take a few weeks longer.

Point to the scuff mark, or the starting point, but do not put your hand ahead of your dog's nose where he would get your scent.

The first problem is to get the dog to start using his nose and keep it on the trail. If you have laid your own track, there is not much incentive except his natural desire to please you and the fact that you are continually urging him on, saying "Track" and pointing to the trail. By pointing to the trail and saying "See, Track," the dog will sniff where you are pointing and go on farther.

One way to get the dog to start using his nose faster is to let him find a reward in the glove at the end of the track. Leave a piece of cooked liver in the glove when you drop it at the end of the track; then, when the finds the glove and brings it to you, praise him excitedly and say "See, see," and give him the liver. He will catch on very quickly and will be more than eager to find the glove. Do not let him take the liver from the glove himself; make him bring the glove to you and then hand him the liver. This method works fine if you are laying your own tracks. When your dog has had enough experience and is using his nose at the beginning of the track, stop giving him food. He will be interested enough to work now and will not need food as an incentive. This just gets him off to a fast start.

The best way to teach a dog Tracking at the very beginning is to have someone he loves lay the track, leave his glove, and hide either on the ground or behind some object about twenty feet beyond the end of the track. The dog will be so eager to find his friend that he will start working naturally with little urging.

Find a good field where the grass is from eight to twelve inches high and, if it is possible, lay the early tracks out in the open away from natural boundaries. Try to practice in the early morning or evening when it is less windy. Take your dog to the field on the leash and do not put his harness on him until you get there so he will associate the harness with Tracking. Use a twenty-foot leash and clip it to the harness. Let your dog sit and watch the tracklayer lay the track and disappear out of sight. Before he starts he should pet your dog and tell him to be a good boy, or say something he understands. At the start of the track he should plant a stake in the ground and scuff his feet for the first twenty feet and then plant another stake. He should then walk in a straight line about two hundred feet, plant another stake, continue on another ten feet, and then take a slight turn to the right, like the hands of a clock pointing to five past six. He should go straight for fifty feet, drop the glove, continue straight on for twenty feet to a hiding place and just lie and wait for you.

When he is laying the first 200 feet of track, he should stop occasionally to wave to your dog and say something to arouse the dog's interest, such as "Good-bye, Hussan," using your dog's name. Your dog would be sure he was missing something and want to follow him.

In order for the tracklayer to walk a perfectly straight track he should keep his eye on some tree or object on the horizon and walk toward it. If he looks at the ground his track will weave all over the place. The tracklayer's job is important — try to impress this upon him.

After waiting five minutes, take your dog up to the first stake, make him lie down with his nose close to the scuffed earth. Point out the spot without putting your hand in front of his nose where he would get your scent, and say excitedly, "See, Track." As soon as the dog takes a good sniff, let him start Tracking. Keep him about ten feet in front of you and encourage him to go out and pull you. If it is necessary, keep urging him to go Track. When he reaches the glove, insist that he pick it up and bring it to you, and then send him on again to find his friend. If he is terribly excited when he reaches the glove, let him pick it up and carry it on to his friend. At this point, you should both make a tremendous fuss over him.

By working on tracks of this kind with either a left or right turn for a few days, the dog will think it is great fun. It is not necessary to give your dog food if you use this method, for he has all the incentive he needs — he is finding someone he loves, and this is what he wants to do.

Now try a track with a slightly sharper turn, say, at ten past six. Many dogs zigzag back and forth across a track when they are following a scent. Repeat this type of track several times until your dog sees it well without your help.

Next day try the same track with a left turn. This would be like the hands of a clock pointing to ten minutes to six.

Practice tracks of this type with either right or left turns and age them for different periods. Start with five-minute tracks and go on to ten- and fifteen-minute tracks as your dog improves.

Slight angle turn to right.

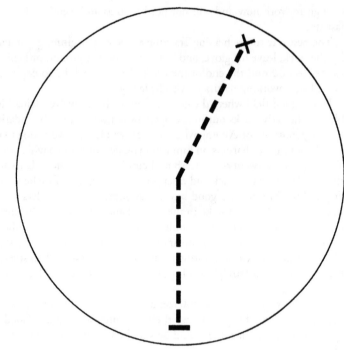

Slight angle turn to left.

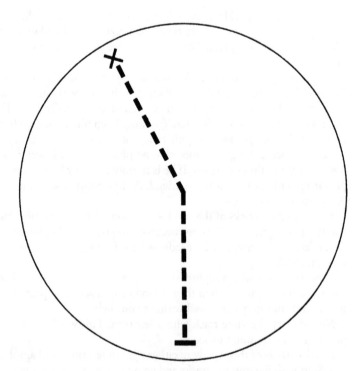

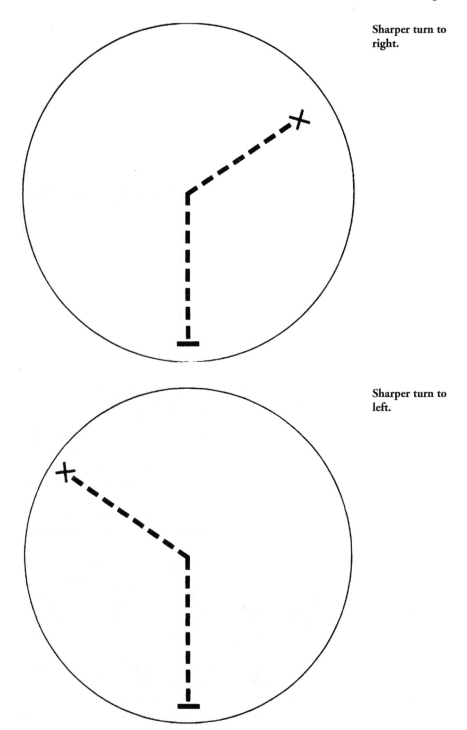

Sharper turn to right.

Sharper turn to left.

Right-angle turn to right. Scuff the track at the beginning and at the center turn.

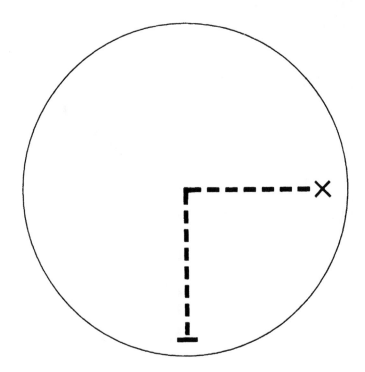

Now you should be able to try your first right-angle turn which, on the clock, would be at a quarter past six. Encourage your dog to work at the end of the leash. When he approaches the corner, be prepared to give him enough leash so he can overrun the turn, come back, circle around until he finds the track, and continue on. Do not let him pass you and retrace his steps back to the starting point. If you stand about twenty feet from the turn, your dog should be able to circle and find the continuation of the track. Later, when you are following a blind trail, you will recognize a turn by the individual manner in which your dog searches for it. Dogs differ a great deal in this respect. Study yours so you can eventually recognize a turn by the signal he gives you. He may whine, lift his head, drop his tail, circle, or give you some other indication of a change in direction. Praise him when he takes the turn correctly.

Do not always expect him to make a turn at the exact point of the right angle. Most dogs overrun the turn about twenty feet before they realize they are no longer on the track. Then they return to the turn and start checking before striking out again on the right track. If the wind is blowing toward you, your dog will probably pick up the turn much sooner than you expect, and will then work parallel to the actual track. When he is opposite the tracklayer's wallet or glove, he will pick up the scent in the air and make a left turn toward it. If you have a cross wind, the dog will work alongside the actual track, and the distance will vary according to the wind direction, wind velocity, and the terrain. If he turns with his tail to the wind he will stay close to the track.

The exception to this is the perfect Tracking dog who keeps his nose down on the track every inch of the way. Wind makes no difference to this dog, for he is working close to the ground with his nose in the grass. I have seen dogs like this take right-angle turns without any hesitation whatever. The work was so flawless that they did not have to stop at any point to double-check. Dogs can be taught to work close by starting on closely cropped grass and by working on a ten-foot lead. When the dog has become accustomed to keeping his nose to the ground, you can lay tracks in fields where the grass is longer. You can gradually play out your Tracking leash until you are thirty feet back. The important thing is to wait until the dog is doing an excellent Track on the ten-foot lead. This type of training takes longer and requires an experienced handler.

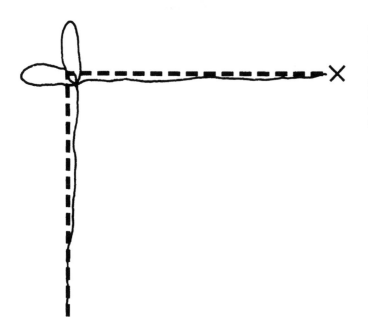

A dog may overrun the turn, come back to it, and then strike out in another direction before he again returns and finds the track.

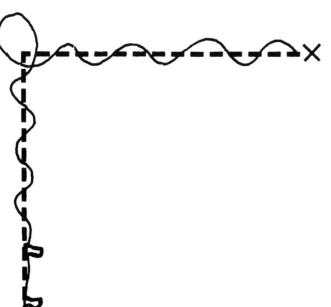

A dog may cross the track repeatedly all the way to the article.

Some of the tracklayer's scent is still on the actual track, but most dogs will follow the scent that the wind has carried some distance from it. These examples illustrate what could happen.

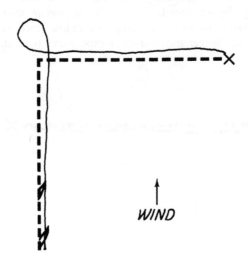

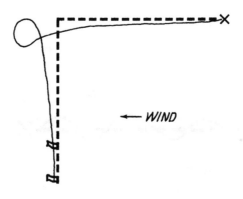

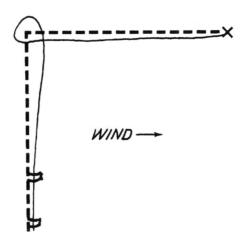

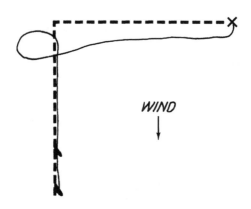

**Right-angle turn
to left.**

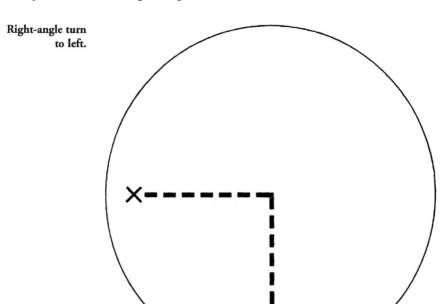

When you feel that your dog has mastered the right-angle turn, follow the same procedure to teach him the left-angle turn. Picture a clock again; the track will look like a quarter to six. Spend a week or more on this until you are certain your dog understands. If you get this down perfectly before you go on to the next step, you will save yourself trouble later on. Practice these right- and left-angle turns when the track has aged five minutes, ten minutes, and fifteen minutes.

From now on, your tracks should be 300 yards in length and should incorporate at least three turns. Practice this type of track, and use different turns each time. Start practicing when the track is five minutes old, and gradually work up to a track that has aged twenty minutes. Use a forty-foot leash, put a knot at twenty feet and one at thirty feet. Try to work at thirty feet, holding the rest in abeyance in case you need it on a turn.

Discuss the track with the tracklayer before he starts. If there are any landmarks such as a tree, shrub, large boulder, and so on, that are visible at a distance, use them for turning points instead of stakes. Use stakes only when there is nothing else to mark the turn. Never turn precisely at the landmark, as the dog would eventually get wise to this. Make your turns about twenty feet past the landmark and have your tracklayer follow the proposed track accurately so you can guide your dog correctly.

Your dog must be convinced that you know where the track leads, for this will encourage him to try harder. It isn't any different than throwing a dumbbell that lands hidden in a hollow. If the dog doesn't see it, he might quit, so you show him where it is and the next time this happens he will look around for it. In Tracking he will occasionally go off the track, and it will be up to you to show him where it is (and be sure you point to a portion of the track that is heavy with scent) so he can continue by himself. He is depending on you to help him when he gets confused, so it is of the utmost importance that you always know where the track lies, where each turn should be made, and when to find the glove.

At the start of each track you should now use two flags just as in an actual Tracking Test. (Tack a twelve-inch square of material on one end of a three-foot pole and sharpen the other end with a knife so it will stick firmly in the ground.) The flags should be placed thirty yards apart, and the tracklayer should scuff the ground near the first flag. The dog should be encouraged to take the scent at the first flag and keep his nose to the ground up to the second flag. This distance should be sufficient for the dog to retain the scent and follow the trail. A dog is permitted to return to the first flag to take the scent again, providing he has not gone beyond the second flag. Do not let your dog retrieve the flag or play with it. At first, when laying tracks, scuff your feet along the ground between the two flags.

When your dog is doing this well, increase the length of the track to 550 yards and incorporate seven or eight turns. You will have to plan your track carefully so you will end up near an exit from the field. Don't become so engrossed in laying the track that you find yourself stuck in a corner of the field with no way out except over the freshly laid track. Never make a turn narrower than a right-or left-angle turn, or the dog will cut over to the other portion of the track. Your objective is to keep the dog as close to the actual track as possible. Therefore, avoid laying any tracks that prevent this.

Tracking fields are generally to be found in the country, and it is quite probable that your dog will flush a pheasant or some other game while he is Tracking. Caution him to "Track" and insist that he continue to work and ignore the interruption. When you lay a track you may come across woodchuck holes or rabbit nests, and many of these creatures are bold enough to sit there and watch you approach. However, when you take your dog out they will be nowhere in sight. Try to give your dog the experience of working near cows or horses. Some tracks are laid in fields that adjoin cow pastures. If there are cows or horses grazing in a nearby field, they will all come over to the fence to watch you and your dog Track. They are naturally inquisitive, and they will clop noisily up and down the fence or stick their heads over and create a general commotion. A dog must be well trained to resist the temptation to dash over and inspect them; it is good experience for him to get this kind of thing during a practice session. The dog that can work under try-ing conditions is the dog that will pass.

If you wish to lay tracks on private property, have the courtesy to obtain permission to do so. Do not trespass on anyone's property; it may be freshly planted, animals may be loose, or you simply may not be welcome. As a rule, however, you will find that owners are willing to let you use their fields, provided you keep your dog under control.

When the tracks you use are twenty minutes old, then it is advisable to have a stranger lay them for you. Your dog will pick up the stranger's scent between the first two flags; encourage him to follow it with the verbal command "Track," Because there will be just one human scent on the field, your dog will readily follow it. Once you find someone who is willing to lay the tracks, you must teach him how to do it, and then you must watch carefully to be sure he does it right. A poorly laid track will not only confuse your dog, but so discourage him that he will not even try. Your friend must lay the track carefully so that no part of the line crosses another part, and the turns should either approximate a right angle or be wider. The track should not cross a road, brook, body of water, or fol-low a fence or boundary within fifteen yards of it.

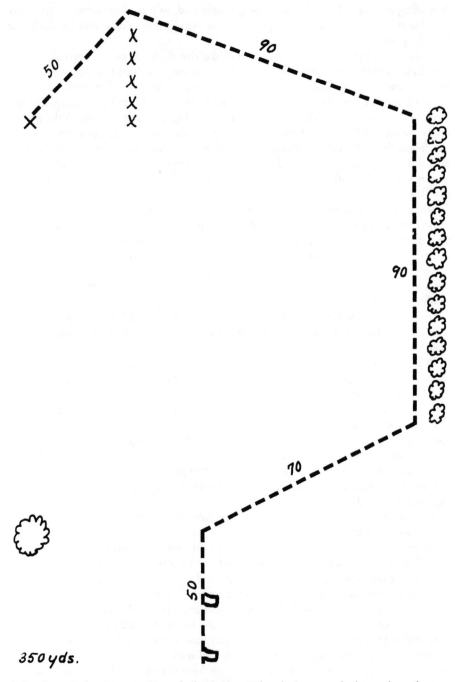

350 yds.

A simple track that you can use at the beginning. When laying a track along a boundary, such as a row of trees, do not work within fifty feet of it.

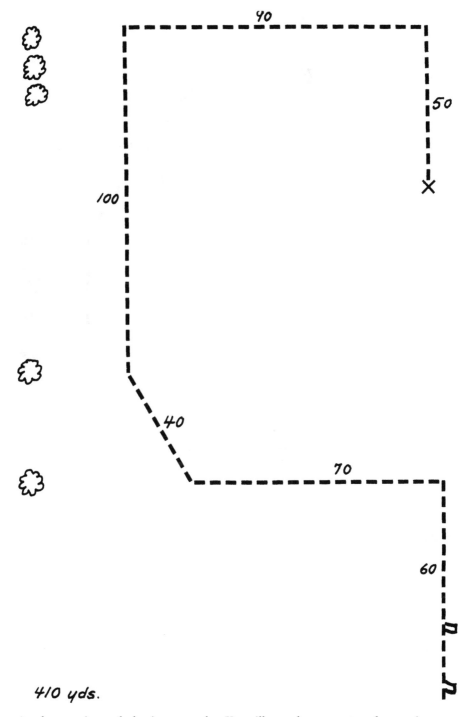

410 yds.

Another practice track that is easy to plan. You will note the turns are made opposite trees, a row of shrubbery, or weeds. When you lay a track, walk toward a distant tree or object, and that will keep your line straight.

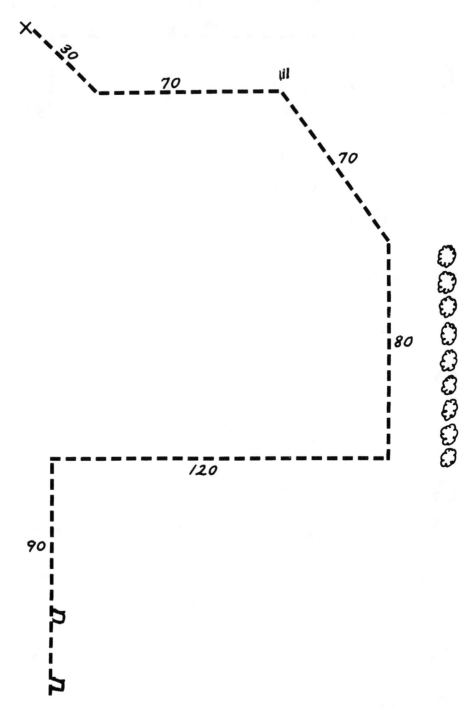

460 yds.

Another example of a well-planned track. This is the type of track you might find at a Tracking Test.

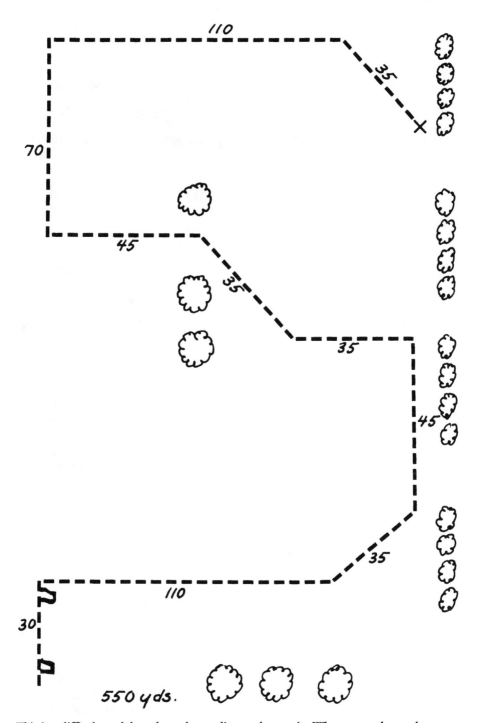

This is a difficult track but planned according to the terrain. When you and your dog can follow a blind track like this, you are ready for a Tracking Test. The actual test will be much easier than this.

Play out your leash slowly and hold your dog back so he will take the time to keep his nose to the ground and get a strong scent. The leash will be taut when the dog is working the track.

Your tracklayer should also be extremely careful to note landmarks and the direction of the wind so you know the exact conditions before you take your dog out on the track. When you are teaching your dog to Track, you must be in complete control of every situation that arises. Your dog must have the utmost confidence in you, and you must strive to impart your knowledge to him in the most subtle and astute ways. He cannot realize that you cannot smell the track, and he fully expects you to show him where it is if he misses a turn. At first encourage him with your voice and guide him with the leash. As you progress and your dog becomes interested in Tracking, you should gradually fade into the background and let him take the initiative to forge ahead and find the track in his own way. Your part will be to interpret his signals correctly and try to prevent him from Tracking too fast. A good Tracker gets excited when he knows he is on the trail and is apt to want to rush ahead exuberantly. Try to check your dog's speed from the beginning so he will not overrun the turns. Have your tracklayer leave his own glove or wallet.

When you check the wind direction, be sure to do so at the dog's height and not your own. Unevenness in the terrain cuts down the wind velocity. Test this fact by standing in a field on a windy day and note the degree of wind at your height. Then lie down and note the amount of wind about fourteen inches off the ground. Most dogs will be taking the scent at a height of fourteen inches or less from the ground.

For the first week only, have the tracklayer scuff the ground on the sharp turns. Start with fifteen-minute tracks and gradually work up to sixty minutes. At the end of the track, have the tracklayer continue straight on for about fifty feet beyond the article, then leave the field without approaching within 100 yards of any part of the track. Your dog should practice four days a week with two or three tracks at each lesson. Try to get a few friends to lay tracks for you.

Stand at the second flag and let twenty feet of your leash play out. Place a knot in your leash at thirty feet also, so you may hold the remainder in abeyance until you need it.

The final stage in teaching your dog to Track is to follow a blind track. Have an experienced tracklayer lay at least five tracks a week for you without your observing him. Get used to relying upon your dog's nose. The tracklayer may follow you at a discreet distance and advise you if the dog goes astray. When you have conquered this last stage, you are ready for a Tracking Test.

I hope you get the enjoyment from Tracking that I have. Topper and Hussan were entered in the same Tracking Test, and both passed that day. I was so excited and pleased that my expression for the next two days was a very wide grin.

Topper had made several turns when suddenly the leash dropped off his harness. It was the type of snap that closes with a tiny bar, and some dirt had gotten into it so that it didn't close. With the permission of the judges, I called him back and snapped the leash on again. I thought we were finished because I had to interrupt his Tracking to do it, but he got right back to business and completed the track.

Half an hour later, Hussan started on his track. He weighed almost as much as I did — there was five pounds' difference — and he loved to Track. When he got started, he made me run to keep up with him. He was so strong that he got going like a freight train and didn't stop until he had the article. It was all I could do to keep my footing, and I remember splashing through a wide puddle and laughing aloud at the amusing spectacle we made. It was a very happy occasion.

Arry was working fast the day he passed his Tracking Test. I remember his taking a left turn into a grove of trees, and as he threaded his way between them, I hoped he knew what he was doing. At the end of the track he headed for some tall grass, and then I was sure he was wrong, for we had been working on very short grass, but he dashed right along and found the article without any trouble.

Wynn Strickland and OTCH, OV Wynthea's Tony, UD, going High in Trial.

All this proves that it is better to leave the Tracking to the dog on the day of the test. When you get out there, it may seem to you that the dog is mistaken in his judgment, but it is wiser to let him prove that he is right.

The day that Max passed his Tracking Test, he was very businesslike and checked all the turns carefully. He didn't hesitate along the way, but went straight to the article. Each dog has his own way of Tracking, and whatever that way is, it is most exhilarating to be on the other end of the leash.

Don't try to help your dog on the day of the test. You will not be able to see the track, so make up your mind to let him take the initiative and do the work. All you have to do is hold on to the leash and make sure that it does not get tangled up in rocks or shrubs.

Judges plan the tracks the day before the Tracking Test, using Tracking poles on the turns and at the end of the track. On the day of the test, the poles are removed by the tracklayer as he lays the actual track and leaves an article of his own at the end of the track for the dog to find.

It takes a great deal of time and effort on the part of the judges to prepare a Tracking Test. Therefore, be quite certain that you and your dog can follow a blind track before you enter him in a Tracking Test.

The Tracking method described here will enable you to pass an AKC Tracking Test and get your Tracking title. This is the preliminary work necessary if you wish to teach your dog the more serious business of finding lost persons (see chapter 24, "Advanced Tracking," for more information). It is a good foundation on which to build, as your dog now realizes that he must follow the given scent until something is found.

It is not too difficult to continue from here and give the dog an article of clothing belonging to the lost person and let him search for him. If you try this out with members of your family, your dog will be eager to cooperate. The "lost" person should always make a big fuss over him when "found" to create more interest and excitement. This type of Tracking is fun and good exercise for all concerned.

Chapter 24

Advanced Tracking

The purpose of this Tracking is to teach your dog to find lost persons. That person might be a child who has wandered away from his home, a camper who has become lost in the woods, or an escaped criminal. In most cases, a search is started by the interested parties, and they only succeed in fouling the ground with assorted scents. After several hours have elapsed, a dog is brought in to help with the search. There are so few reliable tracking dogs in the country that one generally has to be flown to the scene from another state. If there were more dogs situated throughout the country who were qualified to do this type of work, it would save many hours of valuable time in starting the search, and more lives would be saved.

In order for a dog to find a lost person successfully, he must be able to distinguish between the tracklayer's scent and all the other distracting scents that are both confusing and tempting to him. An Advanced Tracking Test should include any problems a dog would have if he were actually tracking a lost person. Any test that fails to do this is neither practical nor realistic.

The American Kennel Club currently offers a Tracking Dog Excellent (TDX) Test that includes a track at least 800 yards long, five to seven turns, cross-tracks and obstacles. It also offers a Variable Surface Tracking (VST) Test that is at least 600 yards long and includes a minimum of three different tracking surfaces and scenting conditions. I have also devised my own test of a dog's practical Tracking ability. If your dog can pass the following test, he deserves to receive what I would call an AT (Advanced Tracking) title.

The test will require one stake, one tracking flag, four tracklayers, and one companion dog. The track will be no less than half a mile and no more than three-quarters of a mile in length, and it will cross open fields, a dirt road or footpath, a shallow brook no less than four feet wide and no wider than eight feet, and end in some woods where the dog will find the tracklayer. There will be at least one ninety-degree turn out in the open field, and the track will be laid in such a manner that no portion of it will cross any other portion.

The main track laid by Tracklayer Number One will be no less than six hours old and no more than seven hours old. The first diversionary track laid by Tracklayer Number Two will be two hours old, the second diversionary track laid by Tracklayer Number three will be one hour old, and the third diversionary track laid by Tracklayer Number Four and his dog will be one-half an hour old. The tracklayers and this dog will be strangers to the handler's dog.

Joll finding the track across the brook.

The tracks will be staked out by the judges two days before the test, and the stakes will be numbered so the tracklayer can collect them in numerical order on the day of the test. The stakes for Tracklayer Number One will be painted bright red, Tracklayer Number Two will have yellow stakes, Tracklayer Number Three will have blue stakes, and Tracklayer Number Four will have orange stakes. The stake marking the 100-yard point will be alternately striped black and white.

The dog will work on a harness or a leather collar, and the leash will be ten feet long. The dog will be given the scent from an old shoe that has been worn that week by Tracklayer Number One. It must belong to him. The dog may be given this scent before he reaches the starting flag, and once more (if the handler deems it necessary) before they reach the 100-yard stake. At this point the handler must then leave the shoe on the ground and continue on without it. The handler may encourage the dog at any time with his voice or restrain him if he thinks he is working too fast; however, if the dog is not working, or if the handler is trying to aid his dog forcefully, he will be marked "Failed."

One tracking flag will mark the starting point. Tracklayer Number One will lay a straight track for the first 100 yards. The 100-yard stake will not be placed on the main track. When the main track is four hours old, Tracklayer Number two will lay a semicircular track that will start some distance to the right of the starting flag, cross the main track within fifty yards of the flag, and end some distance off to the left. It will not parallel the main track at any time by fifteen yards. Nor will tracks three and four.

When the main track is five hours old Tracklayer Number Three will lay a semicircular track that will start at some distance to the left of the starting flag, cross the main track within eighty yards of the flag, and end some distance off to the right. It will not parallel the main track at any time.

As soon as the main track is five-and-a-half hours old, Tracklayer Number Four and his dog will enter the field that contains the main track, and they will walk over it, crossing the main track without walking parallel to it, and leave the field from the other side. The tracklayer's dog will be kept on leash at Heel.

This test is designed to teach a dog to differentiate between the lost person's tracks, those of people walking around the beginning of the track, or those made by a stranger and his dog when they cross the track at a later time. It will teach your dog to recognize the difference between an old track and a new one. If you train your dog to do this correctly, you will be able to rely on him if his services are actually needed in an emergency.

Your dog should be quite reliable on an hour track before you start. Try several very long tracks that are one hour old, and generate a little more excitement by having someone the dog loves lay the track. Gradually work the age of the tracks you use up to eight hours and confine the tracks to fields.

Now take your dog to a wooded area that is not too overgrown with brush or briars. The first track you lay should age about twenty minutes. You will see why anything more than a ten-foot leash is impractical when you try this. Be patient with your dog, for he will encounter all kinds of interesting animal and vegetation odors in the woods that may distract him. You will probably find it necessary to keep urging him on. Always show him the track by pointing to it; let him think you know where it is. I have found that a good way to mark the trail in the woods is to have the tracklayer stick feathered darts into the trees at least five feet from the ground. The feathers should be painted a bright orange so they will be visible from a distance. Work these tracks until the dog is doing it well, and then combine the tracks in the open fields with these.

At this point the tracks will be half-a-mile long and six hours old, and I believe it is best for the tracklayer to be someone the dog loves until he has this work down perfectly. When you feel he understands it, take him down to a brook.

Work on the brook crossing separately until your dog will search around eagerly for the track. Start with a short track leading to the brook and crossing over it, and have the tracklayer hide behind a tree some fifty feet beyond the brook. Make a tremendous fuss over the dog when he finds the tracklayer. Start with a twenty-minute track to make it easy for him and work the time up again when he responds. You will have to show the dog the track until he realizes he must cross the brook in order to find the tracklayer. This is really not too difficult, because most dogs love the water and will not hesitate to go in it. You must keep your dog's mind on the track at this time and not let him play in the brook. Any time the dog seems confused when you are teaching him Advanced Tracking,

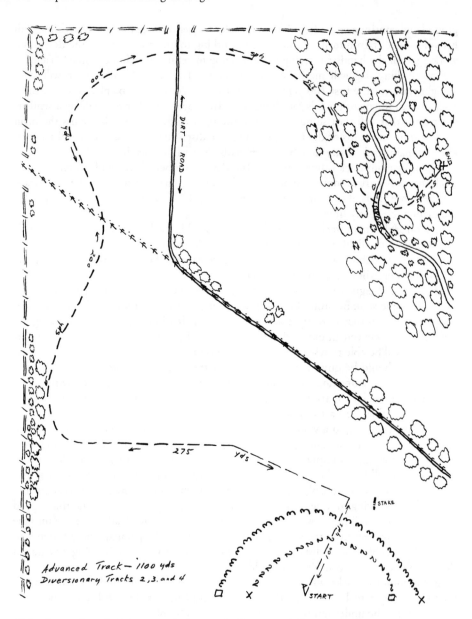

This advanced track is 1,100 yards long and offers several diversions.

give him a sniff of the tracklayer's shoe which you should be carrying in a plastic bag. This will remind him of the scent he is following. In the beginning you will have to show it to him quite frequently, but these instances will lessen as his proficiency increases.

Now try a combination of the three kinds of tracks. Lay a half-mile track through the fields, over a brook, and end it in the woods. Try several of these with the same tracklayer until the dog is very steady.

When you have reached this point, it is time to have strangers lay the tracks. It is much more difficult getting a stranger to lay these tracks than it is to teach your dog to track.

Poorly laid tracks can completely confuse your dog, so it is better to spend some time advising your tracklayers how you want the track laid than to assume they will do it right. If you want to be certain they will do it correctly, use the numbered stakes and mark it out yourself two days before you plan to practice.

There is one important thing to remember when practicing tracks that have aged several hours. The tracklayer will not want to wait in the woods for six or more hours while the track is aging, so the spot where he is to wait must be marked with two stakes, then he can leave the woods by walking in a straight line from the track. He should place stakes as he leaves so he can retrace his steps twenty minutes before you start out at the beginning of the track with your dog.

Teaching your dog to follow this type of track is like anything else — if you take it slowly and carefully at first, your dog will learn. If you encourage him from the beginning by showing him what you want, you will build up his confidence in his ability to find the lost tracklayer.

Once your dog will track a stranger successfully on an eight-hour-old track, it is time to introduce the diversionary tracks. It is quite likely that some animals have crossed the tracks during these weeks you have been practicing, but you will never know. Have a second tracklayer cross the track an hour before you start. You should know exactly where this occurs so you can notice your dog's reaction. Give him a second to investigate this new scent, but do not let him follow it more than twenty feet, caution him to "Track," and help him get back on the main track if necessary.

Try a good number of similar tests with different time periods, but always be in command of the situation by knowing exactly where the tracklayer crosses the main track. This is very important, as you must be ready to assist your dog. When he has it down pat, get two or three tracklayers to cross the main track at the beginning. Again you must know where they cross each time.

At this point of the training you will have a great respect for your dog's ability to use his nose. Now you can rely on him to follow a blind track and try a few tests similar to the one in the illustration. It is sometimes uncanny the way a dog can find a person or an object just by scent and intuition. I had an amazing experience with Joll that still fills me full of wonder and admiration whenever I think of it.

I had to go down to Georgia on business, so I decided to fly down and take Joll with me. I had a pilot's license, so I rented a plane at the local airport near my home in Delaware, invited Joll to hop in behind the pilot's seat where he had plenty of room, and off we flew. Joll loves to fly, and he curls up and takes naps unless I talk to him. On take-offs and landings, he sits up and watches the proceedings, and many a person has been surprised to see him watching out his window.

It was sunny all day long, and we had a head wind most of the way. I stopped twice to refuel, and both times walked a considerable distance with Joll to the office to pay for the gas. Both times on my return to my plane I noticed several planes had come in and parked near us. Joll would dash on ahead and wait for me next to our plane, and I thought at the time that he was being rather bright. It happened that none of these other planes were Cessnas.

The plane that I had rented was brand new, I had never flown it, and Joll and I had never seen it before. It was an all-day flight to Atlanta, and we touched down at 6:00pm After landing, I taxied up to the hangar and asked the attendant to fill the plane with gas. He advised me to lock the plane and take the key, and he would fill it with gas and park it somewhere else later on. It is quite simple to move a plane by rolling it, not like trying to move a locked car. So I got my luggage, asked Joll to jump out, locked the plane, and left it parked there near the hangar office.

This was a Friday night, and the next day it was very hot and sunny all day long. On Sunday it rained steadily all day but cleared enough in the evening for me to decide to leave the next morning. Monday morning our flight home was delayed until 11:00am because of the poor weather farther north. Finally we got the green light from the weather bureau, and I drove out to the airport with Joll. I left Joll in the car while I went into the office to pay my bill and find out where they had parked my plane. The attendant stood at the door and pointed in the general direction and mentioned that it was in one of the front rows. The whole field was a sea of planes, all sizes and shapes, all private planes, and many Cessnas just like mine. However, I knew the number and color of my plane so didn't anticipate any trouble finding it.

I got Joll out of the car and had him Heel by my side until we got to the hangar office, then I said, "Jolly, let's go home." He got all excited and went dashing off ahead of me, leaving me way behind. I ran to catch up with him and we went the length of a long city block, zigzagging in and out of the rows of planes before I saw him standing near a plane way up ahead of me. I couldn't even read the plane's number from where I stood, and so wasn't sure it was mine. When I got close enough, I saw it was our plane, and Joll was all smiles, hopping up and down and turning in little circles. He was waiting in front of the pilot's door, the only one we had used.

I saw it, but I couldn't believe that he knew *that* was our plane, so I tested him. I said, "No, Joll, that's not the one, it's over *here*," and I walked over to another Cessna that was the same model but a different color. He wouldn't budge, but jumped up against our plane door, wagging his tail like mad and flashing his brown eyes at me with a "Yes, it is; Yes, it is," expression. So I laughed and said, "You're right. That's it." I opened the door, and he jumped in behind the pilot's seat and sat there. His expression said very clearly, "Okay, let's go home."

I've seen dogs do some very remarkable things in my lifetime, but I think this was fantastic. There were over three hundred-odd planes in this field, and what little scent there was on the outside of our metal plane was seventy-one hours old. It had been subjected to high winds, a dry, hot sunny day, and twelve hours of steady rainfall.

I know Joll has a keen nose and a remarkably high degree of intelligence, as he has demonstrated these qualities before. I also believe that dogs can distinguish colors. What astounded me was his ability to combine these talents with his intuition.

So this six-hour track is really just a beginning. I am convinced that a keen dog could follow a three- or four-day-old track if he had the incentive and the proper training.

Chapter 25

Traveling with Your Dog

Whenever I travel anywhere I enjoy taking my dog with me because he is such good company and so well behaved. He takes a great interest in everything I do and as a result of his behavior I get more enjoyment out of whatever I'm doing.

For instance, when I am driving, Joll watches everything going on, somewhat like a back-seat driver but without the nagging. When I apply the brakes he looks down at the brake pedal then quickly looks around to see why I put on the brakes. He has watched me drive for such a long time that I'll bet he could drive the car himself if he were physically able. He nudges my shoulder if I complain aloud when someone makes a left turn from the right-hand lane, etc., as if in complete accord. One time on the turnpike when I was passing someone who was in the middle lane, he suddenly swerved out right into the side of my car, as I was nearly parallel with him. I averted an accident by veering over onto the left shoulder, blowing my horn in protest as I did so. The other driver, realizing he had goofed, swerved back again into the middle lane, thus giving me a chance to get back on the road. Joll had been watching this and got quite upset about the whole thing. He stared out the side window at this driver and, when I passed him, Joll turned around and stared back at him out the back window, came up and nudged me, and stared back up the road again. It was just as if he were saying, "Did you see that dumb driver . . . ?" and started calling him a few choice names that I missed. It made an anxious moment rather funny. Joll does many things to relieve the tension of a long drive.

I can't understand the people who keep their dogs in crates like animals. They miss so much by not treating their dogs as part of the family. I suppose they feel it is less nerve-racking to carry untrained dogs in crates. We generally have anywhere from two to six dogs in our station wagon when we go to a show, and they all lie down and behave themselves. It is so much better to train your dogs so they can travel with you.

When I have to ship a dog to another part of the country, I like to send him by air. I try to choose a flight that is direct, or one that doesn't involve two airlines. When a dog is transferred from one airline to another there is always a chance that someone will goof and forget to transfer the dog to the second flight. If you call the airline and make a reservation, you can be assured of kennel space for your dog. You may take your own crate, buy one from the airline, or in some cases rent one. All dogs must travel in a crate (except guide dogs). You may ship your dog alone, or he may accompany you on the same flight.

If your dog has never been in a crate before, introduce him to one at home by having him walk into one and lie down. Make it a pleasant experience by praising him and petting him

The co-pilot listens to last-minute instructions.

when he is lying down, and don't make him stay in it for more than a few minutes at a time. Be sure that the crate is large enough for your dog to move around comfortably.

You will need a health certificate and proof of rabies inoculation when you ship your dog. If he is an older dog, give him something to eat the morning that he is to be shipped, let him exercise just before you take him to the airport, and offer him a drink of water before you place him in the crate. Stay with him at the airport until the crate is put aboard the plane. Be sure to attach an identification tag to his collar with your name, address, and telephone number on it, and be sure to write "Reward if found."

I have never put identification tags on my dogs because I always keep them with me or in my car when we are traveling. At home they don't need tags, for life is very interesting for them and although my property is completely fenced in, I know they wouldn't dream of leaving it. My dogs are all trained to jump and could scale the fences. The thing is, they are happy here, and a content dog will not run away. When we take them to shows, they are not permitted to have any tags on their collars. However, I strongly advise you to attach an identification tag to your dog dog's collar if for any reason you have to ship him somewhere. The following is a good reason why it is necessary.

I had sold one of my dogs to a woman in Denver, Colorado, who had convinced me that he would be given a good home and would be her companion. This dog meant a lot

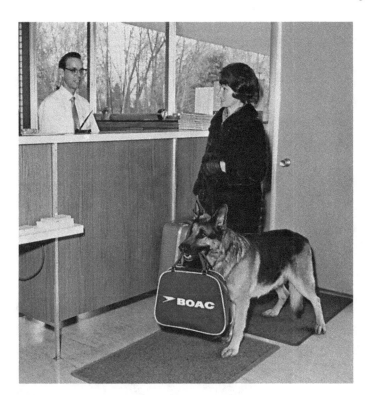

**Dogs can be useful
when checking in
at a motel.**

to me, as I had trained him myself and had handled him to two Highest Scores in Trial with 199 and 199-1/2. The fact that I had his litter brother and sister, and the thought that he would be getting a good home, led me to sell him. I kept reminding myself that a breeder has got to be realistic when running a kennel or he will end up with two zillion dogs. Some inner voice told me to put an identification tag on him, so I attached a red leather tag that held my name, address, etc. I shipped him by air on Friday and stayed with him until his plane left. The next night after I had returned home from a show I called to see if he was adjusting to his new home and was told that he had run away. I was quite upset at this news — a country dog lost in the middle of a large city — and offered to fly out to help look for him, but his new owner didn't like the idea and told me there was nothing I could do. So I took the next plane out there to find him. Upon my arrival I alerted the radio stations, dog pounds, newspapers, and police department. I hired a car and searched all that day and night and again the next morning. The police officials were most cooperative, and I was in their office on the second day when a call came in that a dog had been picked up on the airport grounds. They mentioned that he was a German Shepherd wearing a red leather identification tag. My bright CD dog had decided he didn't want to live in Denver and would go home to his friends. He was right in his decision, too — it wasn't the place for him. He knew the last place he had seen me was at an airport, so he had enough sense to go back to one. Needless to say I was very happy to get him back, Randy was happy to be with me, his would-be owner got her check back in full, and all those fine people in Denver who had been so kind to us were pleased to see us reunited. Randy won't be sold again, and I'll probably end up with two zillion dogs. A month later Randy won Highest Scoring Dog in Show three times.

A well-mannered dog is a joy to own, wherever you go.

Most hotels and motels will accept dog guests if they are well-mannered. Many motels have accepted my dogs when I have shown them my dogs and mentioned their credentials. I am completely sympathetic with the views motel owners have about dogs. Many dog owners take advantage of other people's property and let their dogs do things they wouldn't permit them to do in their own homes. I think every trained dog should have an identification card with his picture on it and his training titles, and a statement signed by his owner that guarantees him to be housebroken, well-mannered, and trained, and these cards should be honored by all motels and hotels everywhere. Then our companion dogs would be welcome wherever we traveled.

Chapter 26

Teaching Your Dog to Be Useful

Now that you have trained your dog and he has earned his Obedience degrees, you can derive both benefit and pleasure from the hard work of all the training. Use your ingenuity and take advantage of these exercises you have taught him. Teach him to be useful.

A dog can easily be taught to retrieve your slippers or shoes if you show him where they are the first few times and praise him for getting them. If you keep your leash and dumbbell in one special place, your dog will delight to retrieve them for you when you wish to use them.

It is my firm belief that dogs learn the names of articles just by hearing them mentioned occasionally. In the case of one of my own dogs, I never taught him what a sweater was, but he knew just the same. One evening when we were having dinner I felt cold and wanted my sweater. I called him over to me and said, "Arry, go get my sweater." He trotted upstairs to my room and came back with it in his mouth. It was something of a shock for the rest of the family who had been betting he would not know what I wanted.

If you have a large dog, you can teach him to carry a basket so that when you go shopping he will help you carry packages. When you get home, let him help you carry the packages in from your car. If you do this frequently, he will soon learn that "shopping" means carrying packages. Arry could carry a ten-pound bag of potatoes with the greatest of ease. He picked up a bag one day and was so pleased with himself for carrying it into the house that he insisted from then on that he be the one to carry in the potatoes.

For several years we lived on a farm that had a long pine-bordered lane leading up to the house. It was quite a walk to get the newspaper or the mail, so I trained my dogs to do this errand.

In the same way, if you are gardening, your dog can help you by carrying the equipment you need.

When I endeavor to improve my golf game by practicing with my short irons, I hit a dozen balls and then let Topper retrieve them. He loves this and waits eagerly for the word so he may dash out and bring the balls back to me two at a time.

At Obedience Trials I always had my dog carry his own bag containing his things in and out of the show. On trips Joll would also carry one of the small suitcases. If I went to the closet to get a suitcase, Joll would select his own bag with the assumption that he would be going. He accompanied me everywhere.

Topper had a quality I admire — initiative. If I sent him after something that was not there, he would substitute another article just to accomplish his mission. Occasionally I would send him after my handbag, thinking it was on a chair, when I had actually put it in a drawer, so he would bring something else instead. I could figure that if he did not return with the correct article, it was locked away somewhere. An amusing incident resulted as a sequel to his never-say-die spirit.

A friend called to say he had lost his wallet and wondered if he had dropped it in my yard. I called Topper and Hussan to aid in the search. They searched diligently, as did we all, without finding a trace of the missing wallet. As we were about to give up, Topper came across the yard to me carrying a huge trash can by one handle. It was larger than he was, but he made a gallant effort to carry it high and off the ground. He carried it some fifty yards and held it until I took it from him. The yard was bare, there was nothing retrievable except the trash can, so, unwieldy as it was, he was determined not to come back empty-handed. I would have considered the feat impossible if I had not seen it. I only wish I could have recorded it on film. The wallet, incidentally, was recovered from a theater where it had been lost.

When Arry finishes his dinner, he picks up his dish and takes it over to the sink to be washed. He has always loved to carry ladies' handbags. He will greet guests at the door and take their handbags and carry them into the living room. They are a little apprehensive at first, but never give him an argument. He always carries them by the handle and relinquishes them upon command. Topper, on the other hand, confines his love for retrieving to my own personal belongings.

Joll, Bar, and Randy help the author carry the groceries.

Joll got mixed reactions from his friends the first time he tried an eight-foot jump over them. It may not be useful, but it sure is fun!

Another great convenience is to teach your dog to carry messages to the rest of your family. If some member is off somewhere, either in or outside the house, give your dog a note and tell him, "Give it to Ron," or whomever you name. Teach your dog the names of the family first and have him deliver messages or articles, at close range, until he becomes adept. This feat has saved me much time and energy. I have lived in the country most of my life, and our family spends a great deal of time out-of-doors. It is much more interesting to use a messenger dog than to search or call for someone.

If you have a big, strong dog, it is great fun to teach him lifesaving in the water. The person teaching him should be himself a strong swimmer; a dog that gets easily excited can climb on you in the water and push you under. Until they are taught water manners, some dogs can be a menace.

Hussan had the ideal disposition and physique for this type of work. He was very calm and deliberate, he could swim like a seal, very fast but effortlessly, he was unusually strong and could swim around for hours without tiring. He hardly rippled the water, and it was a lovely sight to watch his black head gliding along smoothly above the water.

With his natural love for swimming he enjoyed retrieving anything. I taught him to Heel beside me in the water, and we would swim out quite a distance together. On the way back, if I tired, I would put my arm gently around his neck, and he would pull me back to shore.

Next, I tied a cloth around a truck tire tube and had him retrieve it by holding on to the cloth. Then I tied the cloth around my arm and had him hold that and pull me in to shore. When he became expert, I removed the cloth, and he would hold my arm, above the elbow, very firmly but without hurting me, and push me toward shore. I would be in a floating position on my back. The fact that he was so strong and gentle is what made the whole feat possible. I always felt that the children and I were perfectly safe near the water when he was with us.

Nowadays when I have several dogs to train each day, I let Jack be my errand boy. He brings me a leash or a dumbbell whenever I need it. When I am ready to practice a Figure 8, I yell "Figure 8," and Jack and Ace come dashing over to be posts. I also call "Long Sit and Down" when I am ready for those exercises, and all the dogs that are out with me come running over to line up just like a class. They love to do it.

Life has been made richer for me and also for my family because I wanted my first dog to be "obedient." I hope that Obedience Training will be an equal source of enjoyment to you.

Chapter 27

Problems and Solutions

If you are starting out with a new dog, follow the instructions in this book very carefully with close attention to detail. You can avoid mistakes this way.

If you are working with a dog that has been trained by another method and you are having problems with him, read the chapter that pertains to his problem. Study the problem and determine whether the dog is disobedient or just confused. Is it a result of your handling? Do you encourage him to do tasks correctly? Do you pet and praise him whenever you can? You may have to start from scratch so that both of you will benefit from my method.

The following questions and solutions are typical of the training problems that most people encounter. When you try the solution on your dog, repeat the correction until he does it right. Remember to encourage him at the right moment as timing is everything. Pet and praise the dog quickly. It is also important to look your dog in the eye when you are trying to communicate with him.

NOVICE PROBLEMS

Problem: *My dog never pays attention to me when he is heeling.*

Solution: You are not making it interesting for your dog. Encourage him to work with you by talking to him, and occasionally petting him, as you are heeling. Keep making sudden turns, especially when he is looking in the other direction, and jerk his leash as you do so. Then let the leash go slack immediately. Make a quick turn every time he looks away, and he will soon be keeping his eye directly on you to see what you are up to.

Problem: *My dog is so wild I can't control him on leash.*

Solution: Put your fat round nylon choke collar high behind his ears and high under his chin, hold your leash in both hands, hold it short but *do not pull.* Walk briskly and make several turns, including about turns. Each time you turn, *jerk the dog's leash sharply, and then let it go slack. Do not hold a steady pressure on the dog's collar and do not pull him around on a tight leash.* If you do it wrong, he will object. If you do it correctly, you can control him in five minutes. Do not use this method on puppies. This is for wild, strong, rambunctious, hard-headed dogs.

Problem: *My dog Sits one step back when I stop.*

Solution: This is a common error that occurs when handlers jerk their dogs to make them Sit. After a while, the dog backs up a step to avoid the jerk. Reread chapter 14, "The Novice Exercises." Now you must encourage the dog to line his toes up with yours, so hold your leash correctly when you stop, but *don't* jerk up to make him Sit. Instead, show him where you want him, and then praise him.

Problem: *My dog Sits too slowly.*

Solution: You have probably been teaching him to Sit slowly since you started his training by pushing him down slowly. Start giving the dog a quick sharp tap on his croup when you stop, then immediately praise and pet him with your left hand.

Problem: *My dog always Sits with his rear end out to the left.*

Solution: Tap your dog on his left hind leg just as he is sitting. This will quickly make him Sit straight.

Problem: *My dog lags on the outside turn of the Figure 8.*

Solution: This will occur if you train him on a tight lead and pull him around on turns. Move his collar up high, jerk him as you approach the turn, laugh and talk to him, make it fun, and encourage him to work on a loose leash with *no* pressure on his collar.

Problem: *My dog runs away when we heel off leash.*

Solution: This happens when the handler has trained his dog with a tight lead and constant pressure on the dog's collar. Start over again on leash, and this time do not have any pressure on his collar.

Problem: *My dog doesn't Sit straight in front of me when I call him.*

Solution: This is a problem you may encounter through all of the Obedience exercises. Now is the time to work on it. Follow the instructions in chapter 14 very carefully. After you call your dog, remember to hold your hands in front of you, eight inches apart, and encourage him to come to them. When he is close, hold his ruff with one hand very gently, or hold his head up as you pet him and look him in the eye. Praise him.

OPEN PROBLEMS

Problem: *My dog chews the dumbbell, and I can't make him stop.*

Solution: You probably allowed him to chew the dumbbell when you first taught him the exercise. Get a dumbbell with a metal dowel such as a piece of pipe. He won't chew that. In a show, use the wood dowel.

Problem: *My dog either refuses to Drop or walks most of the way to me after I have given him the signal to Drop.*

Solution: Reread the section, "Drop on Recall," in chapter 16, "The Open Exercises." Once your dog will Drop from a Sitting position forty feet away, try this: Call your dog to you and command him to Drop both verbally and with a signal when he is five feet from you. When he does it correctly, increase the distance between you. Go up to him and pet and praise him when he Drops.

A fast way to teach a dog to jump the broad jump is to use fifteen-inch tent stakes with white nylon strings. The taut nylon string will remind the dog not to touch the jumps.

Problem: *I can't praise my dog because he gets too excited.*

Solution: Nonsense. Every dog needs praise. Get him used to it by holding his collar as you pet and praising him quietly. You should let him know he was good at the same time you calm him down.

Problem: *My dog takes a wide turn after he jumps the broad jump.*

Solution: Run the dog over the hurdle on leash. As soon as he lands, jerk him toward you saying "Come." As soon as he starts turning without the jerk on the leash, remove it. Now have him jump off leash and call "Come." As soon as he lands, clap your hands and get him back to you fast. Praise, praise, praise.

Problem: *My dog Sits crooked after returning from the broad jump.*

Solution: Practice angle turns and show him where you want him to Sit. Practice calling him from every possible angle, even with your back to him. Reread chapter 16.

Problem: My dog tics the jump.

Solution: If your dog is physically sound, try this: Put him on a six-foot leather leash, run with him, and call cadence for him. Study him carefully and decide where he should take off in order to clear the jump. Then say "Hup" when he reaches that spot. You should also be teaching him the bar jump at the same time. Start with a low jump and gradually increase the height until he is jumping his required height.

UTILITY PROBLEMS

Problem: My dog creeps a few steps before he goes down on the Signal exercise.

Solution: Drop him five feet from you. If he doesn't Drop immediately, try it again and be quick to help him Drop. Then give him a food reward for doing so. Increase the distance between you gradually, but go up and praise him using the food reward at first. Then, just say "Good," and call him the rest of the way in and give him a reward. Don't give him the food reward every time. Use it as a special treat for good work.

Problem: My dog Drops the article as soon as he brings it to me.

Solution: As your dog approaches you, tell him to "Hold it" in a quiet tone of voice. If necessary, quickly put your hand under his chin gently as you look him in the eye and quietly say "Hold it."

Problem: My dog often gets the wrong glove.

Solution: You may not be turning correctly, or you may be giving the wrong kind of signal. When you give the signal, swish your hand and arm toward the glove as you *look at it.* Be sure the dog is looking at the correct article when you both turn and before you send him. A dog will generally retrieve the glove he is looking at. Practice turning several times so your dog will be precise.

When practicing the Scent Discrimination exercise, place a few toys among the articles as a distraction for your dog.

Problem: *My dog will only Go Out five feet beyond the jumps.*

Solution: Put up a rope thirty feet beyond the jumps, called a ringback. Practice sending your dog to this rope until he will go out quickly. In the beginning, you may find that food will work for you; later, you may have to run out with him many times.

Problem: *My dog looks away just as I give him a signal.*

Solution: Don't ever wait for your dog to look at you. Give him the signal and, if he doesn't obey immediately, run out to him and make him do it. When you are practicing the signals, have a friend throw dog toys and balls in front of him to distract him. Give him verbal praise from a distance when he obeys quickly.

Appendix A

American Kennel Club Obedience Regulations

AKC Obedience Regulations as amended September 1, 2001. For any further amendments to these regulations, please visit the AKC website at www.akc.org or write to the Customer Service Department, American Kennel Club, 5580 Centerview Drive, Raleigh, NC 27606 or phone (919) 233-9767.

OBEDIENCE REGULATIONS
Amended to September 1, 2001
Table of Contents

Purpose

Obedience trials are a sport, and all participants should be guided by the principles of good sportsmanship both in and out of the ring. The purpose of obedience trials is not only to demonstrate the dog's ability to follow specified routines in the obedience ring, but also to emphasize the usefulness of the purebred dog as a companion to man. All contestants in a class are required to perform the same exercises in substantially the same way, so that the relative quality of the various performances may be compared and scored. The basic objective of obedience trials, however, is to produce dogs that have been trained to behave in the home, in public places and in the presence of other dogs, in a manner that will reflect credit on the sport of obedience at all times and under all conditions. The performance of dog and handler in the ring must be accurate and correct according to these Regulations. It is also essential, however, that the dog demonstrate willingness and enjoyment while it is working, and that a smooth and natural handler be given precedence over a handler moving with military precision and using harsh commands.

Chapter 1 — General Regulations

Section 1. Obedience Clubs. An obedience club that meets all the requirements of The American Kennel Club and wishes to hold an obedience trial must apply on the form The American Kennel Club provides for permission to hold such a trial. The trial may be held either in conjunction with a dog show, agility trial or as a separate event. A club that is not a member of The American Kennel Club must pay a license fee in order to hold a trial. The Board of Directors of The American Kennel Club determines this fee. If the trial is not held at the approved time and place, the license fee will be returned.

Section 2. Dog Show and Specialty Clubs. A dog show club, a specialty club or an agility club may be granted permission to hold a licensed or member obedience trial if, in the opinion of the Board of Directors of The American Kennel Club, they are qualified to do so.

Section 3. Obedience Classes. A licensed or member obedience trial need not include all the regular obedience classes, but a club will not be approved to hold Open classes unless it also holds Novice classes, nor will it be approved to hold Utility classes unless it also holds Novice and Open classes. Any club that has been approved to hold a licensed or member obedience trial may offer additional non-regular classes, upon approval of The American Kennel Club. If a non-regular class is one that is not defined in these regulations, a clear and complete description of both the eligibility and performance requirements will appear in the premium list. Dogs must be at least 6 months of age to compete.

Section 4. Tracking Tests. A club may not hold a tracking test on the same day as its show or obedience trial, but the tracking test may be included in the show or obedience trial premium list. If not, the club must provide at the tracking test several copies of all the required catalog information for each dog entered. If the tracking test is to be held within 7 days of the obedience trial, the club may name someone else in the premium list to receive the tracking test entries and the same closing date should apply. If the tracking test is not to be held within 7 days of the obedience trial, the club may name someone else in the premium list to receive the tracking test entries, and may specify a different closing date for entries at least 7 days before the tracking test.

Section 5. Obedience Trial Committee. Any obedience club holding an obedience trial must appoint an obedience trial committee that will exercise all the authority of a dog show's bench show committee. If a trial is in conjunction with a dog show, the obedience trial committee will have some jurisdiction only over the dogs, handlers and owners entered in that trial. If, however, any dog is entered in both obedience and conformation classes, the obedience trial committee's jurisdiction pertains only to the obedience regulations. When an obedience trial is to be held in conjunction with a dog show, the club's bench show committee will include one person designated as obedience chairperson. At this event, the bench show committee has sole jurisdiction over all matters coming before it, whether the matter has to do with the dog show or the obedience trial.

Section 6. Sanctioned Matches. A club may hold an obedience match with approval of The American Kennel Club and under its match regulations. Scores awarded at these matches will not count toward any obedience title and will not be recorded by The American Kennel Club.

All of these obedience regulations apply to sanctioned matches, except for those sections specifying that the provisions apply to licensed or member trials, and except where specifically stated otherwise in the regulations for sanctioned matches.

Section 7. American Kennel Club Sanction. American Kennel Club sanction must be obtained by any club that holds American Kennel Club obedience trials, and for any type of match for which it accepts entries from nonmembers.

Section 8. Dog Show Rules. All the applicable dog show rules will govern the conduct of obedience trials. They will apply to any person and dog entered, unless these regulations state otherwise.

Section 9. Identification. No visible means of identification (badges, ribbons, club jackets, etc.) may be worn or displayed by anyone exhibiting a dog in the ring.

Section 10. Immediate Family. As used in this Chapter, "immediate family" means husband, wife, father, mother, son, daughter, brother, sister, father-in-law, mother-in-law, son-in-law, daughter-in-law, brother-in-law, or sister-in-law.

Section 11. Purebred Dogs Only. As used in these regulations, the word "dog" refers to either sex but only to dogs that are of a breed eligible for entry in American Kennel Club events. A judge must report to The American Kennel Club any dog showing under him or her that appears not to be purebred. This may be done after the show or trial.

Section 12. Unregistered Dogs. Chapter 11, Section 1, of the Dog Show Rules will apply to entries in licensed or member obedience trials, except that a dog with an ILP number may be entered in these events, with the ILP number shown on the entry form.

Dogs approved for entry in the Miscellaneous Class at dog shows, are eligible to compete in Obedience trials and/or Tracking tests provided the dog's AKC identification number appears on the entry form.

Section 13. Dogs That May Not Compete. No dog belonging wholly or in part to a judge or to a show or obedience trial secretary, superintendent, or to any member of such a person's household, may be entered in any dog show or obedience trial, nor may they handle or act as agent for any dog entered at the dog show or obedience trial at which such person officiates or is scheduled to officiate. The official veterinarian will not exhibit or act as agent or handler at the show and dogs owned wholly or in part by him or her will not be eligible to be entered at that show.

No dogs owned wholly or in part by a superintendent or any other employee of that superintendent, or any person residing in the same household as any of the foregoing will be eligible to be entered at any show held 30 days before or after a show which the superintendent has been approved to service by The American Kennel Club, nor may that person exhibit or act as an agent or handler.

For the purpose of this section, the employees of a superintendent would include only those individuals who represent the superintendent or superintending organization at dog shows.

No judge or any person residing in the same household as the judge will exhibit or act as agent or handler at a dog show or obedience trial at which he or she is judging. Dogs owned wholly or in part by such judge, or any member of his or her household, will not be eligible to be entered at such event. This applies to both obedience and dog show judges when an obedience trial is held in conjunction with a dog show.

Subject to the foregoing, members of a judge's immediate family who no longer live in the same household may enter or handle a dog at a show, trial or test if the judge is not officiating over any competition which might involve that dog. If a club does not adver- tise in its premium list who is to judge run-offs between classes, an exhibitor will auto- matically be considered to have lost the run-off of any tie scores between classes if the judge of the run-off is a member of the exhibitor's immediate family. No dogs may be entered or shown under a judge at an obedience trial if the dog has been owned, sold, held under lease, handled in the ring, boarded or has been regularly trained or instructed, within one year prior to the date of the obedience trial, by the judge or by any member of his immediate family or household, and no such dog will be eligible to compete. "Trained or instructed" applies equally to judges who train professionally or as amateurs, and to judges who train individual dogs or who train or instruct dogs in classes with or through their handlers.

No dog may be entered or shown under a judge at an obedience trial if it is owned or handled by any person who has regularly served as a trainer or instructor of that judge within one year prior to the date of the obedience trial, either individually or through classes.

Section 14. Qualifying Score. A qualifying score means that the dog has earned more than 50 percent of the points for each exercise, with a total score of at least 170 points. This score must be earned in a regular class at a licensed or member obedience trial. There is no minimum number of dogs necessary in any class, to earn a qualifying score towards a title.

Section 15. When Titles Are Won. After a dog earns a title, it may continue showing in that class for 60 days.

A dog may compete in a more advanced class if it receives the prerequisite title before the closing date of the trial in which the advanced entry is to be made. Once a dog is entered in Open under this section it may not again be shown in Novice A, and a dog entered in Utility under this section may not be shown in Open A. All entries will be made in accordance with Chapter 11, Section 4, of the Rules Applying to Dog Shows.

Section 16. Disqualification, Ineligibility, Excusal and Change in Appearance of Dogs. If an ineligible dog has been entered in any licensed or member obedience trial or dog show, or if the name of the owner on the entry form is not the person(s) who actu- ally owned the dog at the time entries closed, or if it is shown in a class for which it has not been entered, or if its entry is unacceptable to The American Kennel Club, all result- ing awards will be cancelled.

Any time a judge marks any dog Disqualified or Excused he or she must state the rea- son in the judge's book, and will give the superintendent or show or trial secretary a brief report of the dog's actions which will be submitted to The American Kennel Club with the report of the show or trial.

When a dog has been disqualified under this section as being blind or deaf or for having been changed in appearance for cosmetic reasons or for having attacked or attempted to attack a person in the ring, all awards made to the dog at the trial will be cancelled by The American Kennel Club. The dog may not again compete unless the owner applies for and receives reinstatement.

A dog that is blind or deaf or that has been changed in appearance for cosmetic reasons (except for such changes as are customarily approved for its breed) may not compete in any obedience trial or tracking test and will be disqualified. Blind means without useful vision. Deaf means without useful hearing. The judge will not obtain the opinion of a veterinarian.

The judge will disqualify any dog that attempts to attack any person in the ring.

The judge will excuse a dog that attacks another dog in the ring or that appears dangerous to other dogs in the ring. The owner of any dog which has been excused on two occasions for attacking or attempting to attack another dog in the ring will be notified that the dog is no longer eligible to be shown in obedience classes.

Dogs whose appearance has been surgically altered to correct a congenital or hereditary defect may participate in obedience trials and all tracking tests provided those dogs have been neutered or spayed.

Spayed bitches, monorchid, cryptorchid or castrated dogs, and dogs that have disqualifying conformation faults, may compete in obedience trials, if eligible under these regulations.

A dog that is lame in the ring at any obedience trial or at a tracking test may not compete in that class. Lameness is defined as any irregularity of locomotion. The judge must determine, without a veterinarian's opinion, whether a dog is lame. If so, that judge will not score the dog and will mark his or her book, "Excused-lame."

No dog will be eligible to compete in an obedience trial or tracking test if it is taped or bandaged in any way or if it has anything attached to it for medical or corrective purposes. Such a dog must be immediately excused and under no circumstances may it be judged.

Any dog whose hair over its eyes interferes with its vision may have the hair tied back with up to four rubber bands or small plain barrettes, or as they are normally shown in the breed ring. Any dog whose hair on its ears or beard interferes with the performance of the retrieve exercises may have the hair controlled by the use of up to four rubber bands.

No dog will be eligible to compete if it appears to have been dyed or colored in any way or if the coat shows evidence of chalk or powder, or if the dog has anything attached to it for protection or adornment. Such a dog may be judged later if the condition has been corrected and if the judge desires to do so.

An obedience judge is not required to be familiar with the breed standards or to scrutinize each dog as in dog show judging, but will be alert for conditions that may require disqualification or excusal under this section.

Section 17. Disturbances. Bitches in season are not permitted to compete. The judge of an obedience trial must remove and excuse from competition any bitch in season, any dog which is not under its handler's control, and any handler who willfully interferes with another competitor or that competitor's dog. The judge may also excuse any dog that is unfit to compete, or any bitch that appears so attractive to males as to be a disturbing element. If a dog or handler is excused by a judge, the reason must be stated in the judge's book or in a separate report.

Section 18. Obedience Ribbons. At licensed or member obedience trials the following colors must be used for prize ribbons or rosettes in all regular classes and for the ribbon or rosette for Highest Scoring Dog in the Regular Classes, and for the ribbon or rosette for the dog with the Highest Combined Score in Open and Utility:

First Prize — Blue

Second Prize — Red

Third Prize — Yellow

Fourth Prize — White

Qualifying Prize — Dark Green

Highest Scoring Dog in the Regular Classes — Blue and Gold

Highest Combined Score in Open and Utility — Blue and Green

The following colors shall be used for non-regular classes:

First Prize — Rose

Second Prize — Brown

Third Prize — Light Green

Fourth Prize — Gray

Each ribbon or rosette will be at least two inches wide and a minimum of eight inches long, and will bear on its face a facsimile of the seal of The American Kennel Club, the words Obedience Trial, the name of the placement, the name of the trial-giving club, the date of the trial, and the name of the city or town where the trial is given.

Section 19. Match Ribbons. If ribbons are given at sanctioned obedience matches they will be of the following colors and will have the words Obedience Match printed on them, but may be of any design or size:

First Prize — Rose

Second Prize — Brown

Third Prize — Light Green

Fourth Prize — Gray

Qualifying Prize — Green with Pink edges

Section 20. Ribbons and Prizes. Ribbons for the four official placements and all prizes offered for competition within a single regular class at licensed or member trials or at sanctioned matches will be awarded only to dogs that earn qualifying scores. Qualifying scores will not be required for the awarding of ribbons and prizes in the non-regular classes. Awards for the four placements in these classes will be based solely on the number of points earned. The ribbon and any prizes offered for the dog with the highest combined score in Open B and Utility at a licensed or member trial will be awarded only to a dog that earns qualifying scores in both Open B and Utility.

Prizes for which dogs in one class compete against dogs in one or more other classes at licensed or member trials or at sanctioned matches will be awarded only to dogs that earn qualifying scores.

Prizes at a licensed or member obedience trial must be offered to be won outright, except that a prize requiring three wins by the same owner for permanent possession but not necessarily with the same dog, may be offered for the dog with the highest qualifying score in one of the regular classes or the dog with the highest combined qualifying scores in the Open B and Utility classes.

Subject to the provisions of paragraphs 1 and 2 of this section, prizes may be offered for the highest scoring dog of the groups as defined in Chapter 3 of the Dog Show Rules, or for the highest scoring dogs of any breeds, but not for a breed variety. Show varieties are not recognized for obedience. In accordance with Chapter 3, all Poodles are in the non-sporting group and all Manchester Terriers are in the terrier group. This, however, only applies to all-breed events and breed varieties would be eligible to compete in obedience in their respective all-group event.

Prizes offered only to members of certain clubs or organizations will not be approved for publication in premium lists.

Section 21. Highest Scoring Dog in the Regular Classes and the Dog with the Highest Combined Score in Open B and Utility. The dog receiving the highest qualifying score in the regular classes, and the dog receiving the highest combined score in Open B and Utility, will be awarded the ribbon and any prizes offered for this placement after the announcement of final scores of the last regular class to be judged. The superintendent or show or trial secretary will mark the catalog to identify the dog receiving these awards.

In case of a tie between dogs eligible for either of the above awards, each dog will be tested again, individually, by having it perform the entire Novice Heel Free exercise. The judge for a run-off will be designated by the bench show or obedience trial committee from among the judges of the obedience trial. When a run-off has been completed, the judge will record the results on a special sheet that will identify the dogs taking part in the run-off by catalog number, class and breed. When the judge has marked and signed the sheet, it will be turned over to the superintendent or show or trial secretary who will mark the catalog accordingly and forward the sheet to The American Kennel Club as part of the records of the trial.

Section 22. Risk. The owner or agent entering a dog in an obedience trial does so at his own risk and agrees to abide by the Rules of The American Kennel Club and the Obedience Regulations.

Section 23. Decisions. At the trial the decisions of the judge shall be final in all matters affecting the performance and scoring of the team. Either the obedience trial committee or the bench show committee shall decide all other matters arising at the trial, including protests against dogs made under Chapter 15 of the Dog Show Rules.

Section 24. Dogs Competing. If a dog is excused by the official veterinarian, it must be in writing and must be approved by the superintendent or show or trial secretary and must be submitted to The American Kennel Club with the report of the trial. The judge must report to The American Kennel Club any dog that is not brought back for the group exercises.

Section 25. Judging Program. After the entries have closed, any club holding a licensed or member obedience trial must prepare a program showing the time for the judging of each of the classes before 12:00 noon. Classes after 12:00 noon will be listed "to follow" and must be judged in the order and ring listed. In the case of a Licensed or Member Specialty Show, a starting time for only the first obedience class need be given. In addition, any show where the trial starts after 12:00 noon, a starting time for only the first obedience class need be given.

A copy of this program will be mailed to the owner of each entered dog and to each judge, and the program will be printed in the catalog. This program will be based on the judging of no more than eight (8) Novice entries, seven (7) Open entries or six (6) Utility entries per hour during the published show or trial time.

The published starting hour for judging and the availability of rings must also be taken into consideration. No judge will be scheduled to exceed this limit of dogs per hour and, in addition, may take 45 minutes to one hour for rest or meals at their discretion. No judge will be assigned to judge for more than eight hours in one day, including any breed judging assignment if the obedience trial is held in conjunction with a dog show.

Any non-regular class must be judged after the regular class if it is scheduled to be judged in the same ring.

Section 26. Limitation of Entries. If a club anticipates an entry in excess of its facilities for a licensed or member trial, it may limit entries in any or all regular classes to 64 in a Novice class, 56 in an Open class, or 48 in a Utility class. Non-regular classes, however, may be included, if so desired.

Prominent announcement of such limits will appear on the title or cover page of the premium list for an obedience trial or immediately under the obedience heading in the premium list for a dog show. This announcement must state that entries in one or more specified classes will automatically close when certain limits have been reached, even if this occurs before the official closing date.

When entries are limited in the Open B and/or Utility B classes, a club must designate a UDX class in the premium list. Dogs entered in this UDX class would be entered in both Open B and Utility B and the combined entry fee for these two classes must be paid. Once the limit has been reached in either the Open B or the Utility B class, the UDX class will be considered closed and any subsequent entries for this class will be unacceptable in their entirety.

Section 27. Additional Judges, Reassignment, Split Classes. After the entries have closed, if any judge exceeds the limit established in Section 25, the club will immediately secure the approval of The American Kennel Club for an additional judge, or for reassignment of its advertised judges, so that no judge will be required to exceed the limit.

If a judge was advertised to judge more than one class and receives an excessive entry, at least one of the classes shall be assigned to another judge. Reassignment shall first go to any non-regular classes, and then either the class with the minimum number of entries, or those with the minimum scheduled time. This will bring the advertised judge's schedule as close as possible to the maximum limit.

If a judge with an excessive entry was advertised to judge only one class, the superintendent, show secretary or obedience trial secretary will divide the entry as evenly as possible between the two judges by drawing lots. A notification of any change of judge must be mailed to the owner of each entry affected. The owner will be permitted to withdraw such entry no later than one-half hour prior to the scheduled start of any regular obedience competition at the trial, and the entry fee will then be refunded.

Section 28. Split Classes in Premium List. A club may choose to announce two or more judges for any class in its premium list. In such case, the entries will be divided by lots as provided above. The identification slips and judging program will be made up so that the owner of each dog will know the division and the judge under which his or her dog is entered, but no owner is entitled to a refund of entry fee.

Section 29. Split Classes, Official Ribbons, Prizes. A club that holds a split class will award American Kennel Club official ribbons in each division, even if the split is made after entries close. The four dogs with the highest qualifying scores in each division will be called back into the ring and awarded the four American Kennel Club official ribbons.

Section 30. Stewards. The judge is in sole charge of the ring until his or her assignment is completed. Stewards are provided to assist, but may act only on the judge's instructions. They must not give information or instructions to owners and handlers except when the judge asks them to do so.

Section 31. Ring Conditions. An indoor ring should be rectangular and about 40 × 50 feet for all obedience classes. The Utility ring should never be less than 35 × 50 feet and the Novice or Open ring should not be less than 30 × 40 feet. The floor must have firm footing, using rubber or similar non-slip material at least four feet wide for the takeoffs and landings of all jumps, unless the judge feels the surface does not require it.

At an outdoor show or trial the rings should be about 40 × 50. The ground should be clean and level and any grass should be cut short. For the Open classes, the club and superintendent are responsible for providing an appropriate place, approved by the judge, for the handlers to go completely out of sight of their dogs.

If inclement weather at an outdoor show or trial necessitates the judging of obedience under shelter, the requirements as to ring size may be waived The judge's table and chairs will be of such size and location so as not to interfere with the dog and handler's performance while in the ring.

Section 32. Obedience Rings at Dog Shows. At an outdoor dog show, a separate ring or rings should be provided for obedience. A sign forbidding anyone to permit any dog to use the ring (except during judging) should be set up in each obedience ring by the superintendent or show secretary. It is the duty of the superintendent and/or the show committee to enforce this regulation. At an indoor show where limited space does not permit the exclusive use of any ring for obedience, the same regulation will apply after the obedience rings have been set up. At a dog show the material used for enclosing the obedience rings will be at least equal to the material used for enclosing the breed rings. If the ring has previously been used for breed judging, it must be thoroughly cleaned before the obedience judging starts.

Section 33. Judge's Report on Ring and Equipment. The superintendent and the officials of the club holding the obedience trial are responsible for providing rings and equipment that meet the requirements of these Regulations. The judge, however, must check both the ring and equipment before starting to judge. After the trial, he or she must report to The American Kennel Club any undesirable ring conditions or deficiencies that were not promptly corrected at his or her request.

Section 34. Judges' Education. Obedience judges must attend at least one (1) obedience judges' seminar presented by The American Kennel Club staff in every three-year period, and will be ineligible to accept assignments if this requirement is not met.

To assist in educating prospective judges, they may apprentice under a judge who has been approved to judge the Utility class. The apprentice judge will score dogs and handlers from outside the obedience ring. Proper notification to and consent from the judge must be given prior to the start of the class.

A person who is not currently suspended from the privileges of The American Kennel Club and who has trained and exhibited a dog to the Utility Dog title may be approved to judge non-regular classes.

Chapter 2 — Regulations for Performance and Judging

Section 1. Standardized Judging. Standardized judging is of paramount importance. Judges are not permitted to inject their own variations into the exercise, but will see that each handler and dog execute the various exercises exactly as described in these Regulations. A handler who is familiar with these Regulations should be able to enter the ring under any judge without having to inquire how that particular judge wishes to have an exercise performed and without being confronted with any unexpected requirements.

The judge will inform the first exhibitor in each class what the heeling pattern will be before he or she enters the ring. This may be done vocally, by posting the pattern ringside, or by demonstration. This same procedure will be followed in the event of run-offs.

Section 2. Standard of Perfection. The judge must carry a mental picture of the theoretically perfect performance in each exercise and score each dog and handler against this standard. This perfect picture must be according to the Regulations and shall combine the utmost in willingness, enjoyment and precision on the part of the dog with naturalness, gentleness and smoothness on the part of the handler. Speed alone does not necessarily indicate willingness and enjoyment. Lack of willingness and enjoyment on the part of the dog must be penalized, as must lack of precision in the dog's performance. Roughness in handling, military precision or harsh commands by the handler must also be penalized. There shall be no penalty of less than one-half point.

Section 3. Qualifying Performance. A qualifying score in the judge's book is his or her certification that the dog has performed all the required exercises according to The American Kennel Club Regulations and justifies the awarding of the obedience title associated with the particular class. A qualifying score must never be awarded to a dog whose performance has not met the minimum requirements, or shows fear or resentment, or that relieves itself at any time while in the ring for judging. A handler who carries or offers food in the ring, or disciplines or abuses his or her dog in the ring must receive a non-qualifying (NQ) score.

In deciding whether a faulty performance of an exercise warrants a qualifying score, the judge will consider whether the awarding of an obedience title would be justified if all dogs in the class performed the exercise in a similar manner. The judge must not give a qualifying score for the exercise if he or she decides that it would be contrary to the best interests of the sport if all dogs in the class were to perform in the same way.

Section 4. Judge's Directions. The judge's orders and signals should be given to the handlers in a clear and understandable manner, but in such a way that the work of the dogs is not disturbed. Before starting each exercise, the judge will ask, "Are you ready?" At the end of each exercise the judge will say, "Exercise finished." Each dog will be worked and judged separately except for the group exercises. The judging of an exercise will not begin until the judge has given the first order.

Section 5. No Added Requirements. No judge will require any dog or handler to do anything, nor penalize a dog or handler for failing to do anything, that is not required by these Regulations.

Section 6. A and B Classes and Different Breeds. The same methods and standards will be used for judging and scoring the A and B classes, and in judging and scoring the work of dogs of different breeds.

Section 7. Interference and Double Handling. A judge who is aware of any assistance, interference, or attempts to control a dog from outside the ring, must act promptly to stop such double handling or interference, and must penalize the dog substantially. If the judge feels the circumstances warrant, the dog will receive a non-qualifying (NQ) score for the exercise during which the aid was received.

Section 8. Rejudging. If a dog has failed an exercise, it will not ordinarily be rejudged unless the judge feels the dog's performance was prejudiced by peculiar and unusual conditions. In such a case, the judge may wish to rejudge the dog on the entire exercise. Rejudging of the dog or dogs for the group exercises will be done with the next scheduled group within that class. The limits on the number of dogs allowed in the ring for the group exercise contained in Chapter 3, Section 12, will apply. Should there be no further group within that class, the dog or dogs to be rejudged will immediately do the exercise alone. The dog or dogs involved will be rejudged only on the exercise in question.

Section 9. Ties. In case of a tie for a placement in any class, each dog will be tested again, individually, by having it perform the entire Novice Heel Free exercise. The original scores will not be changed.

Section 10. Judge's Book and Score Sheets. The judge must enter the number of points deducted from each exercise in the official judge's book, immediately after each dog has been judged on the individual exercises. An "NQ" should be recorded in the proper box for any dog who fails to qualify in that exercise, as well as recording an "NQ" in the Total Score column. This is to be completed before the next dog is judged.

Scores for the group exercises and qualifying total scores will be entered in the official judge's book immediately after each group of dogs has been judged.

No person other than the judge may make any numerical entry in the judge's book, and no score may be changed by the judge, except to correct a numerical error or an error in posting.

All final qualifying scores will be entered in the judge's book before ribbons are awarded. Judges may use separate score sheets for their own purposes, but should not give out such sheets, nor give out any other written scores, nor permit anyone else to distribute score sheets or cards prepared by the judge. Carbon copies of the sheets in the official judge's book will be made available through the superintendent or show or trial secretary for examination by handlers, immediately after the ribbons have been awarded in each class.

If a club distributes scorecards after the ribbons are awarded, they must contain no more information than is shown in the judge's book and will be marked "Unofficial."

Section 11. Announcement of Scores. The judge will not disclose any scoring to anyone until the entire class has been judged, nor should anyone else be allowed to do so. Immediately after the group exercises for Novice and Open, the judge will inform the handlers of a non-qualifying score. In Utility, the judge will inform the handler immediately following the last exercise.

After all the scores are recorded for the class, or division of the class, the judge will call the qualifying dogs back into the ring. Before awarding the placements, the judge will inform the spectators as to the maximum number of points for a perfect score. After scores of each placement have been announced, the judge will tell each handler his or her dog's score.

Section 12. Explanations and Errors. The judge is not required to explain his or her scoring and need not enter into a discussion with a dissatisfied exhibitor. After the class is finished and the judge's book has been turned in, however, the judge is encouraged to discuss the scoring with the exhibitors. Any interested person who thinks that there may have been a numerical error or an error in identifying a dog may report the facts to one of the stewards or to the superintendent or show or trial secretary so that the matter may be checked.

Section 13. Compliance with Regulations and Standards. In accordance with the certification on the entry form, the handler of each dog and the person signing each entry form will be familiar with the Obedience Regulations applicable to the class in which the dog is entered.

Section 14. Physically Challenged Handlers. Judges may modify specific requirements of the Regulations so that physically challenged handlers may compete. Such handlers must be able to move around the ring without physical assistance or guidance except that, on the judge's instructions, someone may position a blind handler before, between and after each exercise. Dogs handled by such handlers will be required to perform all parts of all exercises as described in these Regulations, and will be penalized for failure to perform any part of an exercise.

Section 15. Catalog Order. Dogs should be judged in catalog order if it is practical to do so without holding up any judging. Judges are not required to wait for dogs for either the individual or the group exercises. Each handler is responsible for being ready at ringside when required and without being called. The judge's first consideration should be the convenience of those exhibitors who are ready when scheduled and who ask no favors.

If a request is made in advance of the class starting time, a judge may agree to judge a dog earlier or later than the time scheduled by catalog order. If no such arrangement has been made, however, a judge should not hesitate to mark absent any dog and handler not ready to be judged in catalog order.

Section 16. Use of Leash. All dogs must be kept on leash except when in the obedience ring or exercise area and must be brought into and taken out of the ring on leash. Dogs must be kept on leash in the ring when brought in to receive awards, and when waiting in the ring before and after the group exercises. The leash will be left on the judge's table or other designated place except during the Heel on Leash and group exercises. It must be of fabric or leather and need only be long enough to provide adequate slack during the Heel on Leash exercise.

Section 17. Collars. All dogs in the obedience ring must wear a properly fitted collar approved by the judge. No special training collars, such as electronic collars or prong collars, will be permitted. Nothing may be hanging from the dog's collar.

Section 18. Heel Position. The heel position as defined in these Regulations, applies whether the dog is sitting, standing, lying down, or moving at heel. The dog should be straight in line with the direction in which the handler is facing, at the handler's left side. The area from the dog's head to shoulder is to be in line with the handler's left hip. The dog should be close, but not crowding, so that the handler has freedom of motion at all times.

Section 19. Hands. In all exercises where the dog is required to heel free, one of these options should be followed: (1) when the handler is in motion, the arms and hands must move naturally at the sides and must hang naturally at the sides when stopped or (2) the right hand and arm must move naturally at the side, while the left hand must be held against the front of the body, centered in the area of the waist, with the left forearm carried against the body. In either of the above situations the hands and arms may be adjusted during the fast portion of an exercise, in order to maintain balance. There will be a substantial deduction if the hands and arms are not carried in one of the positions stated above. In any exercise in which the dog is required to sit in front, the handler's arms and hands must hang naturally at the sides until the dog has sat in front. The handler must receive a substantial deduction for not doing so.

Section 20. Commands and Signals. When the Regulations mention a command or signal, only a single command or signal may be given and any extra commands or signals must be penalized. When the Regulations specify command and/or signal, the handler may give either one or the other, or both command and signal simultaneously. When a signal is permitted, it must be a single gesture with one arm and hand only, and the arm must immediately be returned to a natural position.

Delay in following a judge's order to give a command or signal must be penalized, unless the judge directs the delay. Lack of prompt response by the dog to a command or signal is subject to a penalty.

Signaling correction to a dog is forbidden and will be penalized. Signals must be inaudible and the handler must not touch the dog. Any unusual noise or motion may be considered to be a signal. Position of the arms and hands and movements of the head and/or body that aid the dog will be considered additional signals. A handler may, however, bend the body and knees to bring his hand on a level with the dog's eyes while giving a signal to a dog in heel position.

Any kind of whistling is prohibited. The dog's name may be used once immediately before any verbal command or before a verbal command and signal when these Regulations permit command and/or signal. The name will not be used with any signal not given simultaneously with a verbal command. The dog's name, when given immediately before a verbal command, will not be considered as an additional command, but a dog that responds to its name without waiting for the verbal command will be scored as having anticipated the command. The dog should never anticipate the handler's directions, but will wait for the appropriate commands and/or signals. Moving forward at the heel without any command or signal other than the natural forward movement of the handler's body will not be considered as anticipation.

Loud commands by handlers to their dogs create a poor impression of obedience and should be avoided. Shouting is not necessary even in a noisy place if the dog is properly trained to respond to a normal tone of voice. Commands which the judge feels are excessively loud will be penalized substantially.

An extra command and/or signal in any non-principal part of an exercise does not constitute a failing score for that exercise.

Section 21. Additional Commands or Signals. If a handler gives an additional command or signal not permitted by these Regulations, the dog shall be scored as though it had failed to perform that particular part of the exercise. This includes giving a signal or command when none is permitted, or using the dog's name with a permitted signal but without a permitted command.

Section 22. Praise. Praise and petting are allowed between and after exercises, but points will be deducted from the total score for a dog that is not under reasonable control while being praised. There will be a substantial penalty for any dog that is picked up or carried at any time in the obedience ring.

Section 23. Handling between Exercises. In the Novice class the dog may be guided gently by the collar between exercises. No other physical guidance is permitted and must be penalized from minor to substantial depending on circumstances.

In the Open or Utility class there will be a substantial penalty for any dog that is physically guided at any time or that is not readily controllable. Minor penalties will be imposed for a dog that does not respond promptly to its handler's commands or signals before or between exercises in the Open or Utility classes.

Section 24. Orders and Minimum Penalties. The orders for the exercises and the standards for judging are set forth in the following Chapters. The lists of faults are not intended to be complete, but minimum penalties are specified for most of the more common and serious faults. There is no maximum limit on penalties. A dog that makes none of the errors listed may still receive a non-qualifying (NQ) score for other reasons.

Section 25. Misbehavior. Any display of fear or nervousness by the dog, or any uncontrolled behavior such as snapping, barking or running away from its handler must be penalized according to the seriousness of the misbehavior, whether it occurs during or between an exercise, or before or after judging. The judge may excuse the dog from further competition in the class.

If the behavior occurs during an exercise, the penalty must first be applied to the score for that exercise. Should the penalty be greater than the value of the exercise, the additional points will be deducted from the total score under Miscellaneous Penalties. If such behavior occurs before or after the judging or between exercises, the entire penalty will be deducted from the total score. Any dog that relieves itself at any time while in the ring for judging must receive a non-qualifying NQ) score and may be excused from the ring.

The judge must disqualify any dog that attacks or attempts to attack any person in the ring. Any dog that attacks another dog or that appears dangerous to other dogs in the ring must be "excused."

Section 26. Training and Warm-up on the Grounds. There will be no intensive or abusive training of the dogs on the grounds or premises at a licensed or member obedience trial or sanctioned match. No practice rings are permitted. Collars must be in accordance with Chapter 2, Section 17. These requirements should not be interpreted as preventing a handler from moving normally about the grounds or premises, nor from warming up his or her dog using any exercise performed in the obedience ring, provided the dog is on a leash being held by the handler. It should be performed as far from the obedience rings as is reasonably possible and must not be disruptive to any dog or person. Physical or verbal disciplining of a dog will not be permitted except to a reasonable extent in case of an attack on either a dog or a person.

All dogs will be kept on leash except when in the obedience ring or exercise area. The superintendent, or show or trial secretary, as well as the members of the bench show or obedience trial committee, shall be responsible for compliance with this section and shall investigate any reports of infractions.

Section 27. Training and Disciplining in the Ring. The judge will not permit any handler to use excessive verbal commands, to move toward the dog to correct it or to practice any exercise in the ring at any time. Any exhibitor who does so may be excused. A dog whose handler disciplines it in the ring will be excused from further competition in the class and must receive a non-qualifying (NQ) score. The judge must immediately report any abuse of a dog in the ring to the bench show or obedience trial committee for action under Chapter 2, Section 29, of these Regulations.

Section 28. Abuse of Dogs. The bench show or obedience trial committee will investigate any report of either abuse or severe disciplining of dogs on the grounds or premises of a show, trial or match. Any person whose conduct is in any manner prejudicial to the best interests of the sport will be dealt with promptly. This will be done during the trial if possible, after the offender has been notified of the specific charges and has been given an opportunity to be heard in his or her own defense. The judge must immediately report any abuse of a dog in the ring to the bench show or obedience trial committee for action under Chapter 2, Section 29, below.

Section 29. Discipline. (See Guide for Bench Show and Obedience Trial Committees in Dealing with Misconduct at Dog Shows and Obedience Trials.) After the alleged offender has been given an opportunity to be heard, the bench show, obedience trial or field trial committee has the right to suspend that person from the privileges of The American Kennel Club for conduct prejudicial to the sport. The committee involved must send written notice to the suspended person by registered mail. A duplicate notice containing full details concerning the suspension must be forwarded to The American Kennel Club within seven days.

An appeal may be made to a decision of a bench show, obedience trial or field trial committee. Written notice of such an appeal, together with a five dollar ($5.00) deposit, must be sent to The American Kennel Club within 30 days after the date of the suspension. The Board of Directors may hear the appeal itself or may refer it to a committee of the board or to a trial board. The deposit will remain with The American Kennel Club if the decision is upheld. If not, the deposit will be returned to the appellant. (See Guide for Bench Show and Obedience Trial Committees in Dealing with Misconduct at Dog Shows and Obedience Trials for proper procedure at licensed or member obedience trials. The committee at a sanctioned event does not have this power of suspension, but must investigate any allegation of misconduct and forward a detailed report of the incident to The American Kennel Club.)

Section 30. Declining Entries. An Obedience Trial Committee may decline any entries or may remove any dog from its trial for cause, but in each such instance shall file good and sufficient reasons for doing so with The American Kennel Club.

Chapter 3 — Novice

Section 1. Novice A Class. The Novice A class shall be for dogs that have not won the CD title and are at least 6 months old. A handler must own the dog entered, or be a member of the owner's household or immediate family, and may not have previously handled any dog that has earned an American Kennel Club obedience title. A person may enter more than one dog in this class, but the same person who handled each dog in the first four exercises must handle that dog in the group exercises. If a person has handled more than one dog in the first four exercises, he or she must provide an additional handler if the additional dog(s) will be judged in the same group. No dog may be entered in both Novice A and Novice B at any trial.

Section 2. Novice B Class. The Novice B class will be for dogs not less than 6 months of age. A CD dog may continue to compete in this class until it receives a qualifying score in an Open class or until it has received one (1) High in Trial award prior to the closing date of the trial. This one (1) High in Trial award is in addition to any obtained before or during the 60-day period after receiving the CD title. The owner or any other person may handle dogs in this class. A person may enter more than one dog in this class, but the same person who handled each dog in the first four exercises will handle each dog in the group exercises. If a person has handled more than one dog in the first four exercises, he or she must provide an additional handler if the additional dog(s) will be judged in the same group. No dog may be entered in both Novice A and Novice B at any one trial.

Section 3. Novice Exercises and Scores. The exercises and maximum scores in the Novice classes:

1. Heel on Leash and Figure Eight   40 points
2. Stand for Examination   30 points
3. Heel Free   40 points
4. Recall   30 points
5. Long Sit   30 points
6. Long Down   30 points

       Maximum Total Score   200 points

Section 4. CD Title. The letters CD may be added after a dog's name when it has been certified by three different judges to have received qualifying scores in Novice classes at three licensed or member obedience trials. That dog will receive a Companion Dog certificate from The American Kennel Club.

Section 5. Heel on Leash and Figure Eight. The principal feature of this exercise is the ability of the dog and handler to work as a team. Orders for this exercise are "Forward," "Halt," "Right turn," "Left turn," "About turn," "Slow," "Normal" and "Fast." "Fast" means that the handler must run, and the handler and dog must move forward at a noticeably accelerated speed. All about turns will be right about turns. Orders for halts and turns will be given only when the handler is moving at a normal speed.

The other orders may be given in any sequence and turns and halts may be repeated. However, the judge should standardize the heeling pattern for all dogs in the class.

The leash may be held in either hand or in both hands, but the hands must be held in a natural position. Any tightening or jerking of the leash or any extra commands and/or signals will be penalized.

The handler will enter the ring with the dog on a loose leash and stand with the dog sitting in the heel position. The judge will ask if the handler is ready before giving the order, "Forward." The handler may give a command or signal to heel, and will walk briskly and naturally with the dog on a loose leash. The dog should walk close to the handler's left side without swinging wide, lagging, forging or crowding. The dog must not interfere with the handler's freedom of motion at any time. At each order to halt, the handler will stop. The dog shall sit straight and promptly in the heel position without command or signal and shall not move until the handler again moves forward on the judge's order. After each halt, it is permissible for the handler to give a command or signal to heel before moving forward again. The judge will say, "Exercise finished" after this portion of the exercise.

For the figure eight, the handler and dog will stand facing the judge, midway between the two stewards, who are standing 8 feet apart. The figure eight in the Novice classes will be done on leash and the handler may go around either steward first. After the judge asks, "Are you ready?" and gives the order "Forward," the handler and dog will walk briskly around and between the two stewards twice. There will be no about turn, fast or slow, but the judge must order at least one halt during this exercise and another halt at the end.

Section 6. Heel on Leash and Figure Eight, Scoring. If a handler is constantly controlling the dog by tugging on the leash or is adapting to the dogs' pace, that dog must receive a non-qualifying (NQ) score for this exercise.

Minor or substantial deductions, depending on the circumstances, will be made for additional commands or signals to heel, or for failure of dog or handler to speed up noticeably for the fast, or slow down noticeably for the slow.

Substantial or minor deductions shall be made for lagging, heeling wide, forging, crowding, poor sits, failure to sit at a halt, and other heeling imperfections. Deductions should also be made for a handler who guides the dog with the leash or does not walk at a brisk pace.

While scoring this exercise the judge should be near enough to observe any signals or commands given by the handler to the dog, without interfering with either.

Section 7. Stand for Examination. The principal feature of this exercise is that the dog stands in position before and during the examination without displaying resentment. Orders are, "Stand your dog and leave when you are ready," "Back to your dog," and "Exercise finished."

On the judge's order, the handler will remove the leash and give it to a steward, who will place it on the judge's table or other designated place. The handler will take his or her dog to the place indicated by the judge and, on the judge's order will stand/pose the dog by the method of his or her choice, taking any reasonable time if he or she chooses to pose the dog as in the show ring. The handler will then stand with the dog in the heel position, give the command and/or signal to stay, walk straight forward about six feet, turn and face the dog.

The judge will approach the dog from the front. Using the fingers and palm of one hand, he or she will touch the dog's head, body and hindquarters. On the order "Back to your dog," the handler will walk around behind the dog and return to the heel position. The dog must remain standing until the judge has said, "Exercise finished."

Section 8. Stand for Examination, Scoring. The scoring of this exercise will not start until the handler has given the command and/or signal to stay, except for such things as rough treatment by the handler or active resistance by the dog to his handler's attempts to have it stand. Either of these will be penalized substantially.

A dog must receive a non-qualifying (NQ) score if it sits or lies down, or moves away from the place where it was left either before or during the examination, or that growls, snaps or displays resentment.

Minor or substantial deductions, even to the point of a non-qualifying (NQ) score, will be made for shyness.

Minor or substantial deductions will be made for a dog that moves its feet at any time, or sits or moves away after the examination has been completed.

Section 9. Heel Free, Performance and Scoring. This exercise will be performed as in the Heel on Leash, but without either the leash or the Figure Eight. The scoring and orders will be the same.

Section 10. Recall. The principal features of this exercise are that the dog stays where left until called by its handler, and that the dog responds promptly to the handler's command or signal to come.

Orders are, "Leave your dog," "Call your dog," and "Finish."

On order from the judge, the handler may give a command and/or signal to the dog to stay in the sit position, and will then walk forward to the other end of the ring, turn to face the dog and stand naturally. On the judge's order or signal, the handler will either command or signal the dog to come. The dog must come directly, at a brisk trot or gallop and sit straight, centered in front of the handler. The dog must be close enough so the handler could touch its head without excessive bending, stretching, or moving either foot.

On the judge's order, the handler will give a command or signal to finish. The dog must go smartly to heel position and sit. The manner in which the dog finishes will be optional provided it is prompt and that the dog sits straight at heel.

Section 11. Recall, Scoring. A dog must receive a non-qualifying (NQ) score if it does not stay without an additional command or signal, or fails to come on the first command or signal, or moves from the place it was left before being called or signaled to come, or does not sit close enough so that the handler could touch its head without excessive bending, stretching or moving either foot.

Substantial deductions will be made for a dog which fails to remain sitting and either stands or lies down, fails to come at a brisk trot or gallop, fails to sit in front, fails to finish or sit at heel and for a handler's extra command or signal to sit or finish.

Minor or substantial deductions will be made for slow or poor sits, finishes which are not prompt or smart, for touching the handler on coming in or while finishing, and for sitting between the handler's feet.

Section 12. Group Exercises. The principal feature of this exercise is that the dog remains in the sitting or down position, whichever is required by the particular exercise.

Orders are "Sit your dogs" or "Down your dogs," "Leave your dogs" and "Back to your dogs."

All the competing dogs in the class perform these exercises together. If, however, there are more dogs competing than can be spaced four (4) feet per dog on one side of a ring, some must be judged in another group. The judge will divide the class into approximately equal sections and the group exercise will be judged after each section.

If the same judge does both Novice A and Novice B and the combined class would not have to be divided into equal sections, the two classes may be judged in one group.

The dogs that are in the ring will be lined up in catalog order along one of the four sides of the ring. Each handler's armband, weighted as necessary, will be placed behind the dog.

Before starting the long sit, the judge will ask if the handlers are ready. When the judge gives the order, the handlers will command and/or signal their dogs to sit, if they are not already sitting. On further order to "Leave your dogs," the handlers will give a command and/or signal to stay and immediately go to the opposite side of the ring, turn and face their dogs.

If a dog gets up and starts to wander or follow its handler, or if a dog moves to interfere with another dog, the judge will promptly instruct the handler or one of the stewards to remove the dog from the ring and/or keep it away from other dogs.

After one minute from the time the judge has ordered the handlers to leave their dogs, he or she will give the order to return. The handlers must go back promptly, walking around and in back of their own dog to the heel position. The dogs must not move from the sitting position until after the judge has said, "Exercise finished." This order will not be given until the handlers are back in heel position.

Before starting the long down, the judge will ask if the handlers are ready. On the judge's order, the handlers will down their dogs without touching either the dog or their collar, so that they are facing the opposite side of the ring. The rest of this exercise is done in the same manner as the long sit, except that the judge will order the handlers to return after three minutes, and the dogs must not move from the down position until after the judge has said, "Exercise finished."

The dogs will not be required to sit at the end of this exercise.

Section 13. Group Exercises, Scoring. A non-qualifying score (NQ) is required for the following: The dog moving a substantial distance away from the place where it was left any time during the exercise, going over to any other dog, not remaining in the required position until the handler has returned to heel position, repeatedly barking or whining.

A substantial deduction will be made for a dog that moves even a short distance from where it was left or that barks or whines only once or twice, or that changes from a sit to a down, or from a down to a sit after the handler has returned to the heel position and before the judge has given the order "Exercise finished."

Depending on the circumstance, a minor or substantial deduction will be made for touching the dog or its collar while getting the dog into the down position.

A dog that is out of position enough to interfere with an adjacent dog must be repositioned by its handler and will be substantially penalized. In extreme cases the dog may be excused. A dog that interferes with another dog on the long sit, should be excused from participating in the long down.

During these exercises the judge will stand so that all the dogs are in his or her line of vision, and where he or she can see all the handlers in the ring without having to turn around.

Scoring of the exercises will not start until after the judge has ordered the handlers to leave their dogs, except for such things as rough treatment of a dog by its handler or resistance by a dog to its handler's attempts to make it sit or lie down. These will be penalized substantially; in extreme cases the dog may be excused.

The judge will not give the "Exercise finished" order until the handlers have returned to heel position.

Chapter 4 — Open

Section 1. Open A Class. The Open A class will be for dogs that have won the CD title, but have not won the CDX title. Anyone who has trained or exhibited a dog that has earned an OTCH may not enter or handle dogs in this class. Each dog must be handled by its owner or by a member of the owner's household or immediate family. Owners may enter more than one dog in this class. The same person will handle the dog in every exercise. However, if a person has handled more than one dog in the first five exercises, he or she must provide a handler for each of his or her other dogs in the same group exercise. No dog may be entered in both the Open A and Open B classes at any one trial.

Section 2. Open B Class. The Open B class will be for dogs that have won the CD or CDX titles. A dog may continue to compete in this class after it has won the UD title. The owner or any other person may handle dogs in this class. Owners may enter more than one dog in this class, but the same person who handled each dog in the first five exercises must handle each dog in the group exercises. However, if a person has handled more than one dog in the first five exercises, he or she must provide an additional handler for each of his or her other dogs in the same group exercise. No dog may be entered in both Open A and Open B classes at any one trial.

Prior to the start of judging, the judge will decide the order of exercises to be performed in that class. This order will not be disclosed to exhibitors until it is posted at the ring, approximately 45 minutes before the start of the class. In future assignments, judges are required to alternate the six orders of exercises so that each will be used approximately the same number of times.

Section 3. Open A Exercises and Scores. The exercises and maximum score in the Open A class:

1. Heel Free and Figure Eight   40 points
2. Drop on Recall   30 points
3. Retrieve on Flat   20 points
4. Retrieve over High Jump   30 points
5. Broad Jump   20 points
6. Long Sit   30 points
7. Long Down   30 points

        Maximum Total Score   200 points

Section 4. Open B Exercises and Scores. The various orders of exercises in the Open B class:

OPEN I

1. Heel Free and Figure Eight   40 points
2. Drop on Recall   30 points
3. Retrieve on Flat   20 points
4. Retrieve over High Jump   30 points
5. Broad Jump   20 points
6. Long Sit   30 points
7. Long Down   30 points

OPEN II

1. Broad Jump   20 points
2. Retrieve over High Jump   30 points
3. Retrieve on Flat   20 points
4. Drop on Recall   30 points
5. Figure Eight and Heel Free   40 points
6. Long Down   30 points
7. Long Sit   30 points

OPEN III

1. Retrieve on Flat   20 points
2. Drop on Recall   30 points
3. Retrieve over High Jump   30 points
4. Broad Jump   20 points
5. Figure Eight and Heel Free   40 points
6. Long Sit   30 points
7. Long Down   30 points

OPEN IV

1.	Drop on Recall	30 points
2.	Heel Free and Figure Eight	40 points
3.	Retrieve over High Jump	30 points
4.	Broad Jump	20 points
5.	Retrieve on Flat	20 points
6.	Long Sit	30 points
7.	Long Down	30 points

OPEN V

1.	Retrieve over High Jump	30 points
2.	Drop on Recall	30 points
3.	Figure Eight and Heel Free	40 points
4.	Retrieve on Flat	20 points
5.	Broad Jump	20 points
6.	Long Down	30 points
7.	Long Sit	30 points

OPEN VI

1.	Broad Jump	20 points
2.	Figure Eight and Heel Free	40 points
3.	Drop on Recall	30 points
4.	Retrieve over High Jump	30 points
5.	Retrieve on Flat	20 points
6.	Long Sit	30 points
7.	Long Down	30 points

Section 5. CDX Title. The letters CDX may be added after the name of each dog that has been certified by three different judges to have received qualifying scores in Open classes at three licensed or member obedience trials. That dog will also receive a Companion Dog Excellent certificate from The American Kennel Club.

Section 6. Heel Free and Figure Eight, Performance and Scoring. This exercise will be executed in the same manner as the Novice Heel on Leash and Figure Eight exercise, except that the dog is off leash. Orders and scoring are the same as in Heel on Leash and Figure Eight.

Section 7. Drop on Recall. The principal features of this exercise, in addition to those listed under the Novice Recall, are the dog's prompt response to the handler's command or signal to drop, and the dog's remaining in the down position until again called or signaled to come. The dog will be judged on the promptness of its response to the command or signal.

The judge will order "Leave your dog," "Call your dog," then give a clear signal to drop the dog, followed by "Call your dog" and "Finish."

On order from the judge, the handler may give a command and/or signal for the dog to stay in the sit position. The handler will walk forward to the other end of the ring, then turn, facing his or her dog and stand naturally. On the judge's order or signal, the handler will either command or signal the dog to come. The dog must come directly at a brisk trot or gallop. On the judge's arm or hand signal, the handler shall give the command or signal to drop, and the dog must drop immediately to a complete down position. The dog must remain down until the judge gives the order or signal for the handler to signal or command the dog to come. The dog completes the exercise as in the Novice Recall.

Section 8. Drop on Recall, Scoring. A non-qualifying (NQ) score should be given to any dog which does not drop completely to the down position on a single command or signal, or for a dog that does not remain down until called or signaled.

Minor or substantial deductions, up to a non-qualifying (NQ) score shall be made for delayed or slow response to the handler's command or signal to drop, and for slow response to either of the recalls. All applicable penalties listed under the Novice Recall shall apply.

Section 9. Retrieve on Flat. The principal feature of this exercise is that the dog retrieve promptly. Orders are "Throw it," "Send your dog," "Take it" and "Finish."

The handler will stand with his or her dog sitting in the heel position in a place designated by the judge. On the judge's order, "Throw it," the handler will give the command and/or signal to stay. If the handler does use a signal, that signal may not be given with the hand that is holding the dumbbell. After the dumbbell is thrown at least 20 feet, the judge will order the handler "Send your dog." The retrieve should be executed at a brisk trot or gallop. The dog will go directly to the dumbbell and retrieve it, returning directly to the handler without unnecessary mouthing or playing. Without touching the handler or sitting between his or her feet, the dog must sit straight, centered immediately in front of the handler, close enough so the handler could touch its head without excessive bending, stretching or moving either foot. On order from the judge to "Take it," the handler will give command or signal and take the dumbbell.

The Finish will be executed as in the Novice Recall.

The dumbbell, which must be approved by the judge, will be made of one or more solid pieces of wood, or of a rigid or semi-rigid, firm, nontoxic, non-wooden material similar in size, shape, and weight to a wooden dumbbell. Metal dumbbells are not permitted. Dumbbells will not be hollowed out. They may be unfinished, coated with a clear finish, painted white or any other color. They may not have decorations or attachments, but may bear an inconspicuous mark for identification. The size of the dumbbell will be proportionate to the size of the dog. The judge will require the dumbbell to be thrown again before the dog is sent if it is thrown less than 20 feet, or too far to one side, or too close to the ring's edge.

Section 10. Retrieve on Flat, Scoring. A dog that fails to go out on the first command or signal, or goes to retrieve before the command or signal is given, or fails to retrieve, or does not return with the dumbbell sufficiently close that the handler can easily take the dumbbell as described above, must receive a non-qualifying (NQ) score.

Minor or substantial deductions will be made for a dog's slowness in going out, returning, slowness in picking up the dumbbell, not going directly to the dumbbell, mouthing or playing with the dumbbell, and reluctance or refusal to release the dumbbell to the handler. Depending on the extent, minor to substantial deduction will be made for dropping the dumbbell. All other applicable penalties listed under the Novice Recall will apply.

Section 11. Retrieve over High Jump. The principal features of this exercise are that the dog goes out over the jump, picks up the dumbbell and promptly returns with it over the jump. Orders are "Throw it," "Send your dog," "Take it," and "Finish." This exercise will be executed in the same manner as the Retrieve on Flat, except that the dog will clear the high jump both going and coming. The handler will stand at least 8 feet, or any reasonable distance beyond 8 feet from the jump, but will remain in the same spot throughout the exercise, and will throw the dumbbell at least 8 feet beyond the jump. (These 8-foot distances should be clearly marked.)

The minimum jump will be set at the nearest multiple of 2 inches to three-quarters the height of the dog at the withers for the following breeds:

Basset Hounds

Bernese Mountain Dogs

Bloodhounds

Bulldogs

Bullmastiffs

Cardigan Welsh Corgis

Clumber Spaniels

Dachshunds

French Bulldogs

Great Danes

Great Pyrenees

Greater Swiss Mountain Dogs

Irish Wolfhounds

Mastiffs

Newfoundlands

Saint Bernards

Skye Terriers

The minimum jump shall be set to the multiple of 2 inches nearest the height of the dog at the withers for all other dogs, with no dog jumping less than 8 inches nor more than 36 inches. Handlers having their dogs jump more than the minimum required height will neither be penalized nor receive extra consideration. For breeds that jump three-quarters the height of the dog at the withers, the minimum jumps will be set in accordance with the following table:

Measured height of dog at withers	Height to be jumped (on the right)
Less than 12½"	8"
12½" to less than 15"	10"
15" to less than 17½"	12"
17½" to less than 20"	14"
20" to less than 23"	16"
23" to less than 25½"	18"
25½" to less than 28"	20"
28" to less than 31"	22"
31" to less than 33½"	24"
33½" to less than 36"	26"
36" to less than 39"	28"

The stewards, based on the handler's advice as to the dog's height, may preset the jumps. The judge will make certain the jump is at least the minimum required height for each dog, and must also be aware that the jump may be set at a higher height if requested by the handler. The judge may, at his or her discretion, verify the height of any dog at the withers.

The high jump will be 5 feet wide and built to provide 2 inch increments from 8 inches to 36 inches. The uprights of the high jump will be 4 feet high. It is suggested that the bottom board measure 8 inches down from its top to the floor or ground. In addition, three other 8-inch boards, a 4-inch board and 2-inch board should be used. A 6-inch board may also be used. The jump will be painted a flat white. The only thing painted on the boards will be their height, written in black 2-inch numbers.

Section 12. Retrieve over High Jump, Scoring. A dog that fails to go over the full height of the jump in either direction, or that uses the jump for any aid in going over must receive a non-qualifying (NQ) score.

Depending on the specific circumstances, minor or substantial deductions shall be made for a dog that touches the jump in going over it or displays any hesitation in jumping. All other penalties listed under the Retrieve on Flat apply.

Section 13. Broad Jump. The principal features of this exercise are that the dog stay where left until directed to jump, that the dog clear the jump on a single command or signal and that the dog return to its handler after it has jumped.

Orders are "Leave your dog," "Send your dog" and "Finish."

The handler will stand with the dog sitting in the heel position, at least 8 feet from the jump, facing the lowest side of the lowest hurdle. (This 8-foot distance should be clearly marked.) On order from the judge to "Leave your dog," the handler will give the command and/or signal to stay and go to a position facing the right side of the jump. The handler may stand anywhere between the lowest edge of the first hurdle and the highest edge of the last hurdle, with his or her toes about 2 feet from the jump.

On the judge's order, the handler will give the command or signal to jump. While the dog is in midair, the handler will execute a right-angle turn, but will remain in the same spot. The dog will clear the entire distance of the hurdle without touching them and, without further command or signal, immediately return to a sitting position in front of the handler, finishing as in the Novice Recall.

The broad jump will consist of four telescoping hurdles, all about 8" wide and painted a flat white. The largest hurdle will measure about 5 feet long and about 6 inches at the highest point. In the ring, they will be arranged in order of size, evenly spaced, covering a distance equal to twice the height of the high jump setting for each dog. Four hurdles will be used for a jump of 48 to 72 inches, three for 28 to 44 inches and two for a jump of 16 to 24 inches. When decreasing the number of hurdles in the jump, the highest hurdle will be removed first. It is the judge's responsibility to see that the distance jumped by each dog is in accordance with these Regulations.

Section 14. Broad Jump, Scoring. A dog that fails to stay until directed to jump, or refuses the jump on the first command or signal, or that steps on or between the hurdle must receive a non-qualifying (NQ) score.

Depending on the circumstances, minor or substantial deductions will be made for a dog that does not return directly to the handler, displays any hesitation in jumping, or that touches the jump. All applicable penalties listed under the Novice Recall shall apply.

Section 15. Open Group Exercises, Performance and Scoring. During these exercises the judge will stand so that all the dogs are in his or her line of vision. Without having to turn around, he or she should be able to see all the handlers as they leave and return to the ring.

These exercises are performed in the same manner as in the Novice classes, except that the handlers must cross to the opposite side of the ring, then leave in a single file and go completely out of the dogs' sight. Counting from the judge's order to "Leave your dogs," the handlers must remain in the place designated by the judge until three (3) minutes have passed for the Long Sit and five (5) minutes for the Long Down. On the judge's orders, the handlers will return to the ring in reverse order, lining up to face their dogs at the opposite side of the ring, and return to their dogs.

Orders and scoring are the same as in the Novice group exercises.

Chapter 5 — Utility

Section 1. Utility A Class. The Utility A class will be for those dogs that have won the CDX title, but have not won the UD title. Anyone who has trained or exhibited a dog that has earned an OTCH may not enter or handle dogs in this class. Each dog will be handled by its owner or by a member of the owner's immediate family or household. Owners may enter more than one dog in this class.

Section 2. Utility B Class. The Utility B class will be for dogs that have won the CDX or UD title. The owner or any other person may handle dogs in this class, and owners may enter more than one dog in this class. No dog may be entered in both Utility A and Utility B classes at any one trial.

Prior to the start of judging, the judge will decide the order of exercises to be performed in this class. This order will not be disclosed to exhibitors until it is posted at the ring, approximately 45 minutes before the start of the class. In future assignments, judges are required to alternate the six orders of exercises so that each will be used approximately the same number of times.

Section 3. Utility A Exercises and Scores. The exercises, maximum scores and order of judging in the Utility A class:

1.	Signal Exercise	40 points
2.	Scent Discrimination Article No. 1	30 points
3.	Scent Discrimination Article No. 2	30 points
4.	Directed Retrieve	30 points
5.	Moving Stand and Examination	30 points
6.	Directed Jumping	40 points
	Maximum Total Score	200 points

Section 4. Utility B Exercises and Scores. The various orders of exercises in the Utility B class:

UTILITY I

1.	Signal Exercise	40 points
2.	Scent Discrimination Article No. 1	30 points
3.	Scent Discrimination Article No. 2	30 points
4.	Directed Retrieve	30 points
5.	Moving Stand and Examination	30 points
6.	Directed Jumping	40 points

UTILITY II

1. Directed Jumping   40 points
2. Moving Stand and Examination   30 points
3. Directed Retrieve   30 points
4. Scent Discrimination Article No. 1   30 points
5. Scent Discrimination Article No. 2   30 points
6. Signal Exercise   40 points

UTILITY III

1. Scent Discrimination Article No. 1   30 points
2. Scent Discrimination Article No. 2   30 points
3. Directed Retrieve   30 points
4. Signal Exercise   40 points
5. Moving Stand and Examination   30 points
6. Directed Jumping   40 points

UTILITY IV

1. Moving Stand and Examination   30 points
2. Directed Jumping   40 points
3. Signal Exercise   40 points
4. Directed Retrieve   30 points
5. Scent Discrimination Article No. 1   30 points
6. Scent Discrimination Article No. 2   30 points

UTILITY V

1. Directed Retrieve   30 points
2. Scent Discrimination Article No. 1   30 points
3. Scent Discrimination Article No. 2   30 points
4. Directed Jumping   40 points
5. Signal Exercise   40 points
6. Moving Stand and Examination   30 points

UTILITY VI

1. Directed Retrieve   30 points
2. Signal Exercise   40 points
3. Directed Jumping   40 points
4. Moving Stand and Examination   30 points
5. Scent Discrimination Article No. 1   30 points
6. Scent Discrimination Article No. 2   30 points

Section 5. UD Title. The American Kennel Club will issue a Utility Dog certificate for each registered dog, that has been certified by three obedience trial judges as having received qualifying Utility scores at three licensed or member obedience trials. The letters UD may then be used after the dog's name.

Section 6. Signal Exercise. The principal features of this exercise are the ability of dog and handler to work as a team while heeling, and the dog's correct response to the signals to stand, stay, down, sit and come.

Orders are the same as in the Novice Heel on Leash, except for the judge's order to "Stand your dog." This order will only be given when dog and handler are walking at a normal pace, and will be followed by the order "Leave your dog." The judge must use signals for directing the handler to signal the dog to down, sit, come (in that sequence) and to finish.

Heeling will be done as in the Heel Free, except that the handler may use signals only and must not speak to his or her dog at any time during this exercise.

While the dog is heeling at one end of the ring, the judge will order the handler to "Stand your dog." On further order to "Leave your dog," the handler will signal the dog to stay, go to the other end of the ring, turn and face the dog On the judge's signal, the handler will give the signals to down, sit, come and finish as in the Novice Recall.

Section 7. Signal Exercise, Scoring. A dog that fails the handler's first signal to stand, stay, down, sit, come, or that receives a command from the handler to do any of these parts of the exercise, must receive a non-qualifying (NQ) score.

Depending on the specific circumstances, minor or substantial deductions will be made for a dog that walks forward on the stand, down or sit portions of the exercise. The deduction could be up to a NQ.

A substantial deduction will be made for any audible command during the heeling or finish portions of the exercise. All applicable penalties listed under the Heel on Leash and the Novice Recall exercises will apply.

Section 8. Scent Discrimination. The principal features of these exercises are the selection of the handler's article from among the other articles by scent alone, and the prompt delivery of the right article to the handler.

The judge will ask, "What method will you be using to send your dog?" The handler must respond with either "After a sit," or "Send directly." The judge will then ask "Are you Ready?" immediately prior to taking the article from the handler. This taking of the article will be considered to be the first order and scoring of the exercise will begin at that time. The remaining orders are "Send your dog," "Take it," and "Finish."

In each of these two exercises the dog must select and retrieve an article that has been handled by its handler. The dog must make this selection based on scent alone.

The articles will be provided by the handler and will consist of two sets, each comprised of five identical objects, which may be items of everyday use. The size of the articles will be proportionate to the size of the dog. One set must be made entirely of rigid metal and one of leather, designed so that only a minimum amount of thread or other material is visible. The articles in each set will be legibly numbered with a different number, and must be approved by the judge.

The handler will present all 10 articles to the judge, who will make a written note of the numbers of the two articles he or she has selected. These articles will be placed on a table or chair within the ring until the handler picks each up separately. The judge or steward will handle each of the remaining 8 articles while randomly arranging them on the floor or ground about 6 inches apart. The closest article should be about 20 feet from the handler and dog. Before the dog is sent, the judge must make sure that the articles are visible to both dog and handler, and that they are far enough apart so that there will be no confusion of scent among articles.

After the articles have been put out, the handler and dog will turn around and will remain facing away until the judge has given the order, "Send your dog." The handler may use either article first, but must hand it to the judge immediately when ordered. The judge will make certain the handler scents each article with his or her hands only.

On the judge's order, the handler will place his or her article on the judge's book or work sheet. Without touching that article, the judge will place it among the others.

On order from the judge to "Send your dog," the handler may give the command to heel and will turn in place, either right or left, to face the articles. The handler will come to a halt with the dog sitting in the heel position. The handler will then give the command or signal to retrieve. Handlers may, on order from the judge to "Send your dog," do a right about-turn, simultaneously giving the command or signal to retrieve. In this case, the dog must not assume a sitting position, but will go directly to the articles. Handlers have the option as to how the dog is sent.

The handler may give his or her scent by extending the palm of one hand in front of the dog's nose, or gently touching the dog's nose, but the arm and hand must be returned to a natural position before they turn and face the articles.

The dog should go directly to the articles at a brisk trot or gallop. It may take any reasonable time to select the right article, but must work continuously. After picking up the right article, the dog will complete the exercise as in the Retrieve on Flat. This procedure should be followed for both articles.

If a dog retrieves the wrong first article, that article and the correct one must be removed. They will be placed on the table or chair and the next exercise will be done with one less article.

Section 9. Scent Discrimination, Scoring. A dog that retrieves a wrong article or that does not complete the retrieve of the right article, or that does not follow the correct method to turn as specified to the judge, must receive a non-qualifying (NQ) score.

Depending on the circumstances, minor or substantial deductions should be made for a dog that is slow, or does not go directly to the articles, or does not work continuously, or for excessive motions by the handler in turning toward the articles. Similar deductions will be made for a dog that picks up the wrong article even though it is immediately put down again, or for any roughness by the handler in giving his or her scent to the dog, or for the handler not turning in place. There should be no penalty for a dog that takes a reasonably long time examining the articles provided it is working continuously.

All applicable penalties listed under the Novice Recall and the Retrieve on Flat will apply.

Section 10. Directed Retrieve. The principal features of this exercise are that the dog stays until directed to retrieve, that it goes directly to the designated glove and retrieves it promptly. In this exercise the handler will provide three cotton work gloves which are predominately white. They must be open and must be approved by the judge. The handler will stand with his or her back to the unobstructed end of the ring midway between and in line with the jumps, with the dog sitting in heel position. The judge or steward will drop the gloves across the end of the ring while the handler and dog are facing the opposite direction. One glove is dropped about 3 feet in from each corner and the remaining glove is dropped in the center, about three feet from the end of the ring.

The gloves will be designated "One," "Two" or "Three" reading from left to right when the handler is facing the gloves. The orders for the exercise are "One," "Two" or "Three," "Take it," and "Finish." When the judge designates the glove by number, the handler will turn in place to face the glove, halting with the dog sitting in heel position. The handler may not touch the dog or reposition it. The handler will give the dog the direction to the designated glove with a single motion of the left hand and arm along the right side of the dog. Either simultaneously with or immediately following giving the direction, the handler must give a verbal retrieve command. The dog must then go directly to the glove, completing the exercise as in the Retrieve on Flat.

The handler may bend the body and knees as far as necessary to give the direction to the dog, but must then stand up in a natural position with his or her arms at the sides.

The judge should decide how to assign the gloves so that each glove will be used approximately the same number of times.

Section 11. Directed Retrieve, Scoring. A non-qualifying (NQ) score is required for any commands or signals to position the dog after the handler turns to face the glove, or a dog that does not go directly to the designated glove, or does not retrieve the correct glove. A handler who does not give a verbal command to retrieve simultaneously or immediately after giving the direction to retrieve, must receive a non-qualifying (NQ) score.

A substantial deduction, depending on the extent, will be made for a handler who does not turn in place or does not face the designated glove. The substantial deduction may include a non-qualifying (NQ) score.

All applicable penalties listed under the Novice Recall and the Retrieve on Flat will apply.

Section 12. Moving Stand and Examination. The principal features of the exercise are that the dog heel, stand and stay as the handler moves away, accept the examination without shyness or resentment, and return to the handler on command.

Orders for the exercise are "Forward," "Stand your dog," and "Call your dog to heel."

The handler will stand with the dog sitting in heel position at a point indicated by the judge. The judge will ask, "Are you ready?" and then order "Forward." The handler will command or signal the dog to heel. After the handler has proceeded about 10 feet, the judge will say "Stand your dog." Without pausing, the handler will command and/or signal the dog to stand, and continue forward about 10–12 feet. He or she will then turn either to the right or left to face the dog, which must stand and stay in position.

The judge will approach the dog from the front to examine it as in dog show judging. The exam will not include either the teeth or testicles.

When the judge orders "Call your dog to heel," the handler will command and/or signal the dog to return to the heel position. The dog should return to heel position in a brisk manner.

Section 13. Moving Stand and Examination, Scoring. A non-qualifying (NQ) score is required for a dog that does any of the following: Displays fear or resentment, moves from the place where it was left, sits or lies down before it is called, growls or snaps, repeatedly whines or barks, fails to heel, stand, stay, accept the judge's examination or fails to return to the handler.

Depending on the circumstances, minor or substantial deductions must be made for a dog that moves his or her feet repeatedly while remaining in place, or for a dog that returns to the handler as defined in the Novice Recall, but not to heel position.

Depending on the extent, minor or substantial penalties should be made for the handler who hesitates or pauses while giving the stand command and/or signal. All appropriate penalties of the Novice Heel Free, Stand for Examination and Recall exercises will apply.

Section 14. Directed Jumping. The principal features of this exercise are that the dog goes away from the handler to the opposite end of the ring, stops, jumps as directed and returns as in the Novice Recall. The orders are "Send your dog," "Bar," "High," and "Finish."

The jumps will be placed midway in the ring at right angles to the sides of the ring, and about 18 to 20 feet apart. The judge must see that the jumps are set at the required height for each dog, as described in the Retrieve Over High Jump.

The handler will stand in the approximate center of the ring with the dog sitting in heel position, about 20 feet from the jumps and mid-way between them. After the judge asks "Are you ready?", he or she will command and/or signal the dog to go forward at a brisk trot or gallop to a point about 20 feet past the jumps and in the approximate center of the unobstructed end of the ring. When the dog reaches this point, the handler will give a command to sit. The dog must stop and sit with its attention on the handler, but need not sit squarely.

The judge will order either "Bar" or "High" for the first jump and the handler will command and/or signal the dog to return to the handler over the designated jump. While the dog is in midair, the handler may turn to face the dog as it returns. The dog will sit in front of the handler and, on order from the judge, finish as in the Novice Recall. After the dog has returned to heel position, the judge will say, "Exercise finished."

When the dog is set up for the second half of this exercise, the judge will ask "Are you ready?" before giving the order for the second part of the exercise. The same procedure will be followed for the second jump.

It is optional which jump the judge first indicates, but both jumps must be included, and the judge must not designate the jump until the dog has reached the far end of the ring.

The height of the jumps and construction of the high jump will be the same as required in the Open classes. The bar jump will consist of a bar between 2 and 2½ inches square with the edges rounded to remove any sharpness. The bar will be painted flat black and white in alternate sections of about 3 inches each. The bar will have the weight of wood. It will be supported by two unconnected 4 foot upright posts about 5 feet apart, and must be adjustable for each 2 inches of height from 8 inches to 36 inches. The jump must be built so that the bar may be knocked off without affecting the uprights.

Section 15. Directed Jumping, Scoring. A dog will receive a non-qualifying (NQ) score if it: Anticipates the handler's command and/or signal to go out, fails to leave the handler, does not go out between the jumps, does not stop and remain at least 10 feet past the jumps, is given a second command to sit, anticipates the handler's command and/or signal to jump, returns over the wrong jump, knocks the bar off the uprights, or uses the top of any jump for aid in going over.

Substantial deductions will be made for a dog that does not stop on command, that does not stop in the approximate center of the ring about 20 feet past the jumps, that does not sit, or for a dog that anticipates the handler's command to sit.

Depending on the extent, minor or substantial deductions will be made for slowness in going out, for touching the jumps, or for any hesitation in jumping.

All applicable penalties of the Novice Heel Free and Recall exercises will apply.

Chapter 6 — Obedience Trial Championship

Section 1. Dogs that May Compete. Championship points will be recorded for dogs that have earned the Utility Dog title. When a dog earns the Obedience Trial Champion title, it may continue to compete and earn points.

Section 2. Championship Points. Championship points will be recorded for those dogs which have earned a First, Second, Third, or Fourth place ribbon competing in the Open B or Utility B class according to the schedule of points established by the Board of Directors of The American Kennel Club. In counting the number of eligible dogs in competition, a dog that is disqualified, or is excused from the ring by the judge will not be included.

Requirements for the Obedience Trial Champion are as follows:

The dog must have won:

1.   100 points;
2.   A first place in Utility B with at least three dogs in competition;
3.   A first place in Open B with at least six dogs in competition;
4.   An additional first place under the conditions of 2 or 3 above;
5.   All three first places under three different judges

One of the required first places may have been won at a Specialty Show.

Section 3. OTCH Title Certificate. The American Kennel Club will issue an Obedience Trial Champion certificate and will permit the use of the letters OTCH preceding the name of each dog that meets the requirements.

Section 4. Dual and Triple Champion. Any dog that has been awarded the titles of Champion of Record and Field Champion may be designated as a Dual Champion.

Any dog which has been awarded the titles of Champion of Record, Field Champion and Obedience Trial Champion may be designated as a Triple Champion.

Section 5. Ineligibility and Cancellation. If an ineligible dog has been entered in any licensed or member obedience trial or dog show, or if the name of the owner on the entry form is not the person(s) who actually owned the dog at the time entries closed, or if it is shown in a class for which it has not been entered, or if its entry is unacceptable by The American Kennel Club, all resulting awards will be cancelled. In computing the championship points, such ineligible dogs will be counted as having competed, whether or not they have received awards.

Section 6. Move Ups. If an award in any of the regular classes is cancelled, the next highest scoring dog will receive that award; if there is no dog to move up, the award will be void.

Section 7. Return of Awards. If The American Kennel Club cancels a dog's win, the dog's owner must return all ribbons and prizes to the show-giving club within 10 days of receipt of The American Kennel Club's cancellation notice.

Section 8. Point Schedule.
NEW POINT SCHEDULE

OPEN B

Number Competing	1st	2nd	3rd	4th
6–10	2	0	0	0
11–15	4	1	0	0
16–20	6	2	0	0
21–25	10	3	1	0
26–30	14	4	2	0
31–35	18	5	2	1
36–40	22	7	3	1
41–45	26	9	4	2
46–50	30	11	5	2
51–56	34	13	6	3

UTILITY B

Number Competing	1st	2nd	3rd	4th
3–4	2	0	0	0
5–7	4	1	0	0
8–10	6	2	0	0
11–13	10	3	1	0
14–16	14	4	1	0
17–19	17	5	2	0
20–23	20	7	2	1
24–26	24	9	3	1
27–29	27	11	4	1
30–32	30	13	4	2
33–36	33	14	5	2
37–40	37	15	6	3
41–48	40	17	7	3

UTILITY B CLASS — HAWAII ONLY

Number Competing	Points for First Place	Points for Second Place
3–4	5	1
5–7	8	2
8–10	10	3
11–13	13	3

(Rest of scale same as regular schedule)

UTILITY B CLASS — ALASKA AND PUERTO RICO ONLY

Number Competing	Points for First Place	Points for Second Place
3–4	3	0
5–7	5	1
8–10	8	2

(Rest of scale same as regular schedule)

Chapter 7 — Utility Dog Excellent

Section 1. Dogs That May Compete. UDX scores will be recorded only for dogs that have earned Utility Dog titles. Dogs who already have the UDX title may continue to compete in Open B and Utility B.

To earn a Utility Dog Excellent title, the dog must have received qualifying scores in both Open B and Utility B at 10 separate licensed or member obedience trials.

Section 2. Utility Dog Excellent Certificate. The American Kennel Club will issue a Utility Dog Excellent certificate and will permit the use of the letters UDX following the name of each dog that meets these requirements.

Chapter 8 — National Obedience Champion

Section 1. Dogs that May Compete. A National Obedience Championship will be awarded annually to the dog that wins the National Obedience Invitational. The National Obedience Association shall run this event only once in any calendar year. The winner of the event shall be entitled to be designated National Obedience Champion of _____(year).

To be invited to participate, each dog must be ranked in the top 25 dogs by number of OTCH points or ranked in the top three of their respective breeds by OTCH points. If the total number of dogs accepting the invitation to be present at the event is less than 125 dogs, invitations shall be extended to a reserve list selected by ratio of dogs qualified by OTCH points in that breed to the number of dogs entered in that breed.

The National Obedience Invitational competition shall be comprised of a varied combination of Open and Utility exercises performed as described in The American Kennel Club Obedience Regulations and Obedience Guidelines for Judges. The winner of the event shall be entitled to be designated National Obedience Champion (NOC) of _____ (year). The title will be placed before the dog's American Kennel Club registered name and will become part of the dog's permanent title.

Chapter 9 — Versatile Companion Dog

Section 1. Versatile Companion Dog Title. Effective January 1, 2001, The American Kennel Club will permit the use of the letters following the name of each registered dog that completes titles as follows:

Versatile Companion Dog 1 (VCD1) — CD, NA, NAJ, TD

Versatile Companion Dog 2 (VCD2) — CDX, OA, OAJ, TD

Versatile Companion Dog 3 (VCD3) — UD, AX, AXJ, TDX

Versatile Companion Dog 4 (VCD4) — UDX, MX, MXJ, VST

Section 2. Versatile Companion Champion Title. Effective January 1, 2001, The American Kennel Club will permit the use of the letters VCCH preceding the name of each dog that completes the titles, as follows:

OTCH, MACH and CT

Note: Explanation of Titles

CD = Companion Dog; CDX = Companion Dog Excellent; UD = Utility Dog; UDX = Utility Dog Excellent; OTCH = Obedience Trial Champion; NA = Novice Agility; NAJ = Novice Agility Jumpers; OA = Open Agility; OAJ = Open Agility Jumpers; AX = Agility Excellent; AXJ = Excellent Agility Jumper; MX = Master Agility Excellent; MXJ = Master Agility Jumper; MACH = Master Agility Champion; TD = Tracking Dog; TDX = Tracking Dog Excellent; VST = Variable Surface Tracker; CT = Champion Tracker

Chapter 10 — Non-regular Classes

Section 1. Ribbons and Prizes. A qualifying score will not be required to earn ribbons and prizes in any non-regular class.

Section 2. Graduate Novice class. The Graduate Novice class is for dogs that have not been certified by a judge to have received a third qualifying score toward a CDX title prior to the closing of entries. The owner or any other person may handle dogs in this class. A person may handle more than one dog in this class, but each dog must have a separate handler for the Long Down exercise when judged in the same group. Dogs entered in Graduate Novice may also be entered in one of the Novice or Open classes.

Judging will be as in the regular classes. The exercises, maximum scores and order of judging:

1.	Open Heel Free	40 points
2.	Graduate Novice Moving Stand and Examination	30 points
3.	Moving Drop on Recall	30 points
4.	Dumbbell Recall	40 points
5.	Recall Over Broad Jump	30 points
6.	Long Down	30 points
	Maximum Total Score	200 points

Open Heel Free. The exercise and scoring will be executed in the same manner as the Novice Heel on Leash and Figure Eight, except that the dog is off leash.

Graduate Novice Moving Stand and Examination. Performed and scored as in the Utility class Moving Stand for Examination except that the judge will approach the dog from the front and will touch only the dog's head, body and hindquarters, using the fingers and palm of one hand. The judge will then order "Back to your dog," and the handler will walk around behind the dog, returning to heel position. The dog must remain standing until after the judge has said, "Exercise finished." Minor or substantial deductions, even to the point of a non-qualifying (NQ) score may be made for any positioning of the dog to stand.

Orders for the exercise are "Forward," "Stand your dog," (given while the handler is walking), and "Back to your dog." All appropriate penalties of the Novice Stand for Examination and Utility Moving Stand and Examination will apply.

Moving Drop on Recall. The principal features of this exercise, are that the dog heel, execute a prompt response to the handler's command and/or signal to down and remain in the down position until called or signaled to come, and come on command. Orders for the exercise are "Forward," "Down your dog," "Call your dog," "Finish."

The handler will stand with the dog sitting in the heel position at a point designated by the judge, who will then ask "Are you ready?" and order "Forward." The handler may command or signal his or her dog to heel, and will walk briskly and naturally. After he or she has gone about 15 feet, the judge will order "Down your dog." Without pausing, the handler will command and/or signal the dog to down. He or she will continue forward to the end of the ring, turn around and stand in a natural manner facing the dog. On the judge's orders or signals, the handler will command or signal the dog to come and to finish. All appropriate penalties of the Novice Heel Free, Open Drop on Recall and the Utility Moving Stand and Examination will apply.

Dumbbell Recall. This exercise will be performed like the Novice Recall, but with the dog holding the dumbbell. In addition to the Novice Recall, the additional features are that the dog promptly take, hold and deliver the dumbbell when commanded.

The orders are "Give your dog the dumbbell," "Leave your dog," "Call your dog," "Take it," and "Finish."

The handler will stand with the dog sitting in the heel position in a place designated by the judge. When the judge orders "Give your dog the dumbbell," the handler will present the dumbbell with one command. The dog must accept it readily and hold it. When the judge orders, the handler may give the command and/or signal to stay while he or she walks forward to the other end of the ring and turns to face the dog. On the judges' order or signal, the handler will command or signal the dog to come. When the dog is sitting in front of the handler, the judge will order "Take it," and the handler will give a command and take the dumbbell. The finish will be done as in the Novice Recall. All appropriate penalties of the Novice Recall and Open Retrieve on Flat shall apply.

Recall Over Broad Jump. The principal features of the exercise are that the dog stay until directed to jump, clear the jump on a single command or signal, and immediately return to sit in front of the handler. Orders are "Leave your dog," "Call your dog," and "Finish."

The handler will stand with his or her dog sitting in the heel position at least eight feet from the jump, facing the lowest end of the lowest hurdle. When the judge orders "Leave your dog," the handler will give command and/or signal to stay, go at least 8 feet beyond the highest edge of the last hurdle, turn and face the dog as in the Novice Recall. On the judge's order, the handler will give the command or signal to jump. The dog must clear the entire distance of the broad jump without touching it and, without any further command or signal, immediately sit in front of the handler and finish as in the Novice Recall.

All penalties in the Novice Recall and the Broad Jump will apply. The distance of the jump will be as required for the Open Broad Jump exercise, as designated in the Obedience Regulations.

Long Down. The Long Down exercise will be performed and scored as in the Open group exercise, except that the judge will order the handlers to return after three (3) minutes.

Section 3. Brace Class. The Brace class will be for two dogs of the same breed that are eligible under these Regulations and capable of performing the Novice exercises. The dogs need not be owned by the same person, but will be handled by one handler. Dogs may be shown unattached or coupled, the coupling device to be not less than six inches in over-all length, and whichever method is used will be continued throughout all exercises. A separate official entry form will be completed in full for each dog entered.

Exercises, performances and judging will be as in the Novice class. The brace should work in unison at all times. Either or both dogs in a brace may be entered in another class or classes.

Section 4. Veterans Class. The Veterans' class will be for dogs that have an obedience title and are at least seven years old on the date of the trial. The exercises will be performed and judged as in the Novice class. Dogs may be entered in another class or classes.

Section 5. Versatility Class. This class will be for dogs that are capable of performing the Utility exercises and that are eligible under the Obedience Regulations. Owners may enter more than one dog. Dogs in this class may be handled by the owner or any other person, and may be entered in another class or classes.

Six exercises will be performed, two each from the Novice, Open and Utility classes, except that there will be no group exercises. The exercises will be performed and judged as in the regular classes. For the purpose of this class, Scent Discrimination Articles Number 1 and Number 2 will be considered as a single Utility exercise. The exercises to be performed by each dog will be determined by the handler drawing one of a set of cards listing combinations of the six exercises totaling 200 points. The trial-giving clubs will furnish these cards. Each handler will provide a dumbbell, Scent Discrimination articles and Directed Retrieve gloves.

Novice exercise No. 1	25
Novice exercise No. 2	25
Open exercise No. 1	35
Open exercise No. 2	35
Utility exercise No. 1	40
Utility exercise No. 2	40
Maximum Total Score	200

Section 6. Team Class. This class will be for teams of any four dogs that are eligible under these Regulations. Five dogs may be entered, one to be considered an alternate for which no entry fee will be required. However, the same four dogs will perform all exercises. Dogs may be handled by the owner or any other person, need not be entered in another class at the same trial, and need not have obedience titles. A separate official entry form will be completed in full for each dog entered.

There will be two judges, one of whom will call orders while the other scores the teams' performance. The teams will be judged one at a time, except for the group exercises, which will be done with no more than four teams (16 dogs) in the ring.

The dogs on a team will perform the exercises simultaneously and will be judged as specified for the Novice class, except that a Drop on Recall will be used in place of the Recall exercise. In all exercises except the Drop on Recall, the teams have the option of executing the judge's orders on the team captain's repeat of the command.

In the Figure Eight portion of the Heel on Leash exercise, five stewards will be used. The stewards will stand 8 feet apart in a straight line. One handler with dog sitting in heel position, will stand about equidistant from each of two stewards, all members of the team facing in the same direction. On orders from the judge, the team will perform the Figure Eight, each handler starting around the steward on his or her left and circling only the two stewards between whom he or she had been standing.

In the Drop on Recall exercise, the handlers will leave their dogs simultaneously on order of the judge. The dogs will be called or signaled in, one at a time, on a separate order from the judge to each handler. The handler will, without any additional order from the judge, command or signal his or her dog to drop at a spot midway between the line of dogs and the handlers. Each dog will remain in the down position until all four have been called and dropped. The judge will give the order to call the dogs, which will be called or signaled simultaneously. The finish will be done in unison on order from the judge.

Section 7. Team Class, Scoring. Individual dogs' scores will be based on the performance of the dogs and handlers individually, plus team precision and coordination. Each dog and handler will be scored against the customary maximum, for a team total of 800 available points. Individual dogs' scores need not be recorded. The exercises and maximum scores:

1.	Heel on Leash	160
2.	Stand for Examination	120
3.	Heel Free	160
4.	Drop on Recall	120
5.	Long Sit	120
6.	Long Down	120
	Maximum Total Score	800

Section 8. Pre-Novice Class. The Pre-Novice class shall be for dogs that have not received a third qualifying score in a Novice class prior to the closing of the trial. The owner or any other person may handle dogs in this class. A person may enter more than one dog in this class, but the same person who handled each dog in the first four exercises will handle each dog in the group exercises. If a person has handled more than one dog in the first four exercises, he or she must provide an additional handler if the additional dog(s) will be judged in the same group.

All exercises will be scored as in the Novice class, except the dogs will perform all exercises on leash, which should be long enough to provide adequate slack.

The exercises, maximum scores and order of judging:

1.	Heel on Leash	45 points
2.	Figure Eight	25 points
3.	Stand for Examination	30 points
4.	Recall	40 points
5.	Long Sit	30 points
6.	Long Down	30 points
	Maximum Total Score	200 points

GLOSSARY OF TERMS

Brisk, briskly — keenly alive, alert, energetic

Command — verbal order from handler to dog

Crooked — a dog that is not straight in line with the direction the handler is facing

Crowding — a dog so close to handler as to interfere with handler's freedom of motion

Directly — immediately, without deviation or hesitation

Drop completely — a down position that would be acceptable for a Long Down exercise

Gently — with kindness, without harshness or roughness

Guiding gently by the collar — control of the dog, by holding any part of the collar, with minimal pressure on the dog's neck

Lame — irregularity or impairment of the function of locomotion, irrespective of the cause or how slight or severe

Minor penalty — ½ point to 2½ points

Mouthing — when a dog chews or rolls the dumbbell in its mouth unnecessarily

Natural — not artificial; free of affectation, and customarily expected in the home or public places

Order — direction from judge to handler, either verbal or nonverbal

Prompt response — without hesitation, immediate, quick

Resentment — resistance, unwillingness

Signal — nonverbal direction from the handler to dog, as described in Chapter 2, Section 20

Smartly — quickly, vigorously

Substantial penalty — 3 points or more

Turn in place — turning in the circle that was occupied by the handler before he or she started to turn

Withers — highest point of the dog's shoulder

OBEDIENCE JUDGES GUIDELINES

These guidelines reflect the policies and practices set forth by the Board of Directors of The American Kennel Club. Judges are expected to conduct themselves in accordance with the guidelines in this booklet. Failure to comply with these guidelines subjects a judge to possible disciplinary action.

Purpose

Obedience trials are a sport and all participants should be guided by the principles of good sportsmanship both inside and outside of the ring. The purpose of obedience trials is to demonstrate the usefulness of the purebred dog as a companion of mankind, not merely the dog's ability to follow specified routines in the obedience ring. While all contestants in a class are required to perform the same exercises in substantially the same way so that the relative quality of the various performances may be compared and scored, the basic objective of obedience trials is to produce dogs that have been trained and conditioned to behave in the home, in public places, and in the presence of other dogs that will reflect credit on the sport of obedience. The performances of dog and handler in the ring must be accurate and correct and must conform to the requirements of the Regulations. However, it is also essential that the dog demonstrate willingness and enjoyment of its work, and that smoothness and naturalness on the part of the handler be given precedence over a performance based on military precision and peremptory commands.

Chapter 1 — The Obedience Judge
Remember, You Make it Work!

As an obedience judge, you are an essential part of the fancy. The obedience trial system needs your dedication and expertise in order to function properly. This booklet is designed as an easy-to-use guide for all American Kennel Club and visiting judges. We believe it will make it easier for you to do your job, and to contribute to the sport of obedience.

You should be thoroughly familiar with this guide, as well as all of The American Kennel Club rules, regulations and policies if you:

- Are an approved or provisional judge,
- Have accepted match or non-regular class judging assignments,
- Are a visiting judge accepting assignments at American Kennel Club events, or
- Plan to apply for provisional judging approval.

This booklet cannot cover all situations, nor can it substitute for common sense.

Whenever you have a question about judging procedure or conduct, remember that at almost every all-breed show an American Kennel Club Field Representative for breed or obedience is present. When at a trial, the field representative is the first person to whom you should turn to discuss questions having to do with your judging. Also, please do not hesitate to call or write the Obedience Department.

Your Responsibilities as a Judge

Judges must understand their responsibilities to the sport.

Responsibility to Exhibitors. Each exhibitor has paid an entry fee for the purpose of competing and having the dog's performance evaluated. Judges are expected to be friendly and courteous to all who enter the ring. Without exhibitors there would be no trials. For every experienced exhibitor there are many newcomers. The future of this sport is in the hands of the novice.

After a judge completes an assignment and has turned in the judge's book, it is appropriate for the judge to discuss an individual dog's performance with the handler, if the handler requests this information. A judge should never continue a conversation with an angry or aggressive person.

Responsibility to Spectators. Spectators form their opinion of the sport through seeing the actions of the judge, the handler and the dog. Care must be taken to avoid any action that might reflect poorly on the sport. Judges should work to maintain spectator appeal in the sport, while keeping foremost in mind the welfare and convenience of the exhibitor and the dog.

Responsibility to the Sport of Purebred Dogs. Approval to judge carries with it the full endorsement of The American Kennel Club. Whether judging at a licensed trial or sanctioned match or engaging in any dog related activity, judges must be cognizant of their responsibility to the sport.

Judges must never ignore or condone any type of abuse of a dog at any time. All judges are expected to take appropriate action when witnessing such conduct.

As a judge, you are required to meet these key criteria:

- **Knowledge.** Through experience and continuing study, you must demonstrate sound knowledge of the dogs you evaluate and score. Good judges never stop learning about the sport of obedience.
- **Procedure.** You must demonstrate sound judging procedure and ring control, plus a thorough knowledge of The American Kennel Club Obedience Regulations and Guidelines. Good procedure is essential. With it, a judge will inspire the confidence of exhibitors and spectators.
- **Impartiality.** It is essential that exhibitors have full faith in the impartiality and competence of judges. There is no room for even the suggestion that anything other than the work of the dogs in the ring is involved in your decisions.

Ethics: Honesty Plus Common Sense

You must possess and project an unwavering air of integrity and ethical behavior that maintains the reputation of The American Kennel Club Obedience Trials as being fair and properly judged. With common sense, judges can easily avoid situations that might raise ethical questions.

Judges are presumed to be honest, competent and dedicated. Nevertheless, it is all too easy to find yourself in uncomfortable or even inappropriate situations. These guidelines cannot cover every situation. They can, however, help you avoid improprieties or perceived improprieties.

Some ethical rules are clear. For example:

- Never solicit or promote assignments.
- Never accept any payments or presents for past or future placements.
- Advise potential exhibitors not to enter under you when their presence, or the presence of their dogs, might give the impression of unfair advantage, such as a person with whom you own dogs, wholly or in part; dogs that have been regularly trained or instructed by you; your employer or employee, or a relative.

These are only examples. The key is to avoid situations that might give the impression of impropriety.

The American Kennel Club recognizes you cannot control who enters. This does not diminish the importance of appearances. Everything possible must be done to keep your reputation above reproach.

Beware of Those Gray Areas . . .

Judges are often singled out for critical observation by exhibitors. Keep in mind that a perfectly innocent action or discussion can be misconstrued.

Attending Shows. If you attend shows immediately before events you are to judge, do not watch the class(es) you are scheduled to judge later.

Training and Exhibiting. All judges start in the sport as exhibitors and trainers. It is natural to want to continue these activities after becoming a judge. The American Kennel Club understands this. It is acceptable to exhibit or have your dogs exhibited at shows at which you are not officiating.

Many judges combine exhibiting and judging without causing complaints. The reason is simple. They are prudent in how and when they exhibit and they demonstrate the utmost in decorum and sportsmanship. Judges who exhibit should expect to be subject to special scrutiny. The American Kennel Club will evaluate all complaints concerning judges who exhibit, on an individual basis. Whatever steps are deemed necessary will be taken in each particular situation.

Exhibiting. Judges (including Provisional) may not handle dogs that are not owned or co-owned by themselves or a family member. It is not proper for a judge to co-own a dog solely to permit the judge to handle the dog. Tracking, agility, obedience and conformation judges may enter the "A" classes, if otherwise eligible.

Social Functions. It is appropriate to attend an affair given by a club holding the show/trial. Judges have the option of attending club dinners and other social functions where exhibitors will be present. In such cases, take extra care in regard to any exhibitor who might appear in your ring.

As an example of those "gray areas," you might find yourself at a social function seated next to someone who mentions exhibiting in the class you will judge. The best way to handle it: Tell everyone you will be judging that class and feel it would be inappropriate to discuss anything concerning your assignment. Tactfully change the subject.

There will be other "gray areas" which could cause problems. Ask yourself if, whatever is happening, however innocent, maintains an outward appearance of propriety. The rule of thumb is: **Would I Be Getting This Treatment If I Were Not A Judge?**

Accepting Assignments

Never solicit or promote assignments. The American Kennel Club's Judges Department will investigate all reports that a judge solicited or promoted an assignment. Appropriate action will be taken whenever needed.

Written Invitations Only. Require all clubs to send you written invitations for assignments. Their request should clearly specify the class(es) you are being asked to judge. Promptly acknowledge all invitations, again in writing, and keep accurate records of assignments you accept.

Avoid Conflicts. It's your responsibility to acknowledge judging invitations promptly. Careful record keeping and prompt acceptance (or refusal) of invitations helps eliminate unnecessary confusion and conflicts for both judges and show giving clubs.

Assignment Limitations. A judge will not be approved to judge the same regular class at all-breed events within 30 days and 200 straight line miles of each other. There are no such restrictions on non-regular classes or tracking tests. Assignments to judge the same class or classes at two breed specialty obedience trials are not considered to be a conflict unless the two specialties are for the same breed. Breed specialty obedience assignments or group shows are not in conflict with an assignment to judge the same class(es) at an all-breed obedience trial.

Travel Between Assignments. Judges cannot do their best work if they are tired from travel. They should not accept assignments on succeeding days where more than a few hours' travel by ground transportation is involved.

Judges should understand that in accepting an invitation, they are committing themselves to the show giving club for the entire day. Their travel plans should not be predicated on arriving late or on leaving early to get transportation home or to another show. Judges should not ask clubs or superintendents to arrange judging programs to accommodate their travel plans.

Judges should not travel to or from shows or stay with anyone who is likely to be exhibiting or handling under them.

Expenses. When you accept an invitation, clearly inform club officials what your expenses and fee, if any, will be, so they will not be surprised by a larger than anticipated bill on the day of the trial. This is a contract between you and the club. The more specific details you and the club include in the contract, the less the potential for misunderstanding. This is an important consideration and a courtesy to clubs. If you sign a contract provided by the club, you and the club are responsible for abiding by its conditions.

Sickness and Fitness To Judge

Fitness to Judge. An Obedience Judge must be capable of performing the functions necessary to properly evaluate the dogs.

This means judges must have:

- The maneuverability to negotiate a ring, indoors and out, with or without mechanical assistance, i.e., a wheelchair, crutches or a cane.
- The flexibility to examine and measure dogs and the retrieval of articles, where applicable.
- The dexterity to move at a sufficient speed to adhere to the schedule of the trial giving club and The American Kennel Club policy.
- Normal vision (correctable by eyeglasses or contact lenses), i.e., be able to judge dogs at a distance.
- The capability to do all the necessary paperwork.

Sickness. Judges are expected to be physically fit. If you find you cannot fulfill an assignment because of illness or other serious occurrence, immediately notify the trial secretary and/or superintendent and the trial chairperson by telephone, overnight letter, telegram or fax. If you are delayed en route to a show, make every effort to contact the trial secretary or superintendent's office immediately.

When a judge can no longer properly perform the duties of a judge because of physical difficulties, he or she does the position and the sport a disservice by continuing to accept assignments. The American Kennel Club has a Judge Emeritus Program to honor judges who have served the sport faithfully and wish to retire. Contact the Judges Department for additional information.

Change of Address. Judges are responsible for promptly notifying the Judges Department at The American Kennel Club of any change in address. The change will be automatically reflected in The American Kennel Club Judges Directory.

Obedience Regulations. The Obedience Regulations are the basic guide to judging, but do not contain explicit directions for every possible situation, only listing the more common and serious faults. The Obedience Regulations clearly define the exercises, their order and the standards by which they are to be judged. The regulations set the standard of perfection by which the performance of each dog is scored. The Obedience Regulations give the judge little choice in deciding how an exercise is to be performed. They require that the judge fulfill his or her responsibility by making competent decisions based on a mental picture of the perfect performance within the framework of the regulations.

The knowledge gained from studying the Obedience Regulations, exhibiting and attending American Kennel Club obedience seminars and then putting this knowledge into practice will permit a judge to make practical the principles of sound judging contained in the Obedience Regulations.

Judges are given full discretionary authority within the framework of the Obedience Regulations. Judges must exercise this authority impartially. A judge is required to make his or her own decisions and to accept the responsibility this implies. If a decision depends on the exact wording of the regulations, the judge is expected to look up the specific regulation prior to making the decision. A judge may not discard, modify or require anything not specified in the regulations.

An obedience title is intended to evoke admiration. To be worthy of this admiration, the title must be based on performances that fully meet the requirements of the regulations. Scores for each exercise must be amply justified by the performance of dog and handler. The owner of any dog that receives a deserved score of 190 points has reason to be very proud of the dog. A score of 170 points should indicate a very creditable performance and fully justify the awarding of a title.

A score of 200 points is possible, but it is extremely rare when the requirements of the regulations are followed. It is a normal occurrence for a dog and handler to earn a perfect score on one or two of the exercises, but it is very rare for a judge to have the privilege of observing and scoring a dog and handler who perform perfectly all of the exercises in a class.

Chapter 2 — Preparation Prior To Judging

Be on Time. Be at your ring at least 30–45 minutes before your judging time. Upon arrival, report immediately to the superintendent or trial secretary to obtain your judge's badge. The judge's book, ribbons and other materials necessary to start judging on schedule will usually be brought to the ring by the stewards.

If you are judging a class on a provisional basis, advise the Field Representative so that you may be observed.

Avoid Contacts. A judge is not permitted to look at a catalog until his or her judging is completed. Do not carry or examine a catalog, discuss the merits of the dogs to be judged, or talk at length with anyone who may be exhibiting under you. When you've completed all assignments for a trial, then such contact is permissible, but be prudent.

Your friends, if they are considerate, should be discreet in making conversation with you prior to judging. It is your responsibility to remind them to do so.

Proper Dress. All judges shall wear business attire (weather permitting). It is important for a judge to maintain a proper and professional appearance. The judge is in the ring to do a job, not to be the center of attention because of outlandish dress or bizarre behavior.

Smoking. Smoking is permissible only between classes, provided it does not delay judging. Judges must comply with all non-smoking regulations.

Judge's Book. The judge alone is responsible for the judge's book. The trial secretary or superintendent may correct an error or omission that has been made in preparing the book for the judge. No one except the judge may enter any other notation in the judge's book. Following the judging of each class, the judge must immediately deliver the judge's book to the superintendent, obedience chairperson or trial secretary. No other person may be entrusted with the judge's book.

Check the Ring. Prior to the scheduled time for judging, the judge inspects the ring, which must meet all requirements of Chapter 1, Section 31, of the Obedience Regulations. Size shall be determined by the judge pacing the ring. If outdoors, the ring must be about 40 × 50 feet and the grass shall be cut short. Indoor rings should be about 40 × 50 feet. Indoor rings for Novice or Open may not be less than about 30 × 40 feet, and indoor Utility rings may not be less than about 35 × 50 feet.

In Open and Utility classes, the jumps are measured by the judge to make sure they meet the requirements of the Regulations. A deviation of one-quarter inch to one-half inch is considered a minor change and is acceptable. If the jumps are made of a material other than wood, they must meet all the requirements of the Regulations, including weight and flat finish. Having checked the jumps, the judge will place the jumps in the ring, giving special attention to lighting and ring enclosures, and make an observation from a dog's line of sight. For Utility classes, the jumps shall be located midway in the ring, at right angles to the longest sides of the ring and about 18 to 20 feet apart. If mats are placed under the jumps they should be at least four feet in width.

If there are ring or equipment deficiencies, the judge shall bring them to the attention of the trial secretary or superintendent so that they may be corrected in accordance with the provisions of Chapter 1, Section 33, of the Obedience Regulations. If the deficiencies cannot be corrected quickly, the judge will note this fact on the inside front cover of the judge's book and proceed to judge the class, under the deficient conditions. In extreme cases, where the deficiencies, in the opinion of the judge, are of such major proportion as to seriously affect the dog's performance or safety, the judge will give each handler the option of not competing, and if the handler's decision is not to compete, he or she will be referred to the trial secretary or superintendent for a refund of the entry fee. Under no condition may a judge refuse to judge a class.

Stewards. The judge shall review with the stewards their duties and the manner in which they are to be performed. Stewards are to be instructed that they are in the ring only to assist the judge. Any request from an exhibitor for special consideration must be directed to the judge.

Catalog Order. The Obedience Regulations require that dogs be judged in catalog order to the extent that is practical to do so without holding up the judging in any ring. A judge need not mark the absentees in the judge's book until the end of the class. Judges are not required to wait for dogs for either the individual or the group exercises.

Veterinarian. The only situations which would require the judge to request the services of the veterinarian would be when a dog in the ring required immediate medical attention or when a judge needed the veterinarian's recommendation concerning the health of the dog in the ring.

Chapter 3 — Procedures in the Ring

Judging the Dogs. The judge has absolute control and unquestioned authority over all persons and dogs in the ring. With this authority comes the responsibility to be courteous and considerate. Be as systematic in your ring procedure from dog to dog as conditions permit.

A judge's comments, other than orders to the handler of a dog, shall be limited to a brief greeting, instructions on positioning the dog and instructions covering the group exercises. A judge will never ask a handler about club affiliations, his or her opinion or about the past performances of the dog. The handler should be informed immediately following the directed jumping exercise in Utility and the group exercise in Novice and Open of a non-qualifying performance.

The actual judging procedure may vary from judge to judge, but performance requirements must remain the same. Position is important for two reasons; first, to establish consistency of judging in the minds of exhibitors and spectators and second, to properly evaluate the dog and handler.

Being in the right position to observe a dog's performance is essential. There is no perfect position, but this does not mean that some positions are not better than others. All dogs shall be viewed from the same relative position. When viewing the dog and handler from the side, try to observe from the dog's side without the handler in between. Handlers should expect and train for a reasonable amount of movement by the judge while the dog is working. Judges must not move quickly toward a dog as it is moving, stand closely behind a dog or follow a heeling dog too closely. The judge shall always be in a position to see both the dog and handler at the same time without having to turn his or her head.

Judges shall stand with their attention on the dogs and handlers during group exercises. During the Open group exercises, Judges shall be in a position to see both the dogs and the handlers as they leave and enter the ring. Fronts and finishes are to be judged from a position in front of the handler.

The judging of an exercise normally begins when the judge gives the first order, except for the unusual circumstances as stated in the regulations.

Corrections, loud repeated directions, a harsh tone of voice toward the dog to get it into position and handling the dog at any time in the ring between exercises, other than gently guiding a dog by the collar in the Novice classes, is to be substantially penalized under Miscellaneous Penalties.

Philosophy of Scoring. It is the judge's responsibility to qualify all the dogs that should qualify and to non-qualify all the dogs whose performance did not meet the standards for a qualifying performance. From the qualifying group of dogs, it is the judge's responsibility to place the top four dogs in order of their performance. The remainder of the qualifying dogs are ranked in order by their scores. Using clickers to score, although permissible, puts judges at a disadvantage when asked to explain decisions.

Natural Manner. The Obedience Regulations place emphasis on naturalness in handling. Chapter 3, Section 5, as described in the Heel on Leash and Figure Eight exercise, specifically states that the hands must be in a natural position but do not require that they be at the handler's side while heeling on leash. It is up to each judge to decide when, and to what extent, the performance of any particular handler is lacking in naturalness, and when the hands of the handler are not in a natural position. A judge is expected to penalize a handler if, in the judge's opinion, the handler's manner or handling is unnatural. On the other hand, no judge should consider that a handler is unnatural just because he or she does not perform with the hands and arms in the same position for each exercise. Nor should the judge require that the hands hang at the handler's sides except when the dog is coming in and until it sits in front of the handler. The Obedience Regulations do not require this. Chapter 2, Section 5, prohibits a judge from requiring anything that is not required by the Regulations. Any motion that the judge considers to aid the dog's performance should be penalized.

Collars. Dogs in the obedience ring must wear a properly fitted collar approved by the judge. No special training collars, such as electronic collars or prong collars, will be permitted. Nothing may be hanging from the collars.

No dog may enter the ring, either for judging or for awards, with unacceptable equipment. Handlers are not permitted to wear such things as waist packs/pouches or any item that, in the judge's opinion, appears to be a training device or aid.

Disqualification and Excusal. The Obedience Regulations, under the provisions of Chapter 1, Sections 16 and 17, and Chapter 2, Sections 25 and 27, cover the conditions and procedure for handling situations requiring the disqualification or excusal of a dog and its handler. A dog which has been disqualified may not compete again, unless and until, following an application by the owner to The American Kennel Club, and the owner has received official notification from the American Kennel Club that the dog's eligibility has been reinstated. There are only four reasons for disqualifying a dog at an obedience trial:

- Blind — without useful vision;
- Deaf — without useful hearing;
- Changed in appearance by artificial means for cosmetic reasons;
- Attacks or attempts to attack a person in the ring.

A dog is excused if it is brought into the ring with bandages, stitches or taped in any manner. The judge must excuse the dog and may not judge the dog later in that class, even if the bandages, tape or stitches have been removed.

A dog which is lame in the ring may not compete in that class and shall not be judged. It is the sole responsibility of the judge to determine whether or not the dog is lame. The judge shall not obtain the opinion of the veterinarian.

The judge must excuse from the class as "unfit to compete" any dog that demonstrates sickness, such as vomiting, in the ring.

Obedience Regulations, Chapter 2, Section 3, states, "A qualifying score must never be awarded to a dog that relieves itself at any time while in the ring for judging. " In some cases, judges have allowed a handler to leave the ring temporarily when it appeared that the dog might foul the ring. A judge may permit this to prevent soiling the ring. However, the judge must consider that had such permission not been given, the ring probably would have been fouled. Therefore, the dog shall be considered as having relieved itself in the ring and is given a non-qualifying score.

If a judge determines that the bitch in the ring is in season or appears to be so attractive to males as to be a disturbing element, the bitch is excused. The judge shall not obtain the opinion of the veterinarian.

If it is reported to the trial secretary or the superintendent that the bitch is in season before the bitch enters the ring for either the individual or group exercises, the matter is to be brought to the attention of the Trial Committee. The committee must examine the bitch and may consult with the veterinarian if desired. If the Trial Committee finds the bitch to be in season, they shall excuse the bitch and so inform the judge, who marks the book accordingly.

If a report is made to the trial secretary or superintendent after the judging of the bitch is completed that the bitch is in season or so attractive to males as to have been a disturbing element, the matter shall not be investigated. There would be no basis for changing the scoring of the bitch. The judge made the decision as to the condition of the bitch at the time of judging and the judge's decision is final.

Eligibility. When the eligibility of a handler or a dog to compete is in question, the matter should be referred to the Trial Committee. When the Trial Committee determines, from the information available, that a dog or a handler is ineligible to compete in the class, the handler is to be informed of the requirement of the Regulations which make him or her ineligible to compete. If any alternative exists (such as substituting an eligible handler to replace the handler who is ineligible to take the dog into the ring), it should be suggested. If the handler insists on competing, regardless of his or her or the dog's eligibility, then it is the duty of the secretary or superintendent to point out to the handler that the judge will be requested to judge the dog "under protest" and the dog or handler's eligibility to compete will be reviewed by The American Kennel Club. The secretary or superintendent should inform the judge of the situation, requesting that the dog and handler be permitted to compete.

The judge then permits the dog to compete and makes a brief notation in the judge's book. It is the responsibility of the trial secretary or superintendent to provide a concise, factual statement of the problem in the official The American Kennel Club show/trial report. The American Kennel Club will make a determination based on what has been reported. If it is determined that the dog is not eligible, the dog's score will be disallowed.

Measuring. In the Open and Utility classes the judge may, at his or her option, verify the height of the dog at the withers as it is brought into the ring. Withers, as defined in the Glossary of the Obedience Regulations, are the highest point of the dog's shoulder. The measurement is made using an ordinary folding rule or steel tape which may be calibrated to show the correct jump height, but nothing may be attached to determine level position. No other measuring device is required or acceptable in the ring. The ruler or tape is held by the judge. Measurements made by the judge are final and are not subject to verification.

Misbehavior. A dog which demonstrates uncontrolled behavior must be penalized according to the seriousness of the misbehavior. There is no reference in the Obedience Regulations to leaving the ring, nor is it mandatory to award a non-qualifying (NQ) score to a dog which leaves the ring. If a dog is working smartly and continuously but goes outside of a ring boundary while completing an exercise, (as opposed to a dog which bolts out of the ring or leaves the ring between exercises) the penalty, if any, is left to the discretion of the judge.

Heeling Pattern. Having set up the ring, the judge must determine the exact heeling pattern to be used and the pattern should be shown to the first handler in the class. The same pattern should be maintained as far as practicable for each competing dog. This is a foundation exercise and it determines the standards for all exercises in which the dog is heeling. In scoring this exercise, the judge shall accompany the handler at a discreet distance, so that he or she can observe any signals or commands given by the handler to the dog. The judge must do so without interfering with either dog or handler. The judge should attempt to be in position during the course of the exercise so that the dog and the handler may be observed from the rear, front and side. The minimum heeling requirements for any class are normal heeling, a fast, a slow, a left turn, a right turn, an about-turn, a halt, and a sit. Dogs receiving an extra command during heeling can still qualify, although a substantial deduction must be made for the extra command. Subsequent additional commands could indicate the dog is not under control and is not working with the handler as a team. The judge must determine whether the dog should receive a non-qualifying (NQ) score for heeling, based on the overall performance of the dog and handler during the entire exercise.

The heeling patterns should not be in the area of the table and/or gate and have only one element of an exercise on a leg. (For example, there shall not be a halt and a slow on the same leg of an exercise.) A fast should always be on a long dimension of the ring; slow may be either on the short or long dimension of the ring. The fast and slow shall be of significant length, not just several steps. No pattern shall have more than one fast and one slow. If possible, have one leg of the heeling pattern with no element on it. The "L" pattern is a minimal pattern. Other patterns are acceptable, but excessive complexity should be avoided.

Heel Free. This is to be judged using the same standards and procedures as the Heel on Leash and Figure Eight, except that it is off leash. Except, further, that Chapter 2, Section 19, requires a substantial deduction if the hands and arms are not carried in one of the following positions:

- "When the handler is in motion, the arms and hands must move naturally at the side."
- "The right hand and arm must move naturally at the side, while the left hand must be held against the front of the body, centered in the area of the waist, with the left forearm carried against the body."

In either of the above situations, the hands and arms may be adjusted during the fast portion of an exercise, in order to maintain balance.

Stand for Examination. Chapter 3, Section 7, states that the handler will leave the dog and walk straight forward about six feet, turn and face the dog. The judge must be alert to keep handlers from going more or less than about six feet and must penalize even to the point of non-qualifying the dog whose handler backs away when leaving.

Chapter 3, Section 7, instructs the judge in the specific manner to conduct an examination. The examination shall consist of touching only the dog's head, body and hindquarters with the fingers and palm of one hand and must not include running the hand down the dog's back. The judge should also note in scoring, that the exercise does not start until the handler has given the command and/or signal to stay, except for such things as rough treatment of the dog by its handler or active resistance by the dog to its handler's attempts to make it stand, which must be penalized substantially. In positioning the dog for this exercise, a handler may stand the dog on command and may then also pose it as in the breed ring, or he or she may simply stand the dog and not pose it. The option is left to the handler, and the judge may not penalize a handler for both standing and posing the dog. The dog need not be sitting at the start of this exercise. The Obedience Regulations require different penalties for faults which occur before and after the examination is complete. The examination is complete when the judge lifts his or her fingers and palm from the dog's hindquarters and steps back.

Judges should not expose themselves needlessly to the danger of being bitten. Should a dog in the ring give warning that it may bite you if you proceed with the examination, you should excuse the dog from the ring. If a dog attempts to attack or bites any person in the ring, the judge must disqualify the dog.

Recall Exercises. To have both dog and handler under constant observation in these exercises, a judge should take a position in line and slightly to the rear of the dog, facing the handler but at an adequate distance to one side.

This is a foundation exercise and governs the faults and behavior of a dog in all exercises where the dog is moving toward the handler. The dog is required to move at a brisk trot or gallop and must be penalized for failure to do so.

The handler's hands and arms should hang naturally at his or her sides while the dog is coming in and until the dog has sat in front. A substantial deduction is required for failure to do so. This requirement applies only while the dog is coming in and sits in front of the handler. It does not apply to the moving stand and examination, as the dog does not sit in front.

Finishes are required to be executed promptly, smartly and straight. Further, this applies to faults in all exercises where the dog sits in front, and finishes.

The finish is not a principal part of any exercise. Therefore, failure to finish or extra commands or signals to finish do not require a non-qualifying score for any exercise.

The judge should never ask the handler to touch the dog or otherwise assist the judge in making a decision. A dog must come in sufficiently close so that the handler could touch its head without excessive bending or stretching, or moving either foot. If, in the judge's opinion, the dog is not close enough to the handler, it must receive a non-qualifying (NQ) score.

Drop on Recall. Faults and penalties in judging this exercise are the same as the Novice Recall, except for the drop.

A perfect drop has three characteristics:

- The dog's prompt response to the handler's command or signal to drop;
- No delay or slowness to down;
- The dog must drop completely to a down position.

The dog should be considered as having met the requirement if, in the judge's opinion, a similar down position would be acceptable for the long down group exercise.

Broad Jump. In setting up the broad jump, the judge should make every effort to avoid having the dog jump toward the gate or the table and that adequate room is allowed in front of the jump for the take-off and on the far side for landing and turning. The hurdles are to be positioned so the dog will be turning away from the ring barrier after landing.

Dog and handler must be at least 8 feet in front of the first edge of the jump. It is the judge's responsibility to see that the handler complies, before the exercise begins. In all jumping exercises a handler standing too close or too far from the side of the jump shall be required to move to the proper position. The minor penalties listed under the Recall also apply to this exercise. Dogs that do not return close enough, as in the Recall, must be considered as not having returned to the handler and therefore must receive a non-qualifying (NQ) score.

During the exercise the judge must stand clear of the handler and the dog in order to prevent any interference with the dog's performance. The judge must be positioned so that both the dog and the handler are under continuous observation during the entire exercise.

This exercise is a Novice Recall except for the jump and the position of the handler. The same faults are associated with the Broad Jump as with the High Jump. A dog touching a hurdle must receive a deduction similar to the dog that touches the high jump. All jumps are to be judged the same way.

Retrieving Exercises — Open Classes. As a foundation exercise, the retrieve exercise defines the ability of a dog to work away from the handler and retrieve an object. The dumbbell, which must be approved by the judge, should be made of one or more solid pieces of wood, or of a rigid or semi-rigid, firm, non-toxic material other than wood, similar in size, shape, and weight of a wooden dumbbell which must not be hollowed out. It may be unfinished, or coated with a clear finish, or painted white or any other color. It must have no decoration or attachments, but may bear an inconspicuous mark for identification. The size of the dumbbell should be proportionate to the size of the dog. By strictly enforcing these requirements, a judge will eliminate any problems with dumbbells that do not meet the requirements. No dog should ever be given a qualifying score in the Open classes unless it has performed the retrieve exercises with a dumbbell that fully meets the requirements of the Regulations.

The judge shall require the dumbbell to be thrown again before the dog is sent, if, in the judge's opinion, it is thrown a distance of less than 20 feet, or too far to one side, or too close to the ringside. A judge should not place a dumbbell that is improperly thrown but should require the handler to throw the dumbbell again. A judge will not ask the handler's opinion when deciding whether a dumbbell is to be thrown again or not. It is the judge's sole responsibility to make this decision. Once the decision is made, the judge or steward will retrieve the dumbbell, and under no circumstances should the handler be penalized for a bad throw. Requiring the handler to re-throw the dumbbell signifies that the exercise is being restarted; therefore, the handler may pet, praise and reposition the dog without penalty before the exercise is begun again.

High Jump. In the retrieve over the high jump exercise, a dog that climbs the jump or uses the jump for aid in going over must receive a non-qualifying (NQ) score. This is in contrast to a dog that merely hits or touches the jump in going over.

In the retrieve over the high jump exercise, the handler with the dog in heel position must be at least 8 feet in front of the jump, or any reasonable distance beyond 8 feet. It is the judge's responsibility to see that the handler complies before the exercise begins. Further, the judge must make certain that the handler throws the dumbbell at least 8 feet beyond the jump. During this exercise a judge must stand well clear of both the handler and the dog in order to prevent any interference with the dog's performance. The judge should be positioned so that both the dog and the handler are under continuous observation during the entire exercise.

Once a dog picks up the dumbbell, the exercise is judged as a Novice Recall, except for faults associated with handling the dumbbell such as: not going directly, mouthing or playing with or dropping or reluctance or refusal to release the dumbbell. The retrieve, including the pickup, must be brisk and without hesitation.

Other than the faults associated with the jump, this is a retrieve on flat. Once the exercise begins, the handler may not adjust feet or position.

There are four faults associated with jumps:

- Failure to clear the jump or the height of the jump;
- Using the jump for aid in going over;
- Touching the jump;
- Hesitation or reluctance to jump.

Signal Exercise. Judges should note that heeling is considered a principal part of this exercise, and that all penalties listed under the heeling exercises apply. A judge should bear in mind that only during the stand, drop, sit and come parts of this exercise is it required to score a dog non-qualifying (NQ) for receiving a command or audible signal. It is possible for the dog, although penalized substantially for receiving a command or audible signal during other parts of the exercise, to receive a passing score for the exercise. A dog may non-qualify in the heeling portion using the same standards as in the Novice Heel on Leash and Figure Eight.

Chapter 5, Section 6, requires the judge to have the handler leave the dog at one end of the ring on the stand and then proceed on the judge's order to the other end of the ring. This should place the handler about three to four feet from the opposite end of the ring. All deductions listed under the Recall exercises also apply to this exercise. A dog moving even a minor distance during the performance of the stand, drop or sit portions of the exercise shall be penalized. In the Recall portion of the Signal Exercise, a dog that does not come in close enough has not performed a Recall. Once the signal has been given for the dog to come, the same faults and penalties apply as in the Novice Recall.

An excellent position for judging the stand, drop, sit and come parts of this exercise is at an adequate distance to the side and slightly to the rear of the dog, when the dog is in the stand-stay position.

This exercise is composed of three principal parts, a heeling portion, the signal portion and a Recall portion.

Scent Discrimination. The judge should be certain that the handler and dog are in position to observe the placement of the eight ring articles, that these articles are handled by the judge or steward, that they are about six inches apart and that the closest article is placed about 20 feet from the handler. The judge must take the necessary precautions to ensure the two articles to be used by the handler are not fouled by the judge or any other scent.

The judge must approve the articles before the exercise begins. At this time, the judge shall designate the articles to be used, make note of the number and place them on the chair in the ring or on the judge's table so that they will be ready at the beginning of the scent discrimination exercise.

This exercise consists of four parts:

- Either the turn and sit, or send direct method;
- Going out;
- Searching for the correct article;
- The return of the correct article.

There are two methods for sending the dog and the method to be used must be announced to the judge. If the turn and sit method is designated, the handler may give the command to heel and will turn in place either right or left to face the articles. The handler will come to a halt with the dog sitting in the heel position and will then give a command or signal to retrieve. The other method to send directly will be done with the handler executing a right about-turn, simultaneously giving the command or signal to retrieve. In this method, the dog must not assume a sitting position, but will go directly to the articles. Any excessive movements must be penalized. The go out and return must be judged as in the Novice Recall and the Retrieve on Flat.

Directed Retrieve. Although this exercise is basically judged as a retrieve on the flat, it has an important difference which must be considered in judging. The difference is that the dog is directed to retrieve. The turn and sit are to be judged as in the Scent Discrimination exercise. A dog that finds a glove without being directed to it by the handler, must be given a non-qualifying (NQ) score. A dog whose handler misdirects the dog (under-turns or over-turns) must be non-qualified or penalized depending on the extent of the over/under turn.

The judge should be certain the gloves are visible to the smallest and largest dogs. Prior to the start of judging, the judge shall make the decision to either assign the gloves to dogs so that successive dogs in catalog order will have different gloves, or to assign the gloves as the dogs appear in the ring for judging so that two successive dogs do not receive the same glove. In either case, each glove shall be used approximately the same number of times. The gloves will be designated "One," "Two" or "Three" reading from left to right when the handler is facing the gloves. The judge will give the order "One," or "Two" or "Three" and at the same time may, with the handler's back to the gloves, point to the designated glove.

The direction the handler turns is at the option of the handler, no matter which glove is designated, but the dog should maintain heel position throughout the turn, and sit at heel when the turn is completed. The retrieve portion of the exercise is then completed without any further order from the judge.

Giving the direction must be done with a single motion. When the motion stops, the direction is completed. If the handler does not give the command simultaneously with or immediately following the direction, but delays between the motion and the command, the dog must receive a non-qualifying (NQ) score.

Moving Stand and Examination. This exercise may be judged from the side while the dog and handler are heeling and until the dog is to be examined. For the examination part of the exercise, the dog should be approached from the front and then given a thorough examination as in conformation judging, except that the dog's mouth and testicles are not examined.

Directed Jumping. At the start of this exercise, the judge should be certain the handler and dog are on the center line of the ring, and about 20 feet from the line of the jumps. A dog that does not go out or does not remain at least 10 feet beyond the jumps must receive a non-qualifying (NQ) score. The judge should determine the 10 feet distance before beginning the class.

In the Directed Jumping exercise the dog is not required to go to the other end of the ring, only to a point about 20 feet beyond the jumps and in the approximate center. If the dog stops on command and remains at this point, it should not be penalized for not having gone out far enough.

A dog using the top of the jump for aid in going over must receive a non-qualifying score. The same penalty applies to a dog that knocks the bar off the uprights. All of the penalties listed under the Recall exercise also apply.

A position on the side of the ring opposite the designated jump, parallel to and slightly to the rear of the handler and dog, is excellent for judging this exercise. This is only a recommendation and is not mandated.

There are several key points that require your attention:

- The dog must move at a brisk trot or gallop until commanded to sit.
- The dog must go out about 20 feet beyond the jumps.
- The handler should give the command to sit when the dog is about 20 feet beyond the jumps.
- The dog must stop and sit promptly on command.

When one or more of these conditions is not met, deductions must be made, as well as for slowness or stopping prior to the command to sit.

The judge should not place a mark 20 feet beyond the jumps. The reference to 20 feet beyond the jumps is to require the sit command be given prior to the dog reaching the ring barrier so that the dog may be evaluated on its ability to stop and sit on command.

The jumps should be set up on the longest two sides of the ring.

Grid for Scoring Directed Jumping. When scoring the Directed Jumping exercise, large variations in performance may occur and there is not a great deal of time to consider how far from perfect each variation is. As an aid to maintaining some consistency in the manner in which all dogs in the class are scored, there should be no question that some type of system needs to be adapted in advance of the class. Although the following suggestion may not fit your particular method of scoring, it may serve as an aid in developing your own individual style. A grid is based on the premise that the closer to perfection, the smaller the deduction.

Should the dog go out about 20 feet beyond the jumps, stop on command by the handler and sit in the approximate center of the ring, there is no deduction. (This is represented by an imaginary circle of about 3 feet in the center of the ring at about a distance of 20 feet beyond the jumps.) It should be kept in mind that the handler should stop and sit the dog at about a distance of 20 feet beyond the jump, not precisely 20 feet beyond the jump. If the dog stops and sits on the handler's command at 21 feet or 19 feet beyond the jumps, this is about 20 feet beyond the jumps and no points should be deducted. The key is that the dog stops and sits on command. The dog should not stop and sit without a command from the handler, or stop and/or sit when it arrives at the ring barrier simply because it can go no further. If the dog does either of these, points are deducted because the handler's command did not cause the dog to stop and sit. If the dog stops and sits on the handler's command but the handler has stopped the dog at about the 12-foot distance, a deduction is in order as the handler did not stop and sit the dog at about 20 feet beyond the jumps. Again, the requirement is to stop and sit the dog at about 20 feet beyond the jumps, not precisely 20 feet beyond the jumps.

If the dog goes out about 20 feet beyond the jumps, stops and sits on the handler's command, but its final position is in one of the corners of the ring, a 3-point deduction should be made. If the dog goes out only 10 feet beyond the jumps, stops and sits on command, but the final position is in the center of the ring, a 3-point deduction should be made. If the dog goes out about 10 feet, stops and sits on command, but the final position is next to the side of the ring, a 5- or 6-point deduction is in order.

Once the handler has commanded the dog to sit at a point about 20 feet beyond the jumps and the dog stops, the go out part of the exercise is complete. A dog must receive a non-qualifying (NQ) score for not staying without additional command or signal to sit or for the handler giving a second command to sit. The penalties for the Recall will apply.

Group exercises. If two classes in the same classification such as Novice A and B have different judges, each must judge the group exercises separately. A judge with only a single dog competing in a class would be required to have the dog perform the group exercises alone. However, if the same judge is doing both A and B classes (in the same classification) and the combined two classes do not exceed the limit of dogs based on the size of the ring, the judge may combine the two classes for the group exercises.

Judges should make every effort to equally divide a class for the group exercises and, yet, not have fewer than six dogs in the exercise.

In the Long Down exercise, the dog should lie down on command and/or signal without being touched. In the down position the dog should be lying straight beside the handler, facing the opposite side of the ring. Should the dog lie down facing the dog on either side or in a manner that could interfere with an adjacent competing dog, the handler should be instructed to straighten or reposition the dog and a substantial penalty applied.

When positioning dogs in the ring for the group exercises in the Open classes, judges should make certain that such positioning of the dogs will permit the competing dogs to keep the handlers in their direct line of vision when the handlers leave and return to the ring.

In Open classes, when signaling the steward to bring the handlers back to the ring, do not use a signal (like the waving of an arm) which might cause the dogs in the ring to react.

If a dog gets up and starts to roam or follows its handler and disturbs the other dogs, or if a dog moves so as to interfere with another dog, the judge should promptly instruct the handler or one of the stewards to take the dog out of the ring or to keep it away from the other dogs. If a dog exhibits evidence of disturbing another dog or of being out of control during the long sit, the judge in all fairness to the other exhibitors, must excuse the dog before the Long Down and so mark the judge's book.

Any handler who physically corrects his or her dog before or after any group exercise or while leaving the ring must be penalized under Miscellaneous Penalty.

Chapter 4 — Physically Challenged Handlers

Physically Challenged Handlers. It is perfectly permissible for physically challenged handlers to compete provided they can do so under their own power with or without mechanical assistance, i.e., a wheelchair (self propelled, electric, etc.), crutches or a cane. Chapter 2, Section 14, says that blind handlers may also compete and, subject to the judge's instructions, anyone may position a blind handler before, between and after each exercise. Directions by walkie-talkie are not permitted. Handlers on crutches may compete, and they should not be penalized for any crutch motions considered normal for their disability. However, if, in the opinion of the judge, the handler uses the crutches in a manner unnecessary for his or her movement and as guidance or control of the dog, a scoring penalty must be imposed.

In determining if a modification of the requirements of the regulations for physically challenged handlers is acceptable under the provisions of Chapter 2, Section 14, the judge needs only to determine that if the modification does not aid the dog's performance, it is acceptable. But, as stated in Chapter 2, Section 14, the dog is required to perform all parts of the exercises as described in the Regulations, and shall be penalized for failure to perform any part of an exercise.

Chapter 2, Section 18, requires all dogs to work from the handler's left side. It is proper for a judge to establish in advance a position on the disabled handler's left side that corresponds to the normal heel position for all exercises.

With respect to speed of the handler in the heeling exercises, a physically challenged handler is expected to do the regular heeling at the equivalent of a brisk pace, with significant changes in speed for the slow and fast. A judge must penalize a handler, as he would any other handler disabled or not, who did not perform the regular heeling at the equivalent of a brisk pace, or with a true slow and fast.

In the case of a blind handler, the judge may permit the stewards to utter softly a verbal aid so that the handler may determine the position of the stewards as he or she performs the Figure Eight.

After the judge or another person positions a blind handler for a jump, the judge may permit the handler to leave his or her dog, walk up to the jump to feel it in order to determine its exact location, and then proceed to perform the exercises as required.

Physically Incapacitated. A handler whose disability prevents him or her from throwing the dumbbell the required distance may be permitted to line his or her dog up in the desired starting position and after giving the command to stay, leave his or her dog and proceed away from the dog to throw the dumbbell. The handler should then return alongside the dog to continue the exercise. The same procedure should be followed for the Retrieve over High Jump.

Hearing Deficiency. When faced with the situation where a handler is hard of hearing, a judge should position him or herself so that it will be possible for the handler to continuously observe the judge during the performance of the individual exercises. If such a handler desires, the judge may use prearranged signals to the handler in lieu of verbal commands.

Group exercises. It is permissible for a judge to allow additional space on each side of a disabled handler to permit the handler to work his or her dog without touching it, or without touching the dog on either side. All dogs, however, must be judged in catalog order.

Chapter 5 — The Judge's Book

Marking the Judge's Book. Chapter 2, Section 10, of the Obedience Regulations instructs judges on the correct marking of the book. Judges must be thorough, neat and precise in marking their books. The awarding of obedience titles based on a dog's performance at obedience trials is valueless if the scores are not accurate. Double checking that the score totals are accurate is an absolute must.

When all dogs have been judged and the four official places are determined, then ribbon prizes can be awarded: blue, red, yellow and white or white, yellow, red and blue. Where ribbons or prizes for additional places are offered, the awards for these should be made after the awarding of the four official ribbon prizes. The judge must sign the book, mark the time finished, remove and retain the sheets marked "Judge's Copy," and then return the book (or sheets) for the completed class promptly to the trial secretary, obedience chairperson or superintendent. When the judge returns the book, the trial secretary, obedience chairperson or superintendent should briefly scan the book for obvious omissions or oversights, which can be corrected immediately.

The judge should retain his or her judging records for a period of at least two months. If such records are required to provide information relative to the judging of a particular class, the information will be readily available to The American Kennel Club.

On the following pages are samples of Novice, Open B and Utility A sheets which show the proper procedure for judges in the marking of the judge's book. This procedure is applicable for all classes.

Procedures for Judges to Follow in Marking the Judge's Book

(Use Ballpoint Pen)

- Indicate class.
- Mark the catalog number, the score of the four official placements, the time started, and the time finished. This should be on the first sheet for the class only.
- Where run-off of ties have taken place for any of the four official placements, indicate the winner of the tie by placing a plus sign after its catalog number. In case of a three-way tie, use a double plus for the winner and a single plus for the dog placed second out of the three.
- To correct an error after marking a score under wrong catalog number, cross out error, write correction and initial.
- Non-qualifying scores should be indicated by an "NQ" in the "Total Score" block.
- Carry only qualifying scores down to the "Final Qualifying Score" block.
- If the judge is aware of the reason for an absence in a group exercise, they should mark the dog "Absent" and state the reason. When a judge is unaware of the reason for an absence in a group exercise, the dog must be marked "Absent — reason not given."
- In the case of a dog that is "Disqualified," state the reason and, if more space is needed, use the inside cover of the judge's book. In addition, if a dog is disqualified for attacking a person in the ring, a form available from the superintendent or trial secretary must be completed by the judge and must accompany the judge's book.
- If any dog is excused, state the reason, using the inside cover of the judge's book if more space is necessary.

Note: Judges should use the inside cover of the book for any comments or explanations required. Do not attach or insert a slip of paper for those comments or explanations.

Sign the Book

Name of Club:
(Event #):_____   _____
Judge: _____   Day/Month/Year

NOVICE CLASS _A_ (Indicate A or B)

MAXIMUM TOTAL SCORE — 200 Points

**ENTER POINTS OFF FOR EACH EXERCISE UNDER
APPROPRIATE ARMBAND NUMBER**

Dog Number	101	102	103	104	105	106	107	108
Heel on Leash (40 Points)	1.5	1	0.5	8	4	2	5	1
Stand for Exam (30 Points)	0	0	0	NQ	0	0	0	0
Heel Free (40 Points)	4	4	4.5	6	8	9	3.5	6
Recall (30 Points)	1	0	3.5	1	0	14	2.5	10
Subtotal of Points off	6.5	5	8.5	NQ	12	25	11	17
Long Sit (30 Points)	0	0	0	0	0	0	NQ	*Absent— Reason not given*
Long Down (30 Points)	0	0	0	0	3	0	0	
Miscellaneous Penalties	0	0	0	0	20	0	0	
Maximum Score (200)	200	200	200	200	200	200	200	200
POINTS OFF (Subtract)	-6.5	-5	-8.5	-	-35	-25	-	-
Total Score	193.5	195	191.5	NQ	NQ	175	NQ	NQ
FINAL QUALIFYING SCORE	193.5	195	191.5			175		

	First Place	Second Place	Third Place	Fourth Place
WINNERS:	102	101	103	106
SCORE:	195	193.5	191.5	175

_____   _____

Time Started: 9:00   Time Finished: 9:40

(PLEASE USE BALL POINT PEN)

Name of Club: _____

(Event #): _____   Day/Month/Year

Judge: _____

OPEN B CLASS

MAXIMUM TOTAL SCORE — 200 Points

ENTER POINTS OFF FOR EACH EXERCISE UNDER APPROPRIATE ARMBAND NUMBER

ORDER OF EXERCISES (I-VI)   3

Dog Number	101	102	103	104	105	106	107	108
ROF	1	0	4			2	2.5	.5
DR	1	0	3				1	.5
RHJ	2.5	0.5	3				1	1
BrJ	0	0.5	1				1.5	0
8+HF	4	2	5.5	Disqualified – changed in appearance – Details on inside cover	Absent	Excused – Lame	3	2
Subtotal of Points Off	8.5	3	16.5				9	4
Long Sit (30 Points)	Absent – Reason not given	0	0				0	0
Long Down (30 Points)		0	3				0	0
Miscellaneous Penalties		0	0				0	0
Maximum Score (200)	200	200	200	200	200	200	200	200
POINTS OFF (Subtract)	-	-3	-19.5	-	-	-	-9	-4
Total Score	NQ	197	180.5				191	196
FINAL QUALIFYING SCORE		197	180.5				191	196

Heel Free = 40   Drop on Recall = 30   Retrieve on Flat = 20
Retrieve Over High Jump = 30   Broad Jump = 20

	First Place	Second Place	Third Place	Fourth Place
WINNERS:	102	108	107	103
SCORE:	197	196	191	180.5

Time Started: 9:00   Time Finished: 9:40

(PLEASE USE BALL POINT PEN)

Name of Club:

(Event #):_____   Day/Month/Year

Judge: _____

UTILITY CLASS A

MAXIMUM TOTAL SCORE — 200 Points

ENTER POINTS OFF FOR EACH EXERCISE UNDER APPROPRIATE ARMBAND NUMBER

Dog Number	101	102	103	104	105	106	107	108
Signal Exercise (40 Points)	NQ	1		3	0.5	2.5	2	NQ
Scent Discrimination Article 1 (30 Points)	1	1.5		2	2.5	4	0.5	NQ
Scent Discrimination Article 2 (30 Points)	2.5	1.5		0.5	NQ	0.5	0.5	2
Directed Retrieve (30 Points)	3	1	Absent	1.5	2	0.5	1	2
Moving Stand & Exam (30 Points)	1	1		0	2	1	0.5	NQ
Directed Jumping (40 Points)	4	4		3	7	1	4	6
Miscellaneous Penalties	0	0		0	2	0	0	0
Maximum Score (200)	200	200	200	200	200	200	200	200
POINTS OFF (Subtract)	-	-10	-	-10	-	-9.5	-8.5	-
Total Score	NQ	190			NQ			NQ
FINAL QUALIFYING SCORE		190		190		190.5	191.5	

	First Place	Second Place	Third Place	Fourth Place
WINNERS:	107	106	104	102
SCORE:	191.5	190.5	190+	190

Time Started: 8:30   Time Finished: 11:30

(PLEASE USE BALL POINT PEN)

THE STEWARD IN OBEDIENCE

Planning an obedience trial is an endeavor that involves many months of preparation by the Obedience Trial Committee. The tasks are varied and demanding: Selecting judges, preparing a premium list, compiling a mailing list, soliciting trophies, preparing equipment, making luncheon arrangements, securing admission tickets, and printing a catalog are only some of the details to be completed. One necessary element of an obedience trial often neglected or treated lightly is the selection and training of stewards.

A steward not acquainted with obedience ring procedure requires time consuming instructions from the judge and can severely slow down the entire judging procedure. In order to ensure the smooth operation of a ring by the obedience stewards, clubs should provide at least one training session for them. Use experienced stewards to instruct the training session.

Well in advance of their trial, clubs should appoint a chief steward whose duty it is to invite a sufficient number of experienced persons to act as stewards in the judging rings on the day of the event. Any person invited to serve as a steward must be in good standing with The American Kennel Club. The chief steward should, as soon as practicable, confirm in writing to each person who accepts an invitation to steward, the date and location of the trial, the time at which they are to report for duty, and their particular ring assignment.

No person may serve as a steward with a judge under whom he or she has an entry or under whom, in the course of a day's judging, his or her entry might become eligible to compete.

Stewards must keep in mind that they have been selected to help the judge and not to advise him or her. They should carefully refrain from discussing or even seeming to discuss the dog's performance with the judge, and should not under any circumstances, show or give the appearance of showing the catalog to the judge. When not actively engaged in their duties, stewards should position themselves so that they will not interfere with the judging of the dogs.

Under no circumstances should a steward give information or instructions to owners or handlers unless specifically instructed to do so by the judge, and then only in such a manner that it is clear that the instructions are those of the judge.

Stewarding functions in the obedience ring are broken down in three general categories: gate, table and ring. Under ideal circumstances a club will provide four stewards to perform these functions (there are two ring stewards). However, if the judge's assignment is relatively light, a club could manage quite well with two experienced persons for each ring. The following discussion will explain the specific duties of each function. Although the duties discussed below cover most of the steward's responsibilities, it is absolutely essential that the stewards be at ringside at least 30 minutes prior to the scheduled start of judging to receive any specific instructions from the judge and to assist in setting up the ring as directed by the judge.

The Gate Steward

The primary responsibility of the gate steward is to ensure that the next dog to be judged is immediately available when the judge indicates that he or she is ready. As soon as the judge begins the judging routine of a dog, this steward calls the next dog to be judged and ensures the handler is at ringside when the dog in the ring has completed all exercises. Dogs may not enter the ring until the judge indicates that he is ready for the next dog, and it is the responsibility of this steward to ensure that the judging time of the class is not delayed by having the judge wait for dogs.

Dogs must be judged in catalog order to the extent that it is practical to do so without holding up the judging in any ring. If the dog listed next in the catalog is not at ringside when needed, the steward should not hesitate to call the next dog in order. Stewards are not required to seek out handlers, as it is the handler's responsibility to be ready when his or her dog's number is called. The steward should report the absence to the judge and the judge will decide when the dog is to be marked absent. This procedure should be followed even if the armband for the absent dog has already been issued.

It is normally the duty of the gate steward to distribute armbands. When an exhibitor identifies himself or herself, the steward should check the catalog and ask the exhibitor his or her name and the name of the dog. Then the steward should check that the number of the armband being given to the exhibitor corresponds to the number in the catalog. It is essential that every precaution be taken when giving out armbands.

Very often, exhibitors make requests for special consideration, such as asking to be judged out of catalog order. Any request of this nature must be directed to the judge. It is the judge's prerogative to grant or deny the request and the steward should never consider the matter himself or herself.

When stewarding in the Novice class, upon completion of the Recall exercise, the gate steward should return the leash to the handler before he or she leaves the ring.

The Table Steward

The extent to which a judge uses the services of a table steward varies greatly. Some judges prefer to do their own bookwork and do not feel it is necessary to have their steward perform many of the duties in this area. The steward must receive specific instructions from the judge to ascertain exactly what will be required as table steward.

Many judges use worksheets. The judge may ask the table steward to prepare and have ready the worksheet for the next dog. The steward should ensure that the class, proper armband number and breed of dog are correctly entered on the sheet. If the judge requests it, the table steward must double check to see that the scores on the worksheet are added correctly. The judge, and only the judge, will transfer the scores from the worksheet to the judge's book. The steward should check to ensure that no error has been made. If an error is detected, the steward should bring it to the attention of the judge. Under no circumstances should the steward write in the judge's book.

The table steward usually prepares the group exercise worksheets, if the judge uses them. These should be prepared in advance and according to the judge's instructions. It is essential that these sheets be prepared in catalog order, even if that is not the order in which the dogs were individually judged.

The table steward must review the catalog to see what trophies (if any) are offered, and to ensure that all trophies and ribbons are available at the conclusion of judging. Very often the steward is asked to assist in the awarding of the trophies and ribbons to the winners.

Ring Stewards

Each judge requires two ring stewards. It is particularly important for these two stewards to report to the ring at least 30 minutes prior to the scheduled time for judging, to assist the judge in setting up the ring and equipment and to receive specific assignments from the judge. As the duties of the ring stewards vary with the class in which they are officiating, the remainder of this discussion will be divided by classes.

Novice

The first exercise in the Novice class is the Heel on Leash. After the dog finishes the heeling pattern, the two ring stewards are required to act as "posts" around which the dog and handler will execute the Figure Eight. Both stewards should be ready immediately when the Figure Eight is called. The judge will indicate where he or she wants the Figure Eight performed. When should the stewards go to the assigned position? Probably just after the judge gives the order "Exercise finished" for the Heel on Leash portion of the exercise. This method saves time by not requiring the judge to call the stewards each time they are needed. The stewards stand 8 feet apart, facing each other, with their hands hanging naturally at their sides, or folded in front. Hands should not be placed on hips or in any way extended from the body. It is absolutely essential that stewards do not talk or move while this exercise is being performed. Stewards must resist the temptation to turn their head to watch the dog's performance.

After the completion of the Figure Eight exercise, a steward must be available to take the leash from the handler. The judge will then give the order for the "Stand for Examination." Very often the judge will require the steward to hold his or her clipboard and pencil. Once the steward has these items, he or she should promptly move away from the area where the exercise is taking place, but he or she should be close enough to quickly return the clipboard and pencil when the judging of the exercise is completed and the judge gives the order "Exercise finished." The steward does not return the dog's leash until after the Recall exercise is completed.

Any number of incidents may occur during the group exercises, and stewards must be particularly alert. If a dog breaks or starts to move toward another dog, the steward may be asked to restrain the dog's movement. The stewards' attention should be divided between the dogs and the judge to make sure the stewards are alert to a possible disturbance and be ready to follow whatever instructions the judge may give.

Open Class

When issuing an armband to a handler, the gate steward should record in the catalog beside the armband number the height and distance the dog jumps as stated by the handler of the dog. The gate steward should also take the leash and dumbbells from the handler when the dog is brought into the ring. A discussion of the heights and distance will be described later. It is essential that the steward setting the Broad Jump have a tape measure or steel rule to ensure the accuracy of the jump. The first duty of the judge will be to check that the jumps are properly set. Stewards must arrange jumps quickly and accurately or much time will be wasted.

In the Open class the Figure Eight is performed off lead as part of the Heel Free exercise. The requirements of stewards are the same as in the Novice class. Again, stewards should be immediately available when the order is given.

The Open class has two retrieving exercises — the Retrieve on Flat and Retrieve over High Jump. The gate steward takes the dumbbell from the handler as the dog enters the ring, and places it on the judges' table. When directed by the judge, a ring steward shall deliver the dumbbell to the handler or to the judge as directed by the judge. This should be done immediately so those handlers are not made to wait.

The gate steward will line up the dogs and handlers outside the ring immediately prior to the time the judge has indicated he or she will do the Long Sit and the Long Down exercises. The judge should not be made to wait while the handlers are located. The Long Sit and the Long Down exercises are always done in exact catalog order. As the dogs enter the ring, the ring stewards must line up dogs and handlers along the ringside as indicated by the judge. Ring stewards must make sure that dogs are in catalog order and that they are placed an equal distance from each other. The judge will instruct handlers to place armbands and leashes behind their dogs, with the leash on top of the armband, in such a manner that the number is easily read. One of the two ring stewards in the Open class will be assigned to lead the handler out of sight of the dogs. Prior to the beginning of the exercise access to this location should be checked by the stewards. Once behind the "blind" area, the steward must watch for the judge's signal to return to the dogs and lead handlers back to the ring. The steward is responsible for having handlers return in the same order in which their dogs are arranged. The other steward assists the judge in the ring in the same manner described for the Novice class.

Utility Class

When issuing an armband to a handler, the gate steward should record in the catalog beside the armband number the height the dog jumps as stated by the handler of the dog. The Utility class contains the Directed Jumping exercise, during which the dog must complete a high jump and a bar jump. As in the Open class, one steward immediately sets the high jump while the other steward sets the bar jump. Again, this must be done quickly and accurately. Also, as in the Open class, the judge will make sure that the jumps are properly set.

For the Scent Discrimination exercise, the gate steward will have placed the handler's articles on the judge's table, where the judge will select two — one leather and one metal — and separate them from the rest. The judge may position the remaining articles or may ask the ring steward to perform this function. The articles must be placed so that the closest article is about 20 feet from the handler. The judge or ring steward must touch (not necessary to scent) each of the eight remaining articles, spreading them in a random manner on the floor, or ground, about 6 inches apart. After completion of the Scent Discrimination exercises, the ring steward places the articles in the handler's container and returns them to the judge's table.

The Directed Retrieve exercise utilizes two ring stewards. While one steward is picking up the scent articles, the other steward takes the three gloves from the judge's table and goes to the far end of the ring. After the dog and handler are in position, (midway between and in line with the two jumps) but facing the opposite direction, the steward will drop the three gloves across the end of the ring: one glove in each corner, about 3 feet from the sides and the end of the ring, and one in the center, about 3 feet from the end of the ring. The judge may wish to do this task but it is usually assigned to the steward. The three gloves must be clearly visible to both dog and handler. It is not necessary to "iron" the gloves flat, but they should be open, not closed. After the exercise is completed, the steward retrieves the remaining two gloves and places them on the judge's table.

For the Moving Stand exercise, one ring steward will be needed to hold the judge's clipboard and pencil during the examination and will stand aside as directed by the judge.

The Jumps

Although the gate steward will ask the handler what height the dog jumps, it is conceivable that he or she will know only the height of the dog. Because of this, it is essential that ring stewards be familiar with the Obedience Regulations concerning the setting of the jumps.

The minimum jump shall be set at the nearest multiple of 2 inches to three-quarters the height of the dog at the withers for the following breeds:

Basset Hounds

Bernese Mountain Dogs

Bloodhounds

Bulldogs

Bullmastiffs

Cardigan Welsh Corgis

Clumber Spaniels

Dachshunds

French Bulldogs

Great Danes

Great Pyrenees

Greater Swiss Mountain Dogs

Irish Wolfhounds

Mastiffs

Newfoundlands

Saint Bernards

Skye Terriers

The minimum jump shall be set to the nearest multiple of 2 inches to the height of the dog at the withers for all other dogs, with no dog jumping less than 8 inches nor more than 36 inches.

The broad jump is set at twice the distance of the high jump. The low side of each hurdle and the lowest hurdle shall be nearest the dog. The highest hurdles shall be removed first.

The boards shall be spaced as equally as possible as follows:

1.   For dogs that jump from 16 to 24 inches — use two boards;

2.   For dogs that jump from 28 to 44 inches — use three boards;

3.   For dogs that jump from 48 to 72 inches — use four boards.

Appendix B

Jump Construction Diagrams

SUGGESTED CONSTRUCTION OF HIGH JUMP

FRONT VIEW OF HIGH JUMP

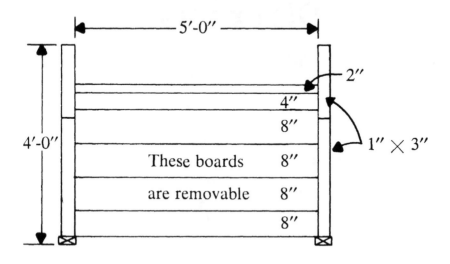

SIDE VIEW OF HIGH JUMP

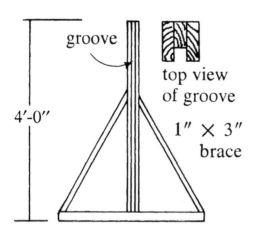

This upright consists of two pieces of 1″ × 3″ and one piece 1″ × 2″, nailed together, with the 1″ × 2″ forming the groove for the boards to slide in.

The high jump must be painted a flat white.

SUGGESTED CONSTRUCTION OF BROAD JUMP

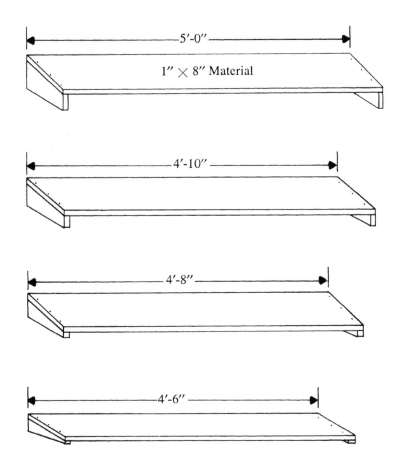

— 5'-0" —

1" × 8" Material

— 4'-10" —

— 4'-8" —

— 4'-6" —

END VIEW OF FOUR HURDLES

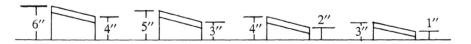

6"   4"   5"   3"   4"   2"   3"   1"

This jump must be painted a flat white.

WINDOW JUMP

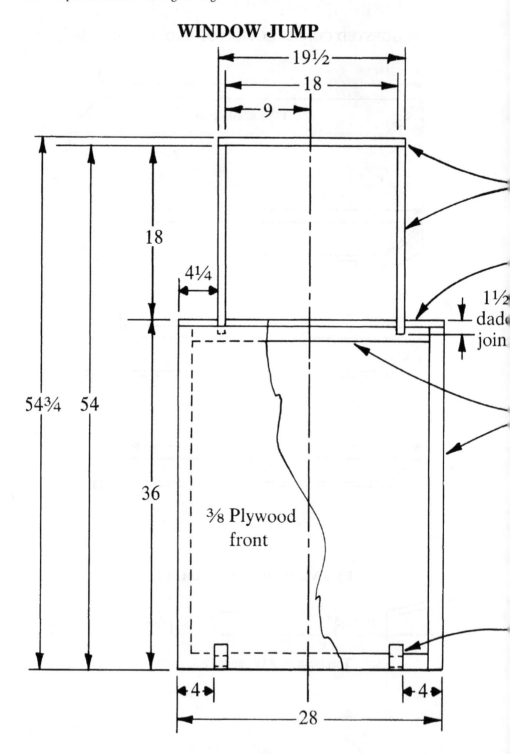

FRONT VIEW

WINDOW JUMP

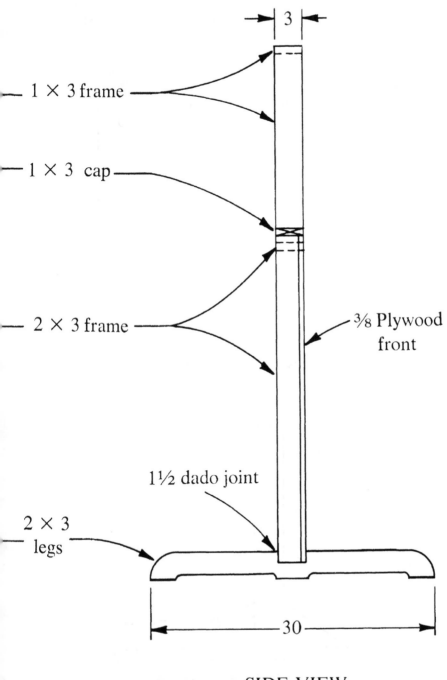

1 × 3 frame

1 × 3 cap

2 × 3 frame

⅜ Plywood front

1½ dado joint

2 × 3 legs

3

30

SIDE VIEW

LONG JUMP
Front View of Long Jump

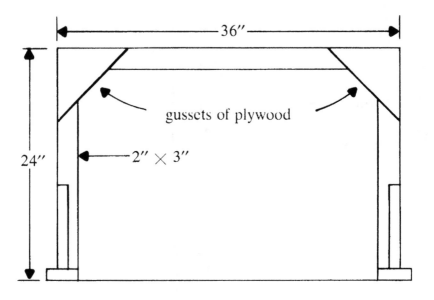

gussets of plywood

36″

24″

2″ × 3″

Side View of Long Jump

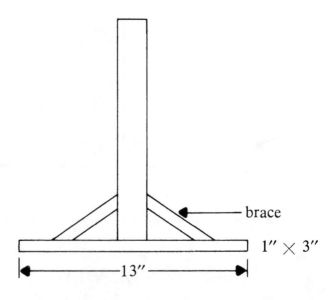

brace

1″ × 3″

13″

Printed in the USA
CPSIA information can be obtained
at www.ICGtesting.com
JSHW051959150824
68134JS00057B/2468

9 781630 269883